This important book challenges some of the foundational categories and assumptions of mainstream international relations theory by insisting that practices that take place in the colonies inevitably travel back to the metropole and transform modes of governance and governmentality at home. By examining the displacement of the camp as a technique of carcerality, surveillance technologies, and neoliberal political economies from "over there" (Iraq, Afghanistan or Latin America) to "over here", Barder brilliantly shows the processes that are central to the imperial management of populations at home and abroad.

Laleh Khalili, School of Oriental and African Studies, UK

In this outstanding book, Alexander Barder provides a powerful and enticing account of the centrality of hierarchy in the international movement of norms and practices. Offering a fascinating analysis of transnational flows of violence, surveillance techniques and neoliberal policy, Barder reveals the multidirectional diffusion of norms, which transforms not only imperial domains but also their metropoles. Especially noteworthy is the focus on the experimentation of the United States in its periphery, experimentation which comes to have ramifications for U.S. democracy. *Empire Within* is a must-read for scholars interested in norm diffusion, globalization [human rights?] and hierarchy in international society

Ann Towns, University of Gothenburg, Sweden

Alexander Barder has returned imperialism to international relations theory, which had long persisted in the view that the world is flat. His geography is more uneven, but with imperial power nonetheless on display here and there. And then what it learns 'there' is not insulated, but makes its way back 'here.' A terrific antidote to the leaden approaches to international power.

Vijay Prashad, author, *The Poorer Nations:
A Possible History of the Global South*

If empire's victims intuitively recognise in the sufferings of the metropoles' peoples a repeat of their own experience of violence and erasure, *Empire Within* unravels the genealogy of this disturbingly common destiny. Barder offers a fascinating, chilling account of empire brought home, and a reminder that knowledges rarely stagnate or dissolve — in the flux of human activity nothing is lost, all is translated. This simultaneously delineates a new horizon of postcolonial solidarity born of a shared experience that can reinvest older knowledges of resistance for today's common struggles.

Inanna Hamati-Ataya, Aberystwyth University, UK

Empire Within

This book explores the reverberating impacts between historical and contemporary imperial laboratories and their metropoles through three case studies concerning violence, surveillance and political economy.

The invasions of Afghanistan in 2001 and Iraq in 2003 forced the United States to experiment and innovate in considerable ways. Faced with growing insurgencies that called into question its entire mission, the occupation authorities engaged in a series of tactical and technological innovations that changed the way they combated insurgents and managed local populations. This book presents new material through three case studies concerning violence, surveillance and political economy, to develop the argument that imperial and colonial contexts function as a laboratory in which techniques of violence, population control and economic principles are developed and subsequently introduced into the domestic society of the imperial state. The text challenges the widely taken for granted notion that the diffusion of norms and techniques is a one-way street from the imperial metropole to the dependent or weak periphery.

This work will be of great interest to scholars of international relations, critical security studies and international relations theory.

Alexander D. Barder is a political scientist at Florida International University in the Department of Politics and International Relations. Barder is the author (with François Debrix) of *Beyond Biopolitics: Theory, Violence and Horror in World Politics* (Routledge, 2011).

Interventions

Jenny Edkins, Aberystwyth University and Nick Vaughan-Williams, University of Warwick

The Series provides a forum for innovative and interdisciplinary work that engages with alternative critical, post-structural, feminist, postcolonial, psychoanalytic and cultural approaches to international relations and global politics. In our first 5 years we have published 60 volumes.

The Series provides a forum for innovative and interdisciplinary work that engages with alternative critical, post-structural, feminist, postcolonial, psychoanalytic and cultural approaches to international relations and global politics. In our first 5 years we have published 60 volumes.

We are very happy to discuss your ideas at any stage of the project: just contact us for advice or proposal guidelines. Proposals should be submitted directly to the Series Editors:

Jenny Edkins (jennyedkins@hotmail.com) and
Nick Vaughan-Williams (N.Vaughan-Williams@Warwick.ac.uk)

As Michel Foucault has famously stated, 'knowledge is not made for understanding; it is made for cutting'. In this spirit the Edkins–Vaughan-Williams Interventions series solicits cutting edge, critical works that challenge mainstream understandings in international relations. It is the best place to contribute post disciplinary works that think rather than merely recognize and affirm the world recycled in IR's traditional geopolitical imaginary.

Michael J. Shapiro, University of Hawai'i at Mãnoa, USA

The series aims to advance understanding of the key areas in which scholars working within broad critical post-structural and post-colonial traditions have chosen to make their interventions, and to present innovative analyses of important topics.

Titles in the series engage with critical thinkers in philosophy, sociology, politics and other disciplines, and provide situated historical, empirical and textual studies in international politics.

Critical Theorists and International Relations
Edited by Jenny Edkins and Nick Vaughan-Williams

Ethics as Foreign Policy
Britain, the EU and the other
Dan Bulley

Empire Within

International hierarchy and its imperial laboratories of governance

Alexander D. Barder

Routledge
Taylor & Francis Group

LONDON AND NEW YORK

First published 2015
by Routledge

2 Park Square, Milton Park, Abingdon, Oxfordshire OX14 4RN
711 Third Avenue, New York, NY 10017

Routledge is an imprint of the Taylor & Francis Group, an informa business

First issued in paperback 2017

British Library Cataloguing in Publication Data
A catalogue record for this book is available from the British Library

Library of Congress Cataloging in Publication Data
A catalog record for this book has been requested

ISBN: 978-1-138-82057-9 (hbk)
ISBN: 978-0-8153-7718-4 (pbk)

Typeset in Times New Roman
by Taylor & Francis Books

Contents

Acknowledgement

A book is at once a solitary endeavor and the product of numerous influences, contributions and generous assistance from a wide range of people. To acknowledge this on paper does in no way extinguish my own feeling of debt and gratitude.

This book is the product of my doctoral dissertation at Johns Hopkins University. I was privileged to work with a generous committee and teachers who have had an enormous influence on me: Siba N'Zatioula Grovogui, Jennifer Culbert, and William E. Connolly. Over the years they have provoked me to think more deeply and to push my arguments in more challenging directions. I am eternally thankful for the brilliant seminars that I participated in and the help that they provided me over the course of completing this project. I am thankful to Beverly Silver and Joel Andreas for their extensive comments.

More generally, I will always be thankful for having pursued my graduate studies in the Department of Political Science at Johns Hopkins University. I cannot think of a more collegial and stimulating environment to work in. I wish to especially thank my colleagues and friends Kellan Anfinson, Willy Blomme, Frankie Clogston, David Dagan, Cara Daggett, Derek Denman, Stefanie Fishel, Tim Hanafin, Meghan Helsel, Jairus Grove, Nicole Sunday Grove, Anatoli Ignatov, Hitomi Koyama, Daniel Levine, Michael McCarthy, Casey McNeill, Benjamin Meiches, Nobutaka Otobe, Akshay Regmi, Chad Shomura, Tarek Tutunji and Drew Walker.

Outside of Johns Hopkins University I would like to especially thank François Debrix, Harry Gould, Ann Towns, and Nicholas Onuf, who have read parts of the manuscript and have been generous with their remarks. I would also like to thank the ASPECT Center at Virginia Tech for giving me the opportunity to present a version of Chapter 2 in March of 2012. I also presented a version of Chapter 4 at the American University of Beirut in April of 2012. I would like to thank my colleagues at the AUB for their hospitality and generosity while I spent 2013–2014 in Beirut. I would like to thank, Samer Frangie, Thomas Haase, Tania Haddad, Waleed Hazbun, Coralie Hindawi, Ohannes Geukjian, Alex Lubin, Karim Makdisi, Sylvain Perdigon, Vjay Prashad, Tariq Tell, Alexis and Livia Wick.

To my dear friend Majid Al-Khalili, who set me on this path so many years ago.

A version of Chapter 4 was published in *Alternatives: Local, Global, Political* in 2013 and is reprinted here with their permission. A shorter version of Chapter 2 will appear in the edited volume by Mark Salter entitled *Making Things International* (2015).

Lastly, I could never have finished this book work without the enormous help of my family. My mother Michelle. My mother and father in law Roza and Robert Mirzoyan. My brother in law Armen and his wife Armine. And of course my precious wife Alla and my son Robert. I hope that you will be proud of this effort.

Introduction

[I]n the outskirts of the world the system reveals its true face.[1]

The title, *Empire Within*, in part comes from Salman Rushdie's 1982 polemical essay "The New Empire within Britain."[2] Rushdie's essay draws the reader's attention to the prevalence of racism in British society. This racism is ineluctably linked to a history of imperialism that leaves its traces at home. As Rushdie writes:

> In short ... it's impossible even to begin to grasp the nature of the beast [i.e. British racism] unless we accept its historical roots. Four hundred years of conquest and looting, four centuries of being told that you are superior to the Fuzzie-Wuzzies and the wogs, leave their stain. This stain has seeped into every part of the culture, the language and daily life; and nothing much has been done to wash it out.[3]

Evidently Britain's empire is formally buried in the past. But the language, culture and reflexive manner of dealing with and thinking about the issues surrounding immigration or race are filtered through an ever-present colonial lens. The "new empire" within Britain internalizes all the racial pathologies accumulated over centuries of expropriation, domination and violence into forms of regimentation and exclusion at "home." Rushdie's essay raised important questions concerning this imperialization of the domestic state. In what ways does the practice of empire or hegemony reflect within domestic state institutions, culture or ways of thinking? How can we understand the effects that the practices of international imperial relations have upon the domestic space?

International theorists have for some time now been interested in understanding how the transnational diffusion of norms, practices and/or forms of knowledge occur and how such processes bridge the divide between the international and the domestic. Yet much of this work remains incomplete. It is incomplete because much of this work looks at diffusion as a set of processes that emanate from an autochthonously constituted "West" that historically socializes the "non-West" into an image of itself. The second reason it is incomplete is because there is a tendency to eschew histories of empire-building or hegemony as constituting the basis for innovation and diffusion. Taking both claims as starting points, my book investigates how international hierarchy (as either imperialism or hegemony) has historically resulted in the experimentation and innovation of various norms and practices that (re)shape the domestic space of various imperial or hegemonic powers. I show that imperial spaces are as much spaces of experimentation and social innovation as spaces of exploitation. These spaces produce norms and practices not only in the periphery but also in the metropole. This happens because empires are constituted as a set of transnational networks and circuits that substantially imbricate both metropole and periphery. This argument explains how under contemporary conditions of American hegemony and the past decade of the Global War on Terror, we can see American experiences abroad reshaping the domestic sphere in various ways.

To illustrate the last point, consider the following concrete example. On March 20, 2003, the United States and its coalition partners launched combat operations to remove the Iraqi leader Saddam Hussein from power. On May 1, 2003, President George W. Bush declared, with great fanfare on the carrier *Abraham Lincoln*, an end to major combat operations. He added, however, a caveat: "We have difficult work to do in Iraq. We are bringing order to parts of that country that remain dangerous."[4] This last comment proved to be a dramatic understatement. For many, it has become somewhat of a truism that United States entered Iraq without adequate postwar planning. The Department of Defense under Donald Rumsfeld long mocked the idea of postwar nation-building as something the US military was not mandated to do nor capable of doing. And yet, while military commanders planned the withdrawal of US forces by September of 2003, leaving a token reserve force, it became increasingly apparent that nation-building was something the US was going to need to do to salvage the ideal of a "free" post-war Iraq.[5]

Iraq proved to be an important "laboratory" for experimentation with novel forms of violence, social control and economic transformation. Faced with a growing insurgency, the US military developed new forms of violent capabilities to track down and hunt insurgent and Al-Qaeda leaders. It experimented with novel mechanisms of social control and surveillance to map out potential threats before they become effective. And it engaged in the radical transformation of the Iraqi economy along "neoliberal" lines by attempting to liberalize Iraqi industry, establishing a flat-tax – long the dream of American conservatives in the US – and removing all tariffs or controls on the flow of foreign capital. By putting this agenda in place, Iraq followed in a long list of laboratories of economic shock therapy that Naomi Klein calls the "disaster capitalism complex."[6]

Many have seen the invasion of Iraq as a contemporary "imperial" moment in American foreign policy.[7] Such a recent imperial moment provokes analogies, as Alfred McCoy argues, with the turn of the nineteenth century and the American takeover of the Philippines. There, as in Iraq, the

United States was faced with a difficult and initially unmanageable insurgency. There, as in Iraq, American imperial authorities were compelled to experiment with new forms of social control and violence. And, moreover, as part of America's civilizing mission the Philippines was a space for socioeconomic experimentation during the so-called Progressive Era.[8] The Philippines proved to be, as McCoy argues, a crucible in which "colonial security agencies fused domestic data management with foreign police techniques to forge a new weapon – a powerful intelligence apparatus that first contained and then crushed Filipino resistance." The crucial point here is that the techniques that were developed in this imperial crucible found their way back to the American homeland. As McCoy observes, "During the country's rapid mobilization for the First World War, these colonial precedents provided a template for domestic counterintelligence marked by massive surveillance, vigilante violence, and the formation of a permanent internal security apparatus."[9] Returning to the Iraq campaign, *Washington Post* journalists Dana Priest and William Arkin investigate the public–private partnerships that adapt and market military technological innovations to local police departments. According to Priest and Arkin, police across the United States are "building ever more sophisticated localized intelligence systems."[10] Such systems integrate and rely on the latest technologies such as "handheld, wireless fingerprint scanners used by US troops to register entire Iraqi villages during the insurgency."[11] Other technologies such as "thermal infrared cameras," "facial recognition equipment" and automatic license plate readers contribute to a growing and interconnected network of surveillance mechanisms to monitor the American public. Add to that the growing call to use unmanned aerial vehicles to monitor US borders and cities and an inchoate image emerges of an intensified militarization of the domestic policing apparatus which sees undocumented immigration, criminality at home, and insurgency abroad as constituting an array of transnational threats that cut across territorially defined boundaries.[12] Such an amalgamation of threat perceptions constitutes an important dimension of what Hugh Gusterson calls the contemporary global "securityscape": "asymmetrical distributions of weaponry, military force, and military-scientific resources among nation-states and the local and global imaginaries of identity, power, and vulnerability that accompany these distributions."[13]

These observations about the "difficult work" the United States did in Iraq provoke questions about the emergence and diffusion of governmental practices across international relations of hierarchy. They force us to think about the ways in which norms, practices and knowledge reverberate across imperial networks, how such imperial zones become "workshops" or laboratories for testing new disciplinary *dispositifs* about managing populations, and how such practices fuse themselves to existing domestic state forms or potentially lead to new ones.[14] Simply stated, my aim in this book is to ask: how can we understand the transnational effects of international hierarchical forms of rule, of which empire constitutes a central frame, on domestic state formation and practice?

To be sure, such a question has been posed by anthropologists, imperial historians, sociologists and literary critics for some time. Many have shown how imperial spaces constituted important "laboratories of modernity." They have also shown how there were significant "tensions of empire" in which European imperial powers were historically as much constituted by their imperial projects as by intra-European or domestic developments.[15] Colonial laboratories emerged for various reasons: either because colonial domains allowed imperial officials much greater leeway in enacting policies perceived to be "modern" (i.e. particularly in the realm of urban planning and public health) or because imperial officials were faced with significant local resistance, a lack of knowledge about the spatial and population identity or generalized lack of administrative capabilities that required innovations in colonial governance. However, as I will argue, international relations theorists have not sufficiently grappled with the implications of seeing imperial spaces and the transnational relations that emanate from them as central features of international politics. This should be considered surprising and unsurprising at the same time. In an era of so-called globalization, the material and ideational flows of capital, knowledge, and technological innovations circulate at increasing speeds, cutting across nation-state boundaries. Such flows continuously affect the socio-political and cultural formations imbricating the developed and developing world under conditions of unequal exchange.[16]

Yet, canonical approaches to international theory continue to be wedded to a specific representation of the international system that obfuscates the reverberating impacts of such hierarchical relations. This representation takes as central the shifting patterns of great power interactions as the dominant features of the international, while leaving to the side histories involving asymmetric or hierarchical relations of rule. The persistence of this representation reflects two ontological commitments. First, is the continued predominance of the concept of anarchy and a notional image of *equal* sovereign states. Second, is a commitment to a Eurocentric understanding of how norms constitute the international *social* world. IR theories continue to privilege a certain Western historical moment and reify it into the fulcrum of socio-political modernity without taking into account the reverse impacts of norms and practices that emerge within the historical crucibles of Western empires.

My purpose in this book is to question these two central working assumptions of mainstream approaches to international theory. Here I would like to justify this by making three central claims.

First, I claim that international hierarchy is historically and today a significant feature of international life. The concept of anarchy in international theory typically refers to the lack of a centralized governmental apparatus that allows for the adjudication of international disputes between states. It is often conceived as a transhistorical condition, particularly in neorealist accounts of international politics, and governs state identity as intrinsic security maximizers. However, the prevalence of forms of international hierarchy can be observed by the ubiquitous feature of empire-building in history.[17] Indeed, David Lake and John Ikenberry take seriously the hierarchies between states to explain the prevalence of international orders.[18] Their work focuses on describing how international hierarchy operates according to relations of authority and legitimacy. Lake, for example, defines hierarchy in relational terms as "the extent of the authority exercised by the ruler over the ruled."[19] Authority becomes a central facet of international politics; its exercise being predicated on the establishment of legitimacy whether in the form of international "rules" (preferable for Lake) or coercion. In other words, we should understand the history of international relations as a patchwork of various forms of hierarchical relations embodying aspects of authority and gradated or disaggregated forms of sovereignty. However, in this work I consider in greater detail the particular cases of formal and informal empire as examples of international hierarchy.

Second, I claim that this condition of international hierarchy is characterized by a diffusion of norms, practices, knowledge and culture that is multidirectional. Here I wish to contest the predominant perceptions within much of international theory, including the approaches to hierarchy established by Lake and Ikenberry, that such patterns of international hierarchy are unidirectional. Their work implies a process of diffusion that occurs from the great powers or core imperial or hegemonic states to a passive and receptive periphery. Instead, I wish to show that imperial domains are important staging grounds for the innovation, experimentation and implementation of techniques of state practice. In essence, they are "laboratories of normalization" that create new objects or targets of governmental practice. Significantly, some of these practices are repatriated in ways that influence and constitute how states govern their own populations.

Third, I claim that state formation is a combination of diffuse and heterogeneous elements and practices about *governing* various kinds of populations (domestic, subaltern, elites, etc.) that coalesce historically into various apparatuses of control. Here I am motivated by Michel Foucault's concept of governmentality.[20] Foucault's histories of governmentality are circumscribed within a European territorial space; I internationalize the applicability of Foucault's concept by looking specifically at the ramifications of transnational and imperial hierarchical relations of governance.[21] My argument is that imperial history cannot remain "outside" the history of international politics and thus inconsequential to an understanding of the development of modern state practice. By contrast, I want to emphasize, following Gary Wilder, the idea that the state, the dominant unit of analysis in international relations theory, was and is in fact an "imperial nation-state," one that is "an artifact of colonial modernity."[22] "[I]mperialism," Wilder continues, "created novel sociopolitical formations that were irreducibly different from those in the West yet were incontestably modern and inseparable from their European counterparts."[23]

To summarize then, I make three arguments in this work: International relations of hierarchy (specifically imperial or hegemonic relations) constitute significant circuits for the multidirectional flow of norms, practices and technologies of governance. These norms, practices and technologies of governance emerge out of imperial laboratories that pioneer new forms of violence, social control and, more generally, *disciplinary* practices. These new forms of violence, social control and disciplinary practice are central for understanding the manner in which modern Western states emerge and govern.

While I began this introduction with a discussion of the recent American foray into Iraq as a way of highlighting how innovations accrued in such neo-imperial domains can reverberate back into the domestic sphere (more on this in the concluding chapter), by no means is the United States the main focus in my work. As I attempt to show, what I am emphasizing are processes of imperial experimentation and innovation that are part of these international hierarchical relations. If I return to the US in various chapters it is mainly for two reasons. First, the focus of this work is mainly tied to specific developments in the late nineteenth century and mid-to-late twentieth century. My interest in the nineteenth century in particular is that many significant developments – such as empire-building – are often not accorded the same importance as intra-European politics. As Barry Buzan and George Lawson argue, international theorists often construe the nineteenth century as simply a data set for constructing parsimonious theories of IR.[24] Moreover, it was during these time periods when the emergence of American power either began to rise substantially or was fundamentally called into question by the set of hegemonic crises of the 1960s and 1970s. In other words, the past century or so marked the US as a significant global power that ultimately had important ramifications for the trajectory of its own domestic sphere. Second, if I turn to the US at multiple points in the book it is because I wish to, in a sense, disabuse "American IR" of an often implicit assumption about the particular uniqueness of American international political development, and to problematize the rigid separation between its own "inside" and "outside." Instead, as I wish to show, the practice of international hierarchy through American hegemony makes it just as prone to patterns of disciplinary innovations and experimentation in the periphery as other imperial powers that have normative ramifications for American liberal democracy. This is something, I believe, that is missing in many discussions of American unipolarity or concerns with the longevity of American hegemony.

Empire as international hierarchy

As I alluded to at the beginning of this introduction, a wide range of scholars have recently challenged how we should think about the ways empires operated.[25] No longer is it adequate to take for granted a "top-down" view of imperial rule, in which a metropole commands and the periphery remains passive. What is emphasized now is the set of imbrications and interactions that have occurred within and throughout imperial "contact zones."[26] Cooper and Stoler problematize the way in which empire is understood to represent a spatial and political ordering of the globe, an "abstract process", that writes out the significant hybridities that emerge through imperial spaces.[27] Not satisfied in seeing the imperial periphery as simply a zone of either capitalist exploitation or perpetual violence, recent scholarship has turned to highlighting and theorizing the manifold ways in which imperial interactions produce novel norms, practices and identities that reconstitute[d] colonizers as much as colonial subjects. Indeed, British and French imperial administrators themselves understood their imperial missions in terms of experimenting with new forms of social and economic practices, which could eventually be merged into the imperial metropole.[28] As far back as 1812, Sir Robert Peel, in his description of the island of Trinidad, wrote:

> Trinidad is like a subject in an anatomy school or rather a poor patient in a country in a hospital and on whom all sorts of surgical experiments are tried, to be given up if they fail, and to be practiced on others if they succeed.[29]

This turn in the scholarship of empire to focus on the intersections between peoples that moves beyond the narrating of empire through its twin poles of colonizer and colonized, should come as no surprise: as J. H. Elliot argues in his review of Emma Rothschild's book *The Inner Life of Empires: An Eighteenth Century History*:

> in an age of self-conscious globalization and of an interconnected world, the traditional dichotomy of center and periphery has come to look excessively stark, and it is the links – between rulers and ruled, colonists and colonized, Europeans and non-Europeans – that are receiving the attention of historians.[30]

This emphasis on transnational links as a consequence of imperial contacts and the novel practices produced through and in such encounters has not been sufficiently addressed by international theorists. Typically, international theorists define empire in monolithic terms: as the embodiment of direct (formal) or indirect (informal) political, economic or social control by a metropole/center over its colonial or imperial domain. Empire becomes judged on the basis of gradations of sovereignty rather than in terms of the productive interrelationships that such formal or informal relations capture. Michael Doyle's classic international theory text on the subject of empire defines it as "a system of interaction between two political entities, one of which, the dominant metropole, exerts political control over the internal and external policy – the effective sovereignty – of the other, the subordinate periphery."[31] Throughout Doyle's text, which is meant to uncover the mechanisms that give rise to imperial domination, there is no attempt to show the multidirectional impacts that such forms of control and discipline give rise to. However, even recent attempts to describe empire as constituting different types of "authority relationships," and thereby recognizing patterns of legitimacy, particularly in cases of informal empire or hegemony, does not shed light on how imperial, or hierarchical, authority maintains itself and evolves over time.[32] For instance, neopositivist explanations of international hierarchy, more generally, foreclose the possibilities of analyzing the social malleability of such imperial relations and the potential for multidirectional norm diffusion. Furthermore, the notion of "discipline" displayed in these explanations is simplistic.[33] When IR scholars speak of international discipline they usually have in mind a range of actions from sanctions through to military intervention. However, in an imperial or hegemonic hierarchical relation, discipline also implies the establishment of vast mechanisms of violence (including structural, cultural and symbolic violence), governmental technologies of social control and the rearrangement of political-economic structures that benefits the imperial or hegemonic power. In addition, discipline also involves the application of "ideological transfers" by non-state actors from core states to subordinated peripheries, transfers that reshape what is deemed legitimate government.[34] There is, in other words, a manifold set of processes occurring within the category of "discipline" that these scholars do not take into account.

At the same time, international theorists have largely shunned empire as a relevant category of analysis. Instead the main theoretical category to describe the international post-Second World War order, and especially post-Cold War, is hegemony. The emphasis on hegemony appears to make hierarchy more innocuous and intrinsically legitimate. It is described as the product of international rules that assure state security for states that accept a trade-off in diminished external (and in many cases internal) sovereignty.[35] Hegemonic states necessarily engage in disciplinary activities, even in "crudely imperial" ones.[36] Nor does it negate the possibility of establishing laboratory-like conditions for socioeconomic experimentation, and the repatriation of the results of these experiments through established transnational circuits.

The significance of this book

It is important to look at the reverberating impacts of transnational hierarchical relations for two kinds of reasons: conceptual and normative. First, by expanding the analytical focus of IR scholarship to encompass the history of these reverberating impacts of transnational hierarchical relations, we can better understand conceptually how domestic changes in state apparatuses occur as a function of international developments. We can then better appreciate the conditions of possibility for how novel norms and practices are generated within historical and contemporary imperial crucibles. Transcending the traditional Eurocentric starting points gives us a different (postcolonial) perspective on the history of international relations. The Eurocentric straightjacket privileges a universal, naturalized Western-centric history which inherently constitutes the periphery as *lacking* "Western" aspects.[37] This conceptually imposed hierarchy also leaves out certain historical events. For example, there is a tendency in the discipline of international relations theory to eschew histories of transatlantic slave trading, nineteenth-century imperialism and its relationship to the non-West, and the various "small" wars fought by imperial powers. Such events tend to remain unexamined because of the much wider concern with interactions between European great powers. This tendency is particularly acute in much of the recently literature on "failed states" and "new wars," which takes for granted the ability of the "West" to offer "solutions" in the form of neocolonial state-building initiatives.[38] By expanding the analytical field of reference by way of observing imperial relations of domination we can probe more deeply into the mutual constitution of the international and domestic spheres. Accepting this wider analytical framework also enables us to challenge assumptions that legitimize certain neo-modernization theories. Such theories take for granted the seamless diffusion and acceptance of domestic Western norms and practices to the global South.

Second, it is important to look at imperial reverberations for normative reasons. Do transnational hierarchical relations have internal detrimental effects for practice of domestic liberal democracy and the ideal of political, social and economic liberty and justice? John Mearsheimer, the dean of offensive realism, strikingly argued that "countries that continuously fight wars invariably build powerful national-security bureaucracies that undermine civil liberties and make it difficult to hold leaders accountable for their behavior; and they invariably end up adopting ruthless policies normally associated with brutal dictators."[39] In other words, he argues that the maintenance of American hegemony requires the persistent "*disciplining*" of subordinate states that in turn legitimizes the emergence of metropolitan authoritarian practices and apparatuses. Achille Mbembe puts it more forcefully, claiming that by uncovering the history of imperial disciplinary apparatuses we would shed light on the authoritarian impulses at work in the management of populations.[40] Such normative concerns relate to a debate among international theorists on the question of the "burdens of hegemony," the costs of maintaining American hegemony and the implications of continuing "imperial overstretch" for us.[41] By considering reverberating impacts of transnational hierarchy, international theorists can broaden their investigations of imperial overstretch to consider its consequences for internal domestic changes.[42]

To be sure, the concern with the manner in which imperial or hegemonic international authority penetrates into the domestic sphere and warps the social and political fabric towards authoritarian ways was traditionally an important *republican* polemic against empire-building.[43] Republican theory reiterates the story of the Roman republic, the expansion of which during the first century BC put enormous stress upon its institutions, which finally gave way to the emergence of the Augustinian *principate*. The story of Rome is told as a cautionary tale about the perils of imperial expansion for domestic republican institutions, specifically about the incompatibility of expanding territorial governance, managing diverse peoples and the stresses it produces for domestic self-rule.[44]

Layout of the chapters

To set the scene, Chapter 1 discusses three main issues in international theory. First, the necessity of moving beyond conceptions of international anarchy to hierarchy. Here I critically examine the work of David Lake and others on the topic of international hierarchy. I show that their approaches to international hierarchy reify the Western state and miss crucial aspects of discipline put in place to maintain imperial and hegemonic international relations. Second, the chapter discusses how social constructivism and English School theorists address the question of imperialism. I turn to these theories because of their emphasis on norm diffusion and socialization. I argue that both approaches remain Eurocentric in their methodological assumptions. Because they emphasize unidirectional norm diffusion they preclude observing domestic imperial reverberations. Lastly, I justify my turn to a Latourian understanding of the laboratory in order to show how we can understand the co-constitution between an imperial laboratory and its metropole.

Chapters 2, 3 and 4 then tackle directly the three themes that I wish to investigate. The first theme is the camp as a novel space of violence. In Chapter 2 I develop a genealogy of the materialization of the concentration camp as a core imperial practice. The camp, I argue, emerged out of this necessity to restrict and control a mass population whose loyalty was in question. Mass rebellions across the imperial periphery in the late nineteenth century imperiled imperial authority, which developed instruments to better control the movement of peoples. As an architectural apparatus, the camp can be traced through the American Midwest, with the push of Native Americans into reservations, the innovation of barbed wire to control the movement of cattle and its adaptation by the British for suppressing insurgency during the Boer War. Lastly, I argue that the camp materialized in Europe during and after the First World War. The collapse of the European state-system in the 1930s, signified by growing transnational, stateless populations, provoked the widespread adaptation of the camp. It would finally become part of Nazi Germany's own imperial project in Eastern Europe during the Second World War.

Chapter 3 concerns the second theme: security through surveillance. In this chapter I argue that the proliferation of surveillance technologies and mechanisms of social control is a significant aspect of modern state formation. Drawing from Michel Foucault's work on discipline which captures the working of modern power and its productive effects on the body, I argue that we need to see the implementation of domestic security and surveillance apparatuses as a consequence of imperial innovations. The point here is not that the modern surveillance state originated in the imperial periphery; rather, I argue that the rise of the surveillance state over the course of the nineteenth century was predicated upon a discursive formation that characterized certain populations within the West as being akin to colonial populations. Consequently, working-class neighborhoods could become perceived as being similar to imperial zones. Thus, imperial innovations such as fingerprinting in British India, or novel American surveillance technologies used in the Philippines, could later be adapted in the metropolitan setting against populations deemed to be a potential threat.

Chapter 4 focuses on the political economy of neoliberalism. The emphasis shifts from instances of formal empire to informal empire or hegemony. I examine the legacy of American hegemony in the post-Second World War context. Departing from the recent work of John Ikenberry, I argue that what proponents of American liberal hegemony miss is the reverberating impact of maintaining such a hegemony. In this chapter I study how the neoliberalization of the US political economy is linked with with the reassertion of US hegemony in Latin America. I turn to the specific case of Chile and its neo-liberalization under General Augusto Pinochet and the Chicago Boys. The implementation of neoliberalism in Chile during the 1970s became a crucial process for normalizing an economic theory of free markets, privatization of state assets, the suppression of trade unionism and worker rights, and the deregulation of financial capital. All of which, I argue, became in one way or another the program of socioeconomic reform in the early 1980s in the United States and the United Kingdom.

The Conclusion ties these three themes together by returning to the contemporary context. I look at how American nation-building efforts in Iraq and Afghanistan impacts domestic American institutions. For example, I show how counterinsurgency methods are being implemented in US inner cities and are pushing forward the militarization of policing across the developed world. This concluding chapter likewise seeks to problematize further the notion of the historical division between core and periphery. In other words, under conditions of global capitalism, we can see the emergence of peripheral zones within metropolitan states in the form of inner cities in the United States or *banlieues* in France. These zones, populated by African-Americans or immigrants, become perceived as internal threats to the established domestic order and the authority of the state. How to govern these zones becomes a central question of the contemporary neoliberal state.

Notes

1 Eduardo Galeano, *Days and Nights of Love and War* (London: Pluto Press, 2000), 170.
2 Salman Rushdie, "The New Empire within Britain," *New Society* 62, no. 1047 (December 1982). Also reprinted in *Imaginary Homeland: Essays and Criticism 1981–1991* (New York: Penguin Books, 1992).
3 Ibid., 130.
4 George W. Bush, "Text of Bush Speech: President Declares End to Major Combat in Iraq" (2003 [Quoted November 18, 2010]); available from www.cbsnews.com/stories/2003/05/01/iraq/main551946.shtml.
5 There is a wealth of sources documenting the transitions in American policies in Iraq since 2003 and especially the fierce inter-governmental debates over what to do with Iraq in the aftermath of the invasion. Particularly on this point is George

Packer, *The Assassins' Gate: America in Iraq* (New York: Farrar, Straus and Giroux, 2005); Michael R. Gordon and Bernard E. Trainor, *Cobra II: The Inside Story of the Invasion and Occupation of Iraq* (New York: Vintage Books, 2007).

6 Naomi Klein, *The Shock Doctrine: The Rise of Disaster Capitalism* (New York: Henry Holt, 2007). By "disaster capitalism complex" Klein means the "orchestrated raids on the public sphere in the wake of catastrophic events, combined with the treatment of disasters as exciting market opportunities," 6.

7 The recent literature across disciplines on the subject of the imperial turn in US policy is vast. Here is a sample of various perspectives on the issue. Julian Go, *Patterns of Empire: The British and American Empires, 1688 to the Present* (Cambridge: Cambridge University Press, 2011); Victor Gordon Kiernan, *America, the New Imperialism: From White Settlement to World Hegemony* (New York: Verso, 2005); David Harvey, *The New Imperialism* (Oxford: Oxford University Press, 2005); Greg Grandin, *Empire's Workshop: Latin America, the United States, and the Rise of the New Imperialism* (New York: Owl Books, 2007); Michael Hardt and Antonio Negri, *Multitude: War and Democracy in the Age of Empire* (New York: The Penguin Press, 2004), George Steinmetz, "Return to Empire: The New US Imperialism in Comparative Historical Perspective," *Sociological Theory* 23, no. 4 (2005); John Agnew, "American Hegemony into American Empire? Lessons from the Invasion of Iraq," *Antipode: A Radical Journal of Geography* 35, no. 5 (2004); Niall Ferguson, *Colossus: The Rise and Fall of the American Empire* (New York: Penguin Books, 2005); Robert D. Kaplan, *Imperial Grunts: The American Military on the Ground* (New York: Random House, 2005); Michael Mann, *Incoherent Empire* (New York: Verso, 2005); Ellen Meiksins Wood, *Empire of Capital* (New York: Verso, 2003).

8 See especially the essays in Alfred W. McCoy and Francisco A. Scarano, *The Colonial Crucible: Empire in the Making of the Modern American State* (Madison: University of Wisconsin Press, 2009).

9 Alfred W. McCoy, *Policing America's Empire: The United States, the Philippines, and the Rise of the Surveillance State* (Madison: University of Wisconsin Press, 2009), 8.

10 Dana Priest and William M. Arkin, *Top Secret America: The Rise of the New American Security State* (New York: Little, Brown, 2011), 147.

11 Ibid., 130.

12 Tyler Wall and Torin Monahan, "Surveillance and Violence from Afar: The Politics of Drones and Liminal Security-Scape," *Theoretical Criminology* 15, no. 3 (2011); See also Donald J. Mihalek, "Urban Combat the Petraeus Way" (2010 [Quoted January 23, 2012]); available from www.tactical-life.com/online/guns-and-weapons/urban-combat-the-petraeus-way/. Mihalek argues that domestic criminality can be understood as being equivalent to a domestic insurgency.

13 Hugh Gusterson, *People of the Bomb: Portraits of America's Nuclear Complex* (Minneapolis: University of Minnesota Press, 2004), xxi.

14 The Foucauldian term *dispositif*, akin to Deleuze's concept of assemblage and usually translated as "apparatus," signifies the array of discourses and practices that constitute how a population is governed. Foucault, himself describes it as "a set of strategies of the relations of forces supporting and supported by, certain types of knowledge." Michel Foucault, *Power/Knowledge: Selected Interviews and Other Writings, 1972–1977* (New York: Pantheon Books, 1980), 196.

15 Frederick Cooper and Ann Laura Stoler, *Tensions of Empire: Colonial Cultures in a Bourgeois World* (Berkeley: University of California Press, 1997).

16 On this point see especially Arjun Appadurai, *Modernity at Large: Cultural Dimensions of Globalization* (Oxford: Oxford University Press, 1997); John Malloy Owen, *The Clash of Ideas in World Politics: Transnational Networks, States, and Regime Change, 1510–2010* (Princeton, NJ: Princeton University Press, 2010);

Sanjeev Khagram, James V. Riker, and Kathryn Sikkink, eds., *Restructuring World Politics: Transnational Social Movements, Networks, and Norms* (Minneapolis: University of Minnesota Press, 2002). Emblematic of this globalized worldview and the connection with empire and imperialism is Michael Hardt and Antonio Negri's classic work *Empire*, which traces what they see as a new form of imperialism beyond the traditional confines of the nation-state. See especially Michael Hardt and Antonio Negri, *Empire* (Cambridge, MA: Harvard University Press, 2000).

17 Tarak Barkawi and Mark Laffey, "Retrieving the Imperial: Empire and International Relations," *Millennium: A Journal of International Studies* 31, no. 1 (2002).

18 G. John Ikenberry, *Liberal Leviathan: The Origins, Crisis, and the Transformation of the American World Order* (Princeton, NJ: Princeton University Press, 2011); David A. Lake, *Hierarchy in International Relations* (Ithaca, NY: Cornell University Press, 2009); Alexander Cooley, *Logics of Hierarchy: The Organization of Empires, States and Military Occupations* (Ithaca, NY: Cornell University Press, 2005); Alexander Wendt and Daniel Friedheim, "Hierarchy under Anarchy: Informal Empire and the East German State," *International Organization* 49, no. 04 (1995).

19 Lake, *Hierarchy in International Relations*, 9.

20 As Foucault argues,

> [T]he state does not have an essence. The state is not a universal nor in itself an autonomous source of power. The state is nothing else but the effect, the profile, the mobile shape of a perpetual statification (étatisation) or stratifications, in the sense of incessant transactions which modify, or move, or drastically change, or insidiously shift sources of finance, modes of investment, decision-making centers, forms and types of control, relationships between local powers, the central authority, and so on.
>
> (Michel Foucault, *The Birth of Biopolitics*, ed. Michel Senellart
> [New York: Palgrave, 2008], 77)

21 There is an increasing literature on global governmentality, of which some key texts are Hans-Martin Jaeger, "UN Reform, Biopolitics, and Global Governmentality," *International Theory* 2, no. 1 (2010); Wendy Larner and William Walters, eds, *Global Governmentality: Governing International Spaces* (New York: Routledge, 2004); Ronnie D. Lipschutz, "Global Civil Society and Global Governmentality: Or, the Search for Politics and the State Amidst the Capillaries of Social Power," in *Power in Global Governance*, eds Michael Barnett and Raymond Duvall (Cambridge: Cambridge University Press, 2005). However, few studies develop the concept within an international hierarchical context.

22 Gary Wilder, *The French Imperial Nation-State: Négritude and Colonial Humanism Between the Two World Wars* (Chicago. IL: University of Chicago Press, 2005), 8.

23 Ibid., 9. Thus Wilder aptly continues:

> the often extreme economic exploitation, social violence, racial hierarchies, and authoritarian politics endemic to colonialism were neither pre-colonial survivals nor symptoms of European regression. They were effects of modern capitalism, rational bureaucracy, scientific administration, normalizing state practices, technological development, urbanization, and the like ... Such an optic ... enables a multifaceted and global (in both senses of the term) view of modernity, not as one composed of plural alternative modernities but as a worldwide if heterogeneous dynamic that works through and on Western societies but is neither possessed nor controlled by them.

24 Barry Buzan and George Lawson, "The Global Transformation: The Nineteenth Century and the Making of Modern International Relations," *International Studies Quarterly* 57, no. 3 (2013), 622.
25 Mary Louise Pratt, *Imperial Eyes: Travel Writing and Transculturation* (New York: Routledge, [1992] 2008); Ann Laura Stoler and Frederick Cooper, "Between Metropole and Colony: Rethinking a Research Agenda," in *Tensions of Empire: Colonial Cultures in a Bourgeois World*, eds Frederick Cooper and Ann Laura Stoler (Berkeley: University of California Press, 1997); David Spurr, *The Rhetoric of Empire: Colonial Discourse in Journalism, Travel Writing, and Imperial Administration* (Raleigh, NC: Duke University Press, 1993); Helen Tilley, *Africa as a Living Laboratory: Empire, Development, and the Problem of Scientific Knowledge, 1870–1950* (Chicago, IL: University of Chicago Press, 2011); Alan Lester, *Imperial Networks: Creating Identities in Nineteenth-Century South Africa and Britain* (London: Routledge, 2001); Kerry Ward, *Networks of Empire: Forced Migration in the Dutch East India Company* (Cambridge: Cambridge University Press, 2009).
26 Mary Louise Pratt defines "contact zone" as that which refers to "the space of imperial encounters, the space in which peoples geographically and historically separated come into contact with each other and establish ongoing relations usually involving conditions of coercion, radical inequality, and intractable conflict." Pratt, *Imperial Eyes: Travel Writing and Transculturation*, 8.
27 Ann Laura Stoler and Frederick Cooper, "Between Metropole and Colony: Rethinking a Research Agenda," 6.
28 To quote the British prime minister Herbert Henry Asquith in 1896: "We look at our colonies and we find in them ... a laboratory in which political and social experiments are every day being made for the information and instruction of the older countries of the world." Quoted in Chandak Sengoopta, "'The Colonial Laboratory': Re-Examining the Metaphor" (unpublished work, London: Birkbeck College, University of London, 2009).
29 Cited in Robert Home, *Of Planting and Planning: The Making of British Colonial Cities* (New York: Routledge, 2013), 7.
30 J. H. Elliot, "How They Made the Empire," *New York Review of Books*, August 18, 2011.
31 Michael W. Doyle, *Empires* (Ithaca, NY: Cornell University Press, 1986), 12.
32 Lake, *Hierarchy in International Relations*, 57.
33 Ibid., 13; Ikenberry, *Liberal Leviathan: The Origins, Crisis, and the Transformation of the American World Order*, 60.
34 See especially Juan Gabriel Valdés, *Pinochet's Economists: The Chicago School in Chile* (Cambridge: Cambridge University Press, 1995), Ch. 2.
35 Jack Snyder contrasts hegemony with empire in terms of the level and scope of control by one state over others. As he writes, "Hegemony, in contrast [to empire], pertains only to the control of the most general pattern of external relations among states." Hegemony, here, appears as the ability to define, implement and enforce international rules that bind states together asymmetrically. Jack Snyder, "Myths of Empires and Strategies of Hegemony," in *Lessons of Empire: Imperial Histories and American Power*, eds Craig Calhoun, Frederick Cooper and Kevin W. Moore (New York: The New Press, 2006).
36 Ikenberry, *Liberal Leviathan: The Origins, Crisis, and the Transformation of the American World Order*, 27.
37 See especially Turan Kayaoglu, "Westphalian Eurocentrism in International Relations Theory," *International Studies Review* 12, no. 2 (2010), 194; emphasis in the original.
38 Tarak Barkawi and Mark Laffey, "The Postcolonial Moment in Security Studies," *Review of International Studies* 32, no. 2 (2006), 342.

39 John J. Mearsheimer, "Imperial by Design," in *The National Interest* (Jan–Feb 2011).
40 "From every point of view, the [Imperial] 'plantation', the 'factory' and the 'colony' were the principal laboratories in which experiments were conducted into the authoritarian destiny of the world that we see today." Quoted in Nathalie Lempereur, Jean-Louis Schlegel and Olivier Mongin, "What Is Postcolonial Thinking? An Interview with Achille Mbembé" (*Eurozine*, [Quoted June 7, 2006]); available from www.eurozine.com/articles/2008-01-09-mbembe-en.html.
41 Paul Kennedy, *The Rise and Fall of the Great Powers* (New York: Vintage Books, 1989 [1987]), 515; By which Kennedy defines as the "sum total of the United States' global interests and obligations is nowadays far larger than the country's power to defend them all simultaneously."
42 Michael Beckley, "China's Century? Why America's Edge Will Endure," *International Security* 36, no. 3 (2011/12), 46–48.
43 Here I use the term republican in its conceptual sense, as a body of theory and tradition on the role of the state in civic life, as a way of living which privileged a certain conception of political and individual freedom. See especially J. G. A. Pocock, *The Machiavellian Moment: Florentine Political Thought and the Atlantic Republican Tradition* (Princeton, NJ: Princeton University Press, 2003); Nicholas G. Onuf, *The Republican Legacy in International Thought* (Cambridge: Cambridge University Press, 1998). Also Daniel Deudney's work on republican security theory is concerned that international competition will inevitably impact domestic American institutions in a way that will undermine individual liberty. Daniel H. Deudney, *Bounding Power: Republican Security Theory from the Polis to the Global Village* (Princeton, NJ: Princeton University Press, 2008). Indeed, as Deudney writes in the preface:

> Many of the friends of freedom in America congratulate themselves on their role as the indispensable nation and agent chosen by History and Providence to spread political freedom in the world. But few seem much troubled by the massive globe-spanning American national security state and its implications for limited constitutional government, political liberty, and global security.
>
> (xiii)

44 Hannah Arendt, *The Origins of Totalitarianism* (New York: Harcourt, 1994), see Ch. 5.

1 International relations theory
Hierarchy and the problem of empire

Introduction

Historical patterns of international hierarchy reveal a multi-directional diffusion of norms, practices and technologies of governance. However, this multi-directional diffusion remains largely unexamined by international theorists because of two main reasons that I explore throughout this chapter: first, the fact that canonical international theory is largely predicated upon an assumption of international anarchy. International anarchy is construed as a timeless feature of international politics, which also implies an ahistorical representation of the state. Second, this multi-directional diffusion of norms remains unexamined because of a continuing Eurocentrism that sees the West as a privileged historical actor. This implies that Western norms travel outbound rather than being the product of interactions with the non-West. It also implies that the reverse flow of norms and practices from imperial and/or hegemonic relations remain hidden. Socialization, when it is theorized in international theory, is conceived as the socialization of the non-West into an already constituted European society of states. What these perspectives imply is in general a lack of importance attached to historical global patterns of imperialism. International theorists have largely ignored histories of domination that have resulted in a set of imperial know-how, practices, cultures and norms – what some have called a "colonial archive" – that has left significant traces upon the historical trajectory of Western state-formation up to the present.[1]

The ultimate goal of this chapter is then to set the theoretical background for the subsequent empirical chapters that detail how the materialization of the camp, surveillance and neoliberalism are fundamentally imbricated in transnational imperial or hegemonic circuits. My concern is first to show why international theory currently lacks the conceptual tools to examine these transnational (as opposed to inter-national, between nations) hierarchical relations that result in novel institutions and apparatuses in the West. Second, I will discuss why and how we can see the imperial domain as a central "space of experience" or a laboratory of political, social, cultural, and economic experimentation that then becomes adapted for implementation within metropolitan domains. Rather than seeing the state as an ahistorical maximizer of security because of the requirements of international anarchy, imperial zones of exploitation and experimentation have left important traces upon metropolitan state development. It is here that I believe that Bruno Latour provides us with an intriguing way of thinking about the role of the laboratory more generally. Though Latour had in mind the scientific laboratory, I believe his sociology of the laboratory holds just as well for the imperial laboratory. For Latour, the translation of scientific facts or discoveries from the laboratory occurs because of the establishment of networks or relays outside the laboratory that make such facts visible and intelligible. In other words, of primary importance is the building of institutions and norms that essentially extends the laboratory into the social world. In an analogous way, the "tools of empire" become legitimated over time as the way of managing subject populations and become extended in response to problems in the metropole.

International hierarchy revisited

The concept of international anarchy has long been the foundational concept for the discipline of international relations. Often understood as the lack of a global mechanism to adjudicate international disputes between nation-states, anarchy implies systemic properties that are distinct from the domestic "hierarchical" level. Whereas the domestic level is governed by a state apparatus that is functionally differentiated (i.e. institutions such as the executive, legislative or judiciary serve different functions) at the international level, according to neorealists in particular, all states must maintain certain capacities of defense and security, making them "like-units".[2] Anarchy implies a system of self-help; it implies the predominance of the pursuit of national interests and, for political realists at least, signifies the realm of a Hobbesian state of nature that demands constant vigilance. Whereas the domestic level implies relations of authority and legitimacy, anarchy implies a lack of those two attributes, rendering international difference a matter of material capability. More importantly, for Kenneth Waltz, investigating the system in which international relations takes place necessitates a level of abstraction removed from the historical specificities of how such units themselves came into being:

> Definitions of structure must leave aside, or abstract from, the characteristics of units, their behavior, and their interactions. Why must those obviously important matters be omitted? They must be omitted so that we can distinguish between variables at the level of the units and variables at the level of the system.[3]

As many have shown, Waltz's theory of international political is itself unable to explain changes in either the structure or system of the international itself, and that it operates by assuming that states are in essence black boxes.[4] Waltz's theory of international politics works by establishing "scientific" generalizations that rest upon unproblematized historical continuities papered over through deductive rationalizations.[5] It is not surprising then that Waltz confidently asserts that "The enduring anarchic character of international politics accounts for the striking sameness in the quality of international life through the millennia, a statement that will meet with wide assent."[6] Indeed not much happens in Waltz's structural realism: there is no norm diffusion, no changes in the constitution of the units, no changes in the system of international relations (only through a switch to global hierarchy would the system change). Only the continuous billiard-ball-like balancing coalitions of great powers, the structural changes in polarity and the occasional great power war appear to mark the flow of its immanent cyclical time.

The lack of concern with historical change, by neorealists in particular, translates into a lack of theorization and historical understanding of state-formation more generally. The state is typically spatially conceived through its Weberian capacity to wield ultimate authority in a designated territory – its intrinsically hierarchical constitution. This representation of two distinct spaces, the orderly/hierarchical inside versus the disorderly/anarchic and hence insecure outside, is often assumed to be the immanent product of a specifically Westphalian (European) narrative (more on this below).[7] This ontological starting point, however, gives primary importance to international theory's methodological need to delineate various "levels of analysis" for coherent theorization to occur.[8] However, defining these levels of analysis often presupposes a certain ability to compartmentalize interactions between levels and implies, for international theory, an essential need to temporally bracket changes in the state apparatus.[9] As R. B. J. Walker argues, the "discourse of eternity" that characterizes much of political realism's vision of the unitary state is rooted in a set of specifically modern questions of particularity versus universality and self versus other, along with specifically modern understandings of space and time. By removing the question of temporality and historicity from theorizing international politics, political realism narrates the:

> conventional story [of the state] as a formal and almost lifeless category, when in fact states are constantly maintained, defended, attacked, reproduced, undermined, and relegitimized on a daily basis ... Again, appeals to state sovereignty serve to maintain the high ground of timelessness (epistème, eternity) against the flux (doxa) of time, and to confirm the existence of the state as something "out there" separate from the ordinary experience of people's lives.[10]

The strict differentiation between anarchy and hierarchy and the timeless representation of the state coexists uneasily with the historical instances of empire-building and the practice of imperialism. Waltz, for example, spends the entirety of Chapter 2 of his magnum opus, *Theory of International Politics*, arguing that theories of imperialism cannot explain the prevalence of war between states – what he sees as the main justification for the discipline of international relations to begin with. In particular, theories of imperialism espoused by early twentieth-century writers such as John Hobson and Vladimir Lenin, along with more recent neocolonial/neomarxist variants, such as Johann Galtung's, are mistaken in that they confuse specific unit-level attributes over structural conditions for the reasons why states engage in unequal exchange and dominion.[11] "Imperialism," for Waltz, "is at least as old as recorded history ... Historically, imperialism is a common phenomenon."[12] It cannot be reduced to a particular domestic configuration such as capitalistic overproduction as it appears to be a transhistorical condition. Nonetheless, Waltz assumes that the genesis of imperialism is also a function of unit-level organization: "Where one finds empires, one notices that they are built by those who have organized themselves and exploited their resources most effectively."[13] Thus Waltz sees imperialism as a combination between unit-level factors and a structural setting, where a lack of balance between states prompts imperial domination of those that are materially weak.[14] However, the point here is that in order to understand the supposedly timeless phenomena of imperialism we need to understand the historical background of how states that came to engage in imperialism organized themselves over time. In other words, we need a theory of the state which Waltz argues is unnecessary for understanding international political outcomes – much as in economic theory we do not need to have a theory of the firm if we are to understand the market. By contrast, for Jane Burbank and Fredrick Cooper, "To the extent that states became more powerful in England and France [for example] in the late seventeenth and eighteenth centuries, *these transformations were a consequence of empire rather than the other way around.*"[15] Missing in Waltz's paradigm is any sense of how the practice of imperialism feeds back into the very constitution and evolution of the imperial state. To put it differently, the crucial tension in Waltz's discussion of imperialism is the manner in which the domestic space becomes imbricated with the international space in such a way that it calls into question Waltz's attempt at creating a systemic theory of international politics abstracted from unit-level characteristics.[16]

International theory's canonical representation of the inherent precariousness of international life, the timelessness of anarchy, the relegation of state-formation to domestic factors and the general lack of a conceptualization of the social malleability and complexity of the international system has been contested from a variety of different perspectives. Liberal international theorists have for some time now argued for the importance of complex economic interdependence.[17] Social constructivists of a variety of ontological and epistemological perspectives have argued for a much deeper and richer ontological view of the social relations between states. Questions surrounding the role of institutions, cultures, norms, knowledge, rules or practices have guided theorists towards an image of the international system as more than the undoubtedly misleading Hobbesian representation of the fictional state of nature. Such schools of thought also open up a need to reinvestigate the historical moments of state-formation as a function of evolving international conditions and the practices of states.[18] In other words, the question of how the modern state came into being cannot be reduced to just internal developments, but must be situated within international historical narratives that illuminate the heterogeneous "systems [that] have been the norm in western civilization."[19] And, indeed, such heterogeneous systems were largely characterized by transnational hierarchical relations of authority and rule that do not fit into this ontological conceptualization of international anarchy as being ubiquitous over time.

Rationalist scholars have recently turned to the question of hierarchy as a way of rethinking issues of authority and legitimacy in a world dominated by American power. David Lake, for example, sees state subordination as being a common feature of international life. He also argues that international hierarchy cannot be simply reduced to the differences of material capabilities, as implied in structural realist formulations, but rather involves relations of authority and legitimacy that bind states in asymmetric ways.[20] Along these lines John Ikenberry claims that the American hegemonic liberal order was inherently hierarchical, beneficial and therefore legitimate for a vast array of subordinate states.[21] Lake and Ikenberry, who have engaged in the most important discussion of international hierarchy in recent years, argue that hierarchy is generated when a dominant power establishes a political order providing a set of public goods beneficial to the wider members of that order.[22] Legitimacy emerges out of this political order when other members acknowledge the authority of the dominant power to "restrict their behavior and extract resources necessary to produce that order."[23] Gradations of sovereignty pervade an international political order in which weaker states bind themselves to stronger states in order to benefit through an increase in their security. "Hegemonic support for an order based on rules and institutions," Ikenberry argues, "signals restraint and commitment – and this makes the order more normatively acceptable."[24] Which rules and institutions make up this political order shifts according to historical periods. Lake understands hierarchy as a variation in the exercise of authority of one state over another. The main issue with respect to hierarchy resides in the restraints imposed on the dominant state in order to limit the potential abuse in the relationship. For Lake, this feature of restraint is inherent in the anti-colonial American history and self-perception: "the United States has effectively used its own anticolonial stance to signal its limited ambition to govern other countries." And as Lake adds, "Norms of human equality and principles of juridical sovereignty may serve to limit the extent of hierarchy, but these same factors may have the effect of making more limited forms even more attractive than in the past."[25] But Lake and Ikenberry are clear that they privilege a specific "consent"-driven post-Second World War American international liberal order that establishes informal relations of authority between the United States and other states.

Be that as it may, both Lake and Ikenberry also turn their attention to the question of imperial rule as a form of international hierarchy. For Lake, empire represents a combination of "security and economic hierarchies" which enables a set of formal (direct) or informal (indirect) relations between two polities.[26] These hierarchies vary in intensity and commitment. Nevertheless, at the heart of these relations lies an exercise of political authority that has some semblance of legitimacy and cannot simply be described as pure domination. For Ikenberry empire signifies "a hierarchical order in which a powerful state engages in organized rule over several dispersed weaker and secondary polities."[27] Like Lake, Ikenberry distinguishes between formal and informal rule. Though he adds that, such an imperial "hierarchy is established and control exercised through various sorts of center-periphery elite networks and relationships."[28] Despite this, both Lake and Ikenberry's formulations still overlook the reverse impacts of imperial (and for that matter non-imperial) relations of hierarchy upon the dominant state. As Ikenberry admits, "The peripheral polities are all connected to the core but disconnected from each other. All roads lead to and from Rome."[29] He does not follow up on the implication that imperial hierarchy creates circuits for the distribution of material resources and potentially ideational forms "to and from." Acknowledging elite networks and relationships as Ikenberry does at least implies the transmission of ideas, norms, practices, cultures or knowledge across imperial networks. That itself implies a process of learning and evolution of imperial rule over time. And importantly, it implies the potential reverberating impact of imperial knowledge into the core and influencing the historical trajectory of the Western state and its domestic sphere. Neither Lake nor Ikenberry explore this possibility.

Critical international theorists, in contrast to rationalists, have been concerned with exposing patterns of hierarchy and hegemony in relations between states and in unequal relations between states and peoples.[30] A prominent feature of critical theoretical attention has been on unequal exchange between the North and global South and how gender hierarchies in theory and practice continue to abound.[31] More recently, postcolonial scholars are turning to race and race-thinking to show their importance for the formation of the discipline of IR.[32] As Robert Vitalis argues, many ideas emanating from early twentieth-century American political science emerged out of a context in which American imperial management in the aftermath of the Spanish–American war proved enormously important. In such a context, Vitalis shows:

> The white social scientists that offered their expertise to the new imperial state, and the handful of critics of the new expansionist wave, all assumed the following: hierarchy was natural, it was biologically rooted, and it could be made sense of best by such concepts as higher and lower races, natural and historic races, savagery and civilization, and the like.[33]

For Vitalis, hierarchy was not simply an observation of how international relations appeared to operate; international hierarchy was also legitimized by a discourse of racial typologies that was deemed by political scientists at the time even more important than nation-state geopolitical interests.[34] Likewise, a recent special issue of the *Cambridge Review of International Studies* on race and IR echoes Vitalis' argument about the nexus between the practice and theory of international racial hierarchy. For Duncan Bell, "International relations was thus a policy science dedicated, in part, to helping 'solve' problems of imperial domination and colonial governance."[35] Though this explicit discourse of race and racial struggle begins to fade, especially in the aftermath of the Second World War, it is never entirely removed from either the practice of international politics or its disciplinary study. As Robbie Shilliam explains:

> IR disavows its intellectual debts accrued from the colonial study of "primitive" political systems; furthermore, the racial differences cultivated by slavery and colonialism are demonstrated to be central to the very formation of modern social and political thought; in the twentieth and twenty-first centuries, principles of racial difference still inform debates on democratization and good governance, likewise the meaning of self-determination and citizenship, so too the attempts by imperial rivals to legalize military intervention; indeed, because our semantic universes are so deeply racialized, race remains a – perhaps the – global idea of our age.[36]

The reification of racial difference and its privileging of a specific Euro-American historical and contemporary vantage point is thus never entirely exuviated even with the formal decolonizations of the twentieth century. This Eurocentric perception, as Meera Sabaratnam argues, that "IR is constructed around the exclusionary premise of an imagined *Western subject* of world politics" remains deeply embedded in an emergent post-Second World War American discipline.[37] It structures a large body of knowledge according to the idea that "something special was indeed done by Europe in the sixteenth to the eighteenth centuries that did transform the world."[38] This very assumption is what needs to be contested in order to observe the myriad historical hybridities and patterns of diffusion.

Eurocentrism in international theory

In 1959 Stanley Hoffmann penned an essay in the journal *World Politics* entitled "International Relations: The Long Road to Theory" in which he cast doubt on the trajectory of the discipline. On the one hand, Hoffmann argues, political realism à la Hans Morgenthau fails to theorize the changing contours of international systems because "it sees the world as a static field in which power relations reproduce themselves in timeless monotony."[39] Hoffmann criticizes Morgenthau's central departing point that individuals are intrinsically and ahistorically motivated by a lust for power. At the same time,

Hoffmann claims that political realism actively reflects a "highly embellished ideal-type of eighteenth and nineteenth-century international relations."[40] The problem of idealizing a specific historical epoch is that it evidently leads to a series of distortions whereby:

> from the point of view of systemic empirical analysis, the theory [of political realism] stresses the autonomy of international relations to the point of leaving beyond its pale the forces which work for change and which, cutting across the states, affect the states' behavior.[41]

On the other hand, Hoffmann argues that the rise of systems theory, exemplified in the work of Morton Kaplan, leads to a kind of disciplinary dilettantism. First, systems theory takes concepts and methods from the physical sciences without adequately understanding whether such concepts or methods are adequate to the study of international relations. Second, the attempt to find regular patterns of behavior reifies the specific properties of the system: "The only processes discussed are processes of maintenance, integration, and disintegration; for the implied supreme value is stability: mechanical stability, since purpose and values other than preservation of the system are left out."[42] Kaplan's systems theory "involves a neglect of the domestic determinants of the national actors, and ... leaves out the forces of change operating within or across actors."[43]

Hoffmann explicitly critiques what underpins much of international theory: its over-reliance on a particular European historical experience. There is a tendency, as Hoffmann argues, to represent eighteenth- and nineteenth-century inter-state European politics as the highpoint of rational international relations and the universal starting point to explain and understand contemporary global politics. State practices such as colonialism, colonial warfare or more generally imperial governance as practiced in the nineteenth century were not deemed to seriously impact state actions within Europe.[44] As J. Marshall Beier puts it, "Owing to the subsumption of the colonies into various European empires, their external relations were not understood to be international."[45] Beier avers that the invisibility of colonized populations in the discipline of international relations is a function of the "hegemonic accounts of the possibilities for political order, in respect of which the state is treated as monopolistic."[46] Furthermore, given the important impact that Thomas Hobbes' fictitious state of nature plays in creating the dividing line between anarchy and hierarchy for political realism, Beier is correct in seeing that such an ontological commitment "does not lend itself well to unequal relations between states," as I noted above.[47]

The assumption that European history is universal history remains pervasive in international theory. Samir Amin defines Eurocentrism as a "culturalist phenomenon" that claims universality and that "imitation of the Western model by all peoples is the only solution to the challenges of our time."[48] Eurocentrism is, Amin continues, a "specifically modern phenomenon," one that "did not flourish until the nineteenth century."[49] Indeed, it is in the nineteenth century that imperialism and colonialism reached its apogee, necessitating a means of self-justifying Western dominion over major parts of the world. This language of self-justification was centered around defining Europe as the natural and progressive civilizational force above all others.[50] It rested on the crafting of world historical narratives that demonstrate the immanent emergence of Europe as wholly the product of internal factors, what usually becomes known as the "European miracle." Thus, as Gurminder K. Bhambra argues, "Eurocentrism is the belief, implicit or otherwise, in the world historical significance of events believed to have developed endogenously with the cultural-geographical sphere of Europe."[51] Eurocentrism then operates by, on the one hand, defining a specific canon or tradition of European political thought as making universal claims of validity. Thus the canonical texts of international theory span from the ancient Greeks (Thucydides) through Machiavelli and Hobbes to more modern European political thinkers in an almost continuous line. To be sure, the claim here of Eurocentrism is not simply that the main thinkers are European – if we assume, for example, that the ancient Greeks were European in the modern sense; rather, it is that readings of this canon reflect an inherent presupposition that the European political experience that such thinkers engage is genuinely universal. The second way in which Eurocentrism works – via the "European miracle" – is explained by James Blaut:

> It is the idea that Europe was more advanced and more progressive than all other regions prior to 1492, prior, that is, to the beginning of the period of colonialism, the period in which Europe and non-Europe came into intense interaction. If one believes this to be the case ... then it must follow that the economic and social modernization of Europe is fundamentally the result of Europe's internal qualities, not of interactions with the societies of Africa, Asia, and America after 1492. Therefore: the main building-blocks of modernity must be European. Therefore: colonialism cannot have been really important for Europe's modernization. Therefore: colonialism must mean for the Africans, Asians and Americans, not spoliation and cultural destruction but, rather, the receipt-by-difference of European civilization: modernization.[52]

Anibal Quijano explains that Eurocentric discourses of exceptionalism:

> [are as well] based on two principle founding myths: first the idea of the history of human civilization as a trajectory that departed from a state of nature and culminated in Europe; second, a view of the differences between Europe and non-Europe as natural (racial) differences and not consequences of a history of power.[53]

It follows for Quijano that contemporary discourses of modernization are fundamentally discourses of the *Europeanization* of non-European populations. Eurocentrism provides a discursive means to rationalize relations of power at the heart of histories of colonial or hegemonic forms of domination. The concept of "coloniality of power" that Quijano develops refers to this very matrix or an ensemble of dominating forces that restructures all aspects of social relations including economic activities, sexuality, identity, and knowledge according to such Eurocentric discourses. The coloniality of power acts especially by closing off Europe or the West from the events and experiences gained through the interactions with the non-West and thereby limiting the need to uncover relations of hybridity that cut across both.

By unconsciously adhering to a self-evident naturalness and universality of the European historical experience, Eurocentric world histories percolate in various academic disciplines. When it comes to Eurocentrism in international theory, Amitav Archarya and Barry Buzan echo Hoffmann's own critique that classical and, by implication, structural, realism "project onto the rest of world history their basic Europe-derived story of international anarchy and balance of power politics as a permanent, universal structural condition."[54] With respect to liberalism and neoliberalism a similar Eurocentric focus is also evident, but with a different notion of temporality. Acharya and Buzan argue that whereas realism extrapolates a structural present condition of power politics from a specific European past, "liberalism reflects a forward-looking one" in order to "improve on past practice and move humankind towards a more peaceful, prosperous and just future."[55] "Justification for this frankly imperial perspective," they add, "is found in the great relative success of the West (in terms of power and prosperity and justice) compared with the rest of the world during the past two centuries."[56] Liberalism abstracts out the historical trajectory of Europe or the West by implicitly claiming its success as the culmination of internal self-organization and by implication constructing the possibilities of universal emancipation in traditional societies.[57]

An important consequence of Eurocentric discourse is that it explicitly creates a hierarchical representation of the world that impacts how international theory conceives of norm diffusion. Norm diffusion may not simply emerge as a result of the legitimate and consensual acceptance of states to bind themselves together and adopt such norms; norm diffusion may also emerge out of transnational relations of imperialism or hegemony reflecting real histories of domination and coercion. The relationship between Europe and its "outside," non-European/non-Western "other," as Turan Kayaoglu explains, is one in which:

> Western states *produce* norms, principles, and institutions of international society and non-Western states *lack* these until they are socialized into the norms, principles, and institutions of international society. In this perspective, international society is a normative hierarchy assumed to reflect the natural division of labor in international relations.[58]

This model of socialization is particularly prevalent in English School and various social constructivist theories. For English School theorists, what constitutes a society of states (as opposed to simply a system of states) is a "set of common rules, institutions, codes of conduct and values which some or all of such states agree to be bound by."[59] Rather than seeing the emergence of the balance of power, for example as neorealists do, as the product of rational interactions given the structural condition of anarchy, the English School theorists ascribe a balance of power to the persistence of common ideas and traditions that render state practices predictable. Of course, the origin of this set of common rules, institutions and codes of conduct and values is decidedly rooted in a specifically European culture.[60] This European culture emerges from the twin historical legacy of Christendom and the Enlightenment; in brief it emerges from a specific European civilization.[61] Kayaoglu argues as well that Hedley Bull's discussion of the evolution of European international society is predicated upon an historical reconstruction of the Westphalian myth of 1648 by German jurists of the nineteenth century.[62] In this historical reconstruction Westphalia engendered novel norms of non-interference between sovereigns and neutralized religious conflict from inter-European state relations.[63] As a result, the Westphalian treaty, Bull argues, allowed for a "a kind of constitutional foundation of international society" that becomes central for its subsequent enlargement in the aftermath of decolonization.[64]

The implication of the English School's Eurocentrism is that the expansion of international society rests upon the socialization of non-Europeans into the European social model. Watson and Bull are aware that this initially occurred through European imperial and colonial domination.[65] Insofar as Bull originally believed that only by spreading European values and cultural practices throughout the world can there emerge a truly just international society, there appears a certain slippage between imperialism and contemporary enlargement of international society.[66] Bull's concern is ultimately how to generate a kind of international society that bound European states in the aftermath of decolonization when there were few – according to him – social and cultural ties between the West and the rest. More recently, even Barry Buzan associates an almost seamless transition between imperialism and the expansion of international society when he argues that:

> [I]nternational society has to provide the layers of governance that weak states cannot yet provide for themselves. In a sense, it has to take over from imperialism as the next phase of the transition to modernism (and its derivatives and successors) that all parts of the world except the West still have to go through not necessarily in the same stages, but somehow having to get to a similar end result, compatible with their cultures.[67]

Buzan's caveat of "compatible with their cultures" remains unclear; moreover, he himself admits that much of the English School's historiography remains "too Eurocentric in its assumptions."[68] Nonetheless, what I want to stress is this slippage when it comes to understanding the global diffusion of norms, rules, institutions, and ultimately culture, as being necessarily derived from a

particular European starting point and expanding outwards. While the English School theorists necessarily admit the prevalence of imperial and colonial
practices as part of the story of the enlargement of international society, there
is no attempt to understand the potential for how imperialism might have
played a role in generating European states and society. European society,
whether of particular states such as Britain or France, or the wider European
order of states, appear to be cordoned off from the outside only insofar as norms
and culture (and obviously overt forms of domination) emanate outwards
from it. Even criticism of English School approaches falls into the trap of
reifying both the European society of states and the exterior non-European/
non-Western space. Edward Keene, for example, largely sees the two spheres
as unrelated, both embodying different practices and configurations.[69]
Though Keene rightly draws attention to the inherent Eurocentrism of English
School representations of international society his account leaves out the
crucial element that, as Kayaoglu argues:

> European self-identification depended on various European other identi-
> fications; the assertion of the complete superiority and exceptionalism of
> the European political and legal order has necessitated the European
> willingness to spread it, even if the process of civilizing non-European
> societies frequently requires some evil.[70]

In other words, European self-identification as a distinct yet universal "standard of civilization" is predicated upon its ability to define and subject the
non-European "Other." To the extent that this is the case, William Callahan
is correct in drawing our attention to what is a central research question
emanating from English School approaches:

> we need to examine how the two world orders [that of Europe and its
> outside under imperialism] are intimately connected and complementary:
> the European self depended on the colonial Other. If this is the case,
> *supplementing* the English School is not enough. A more thorough
> critique is necessary.[71]

In his seminal *Social Theory of International Politics*, Alexander Wendt, in
particular, pluralized how international structures should be conceived by
defining three distinct European ideal-types, what he calls cultures: Hobbesian,
Lockean and Kantian.[72] Wendt defines culture as "socially shared knowledge," that is "knowledge that is both common and connected between individuals." "Culture," Wendt continues, "takes on many specific forms, including
norms, rules, institutions, ideologies, organizations, threat-systems, and so
on ... " Moreover, Wendt adds, "culture is not a sector or sphere distinct from
economy or polity, but present whenever shared knowledge is found."[73]
Wendt places significant emphasis on dyadic relations between self and other
which produces and reproduces shared knowledge that is not reducible to the

structural identities of each. This approach has the benefit of reconfiguring state identity from a specific given identity to one in which understanding of the other conditions behavior. Thus Wendt asserts that the Hobbesian culture cannot then be simply defined by a material condition of anarchy that ensures a rational state identity (i.e. as security maximizers); rather, what fundamentally guides state identity and subsequently the configuration of the international system is a representation of the enemy other.[74] Wendt assumes that pre-Westphalian international culture was decidedly Hobbesian.[75] By contrast, the "Westphalian states system … [is] clearly not Hobbesian" since it has internally managed to inculcate within the actors involved a measure of self-restraint that allows for the mutual recognition of states.[76] Wendt's spectral definition of anarchy has the merit of making structural (i.e. progressive) change possible as a function of how actors develop a "shared understanding of their condition."[77] This notion of shared understanding or culture is crucial for Wendt in order to demonstrate the inherent possibility of mitigating enmity into rivalry (and ultimately into friendship, the Kantian culture).

There are two points that I want to stress with respect to enunciation of Wendt's framework of "cultures of anarchy." The first concerns the relationship between self and other with respect to the condition of imperialism. Wendt is silent about hierarchical relationships within the framework of cultures of anarchy.[78] And yet he admits the ubiquity of imperialism in history as the English School does. For instance, Wendt claims that "in the seventeenth century European states founded a Lockean culture where conflict was constrained by mutual recognition of sovereignty. This culture eventually became global, albeit in part through a Hobbesian process of colonialism."[79] So, on the one hand, we have the traditional English School narrative of the progressive expansion of international society under conditions of imperial domination and on the other, we have a characterization of the initial act of colonial appropriation as "Hobbesian." This characterization implies no recognition of legitimacy on the part of the colonizer for the colonized. Nor is there any indication in Wendt as to what happens in the aftermath of the initial act of colonization. He does not discuss the relation between self and other, the culture that emerges under the hierarchical condition of imperial domination. Implicit in Wendt's theorization of the dyadic relationship between European self and the colonized other is the unstated assumption that this colonized other lacks the attributes necessary to create a condition of mutual recognition and respect.[80] A second point can be made more generally concerning Wendt's implicit historical reconstruction of cultural change. Katalin Sárváry argues that "[Wendt] projects our modern, Eurocentric view of the 'universe' into the past" in the form of reifying a European state.[81] This state is the political organization that is capable of entering into the Lockean or Kantian cultures of anarchy that Wendt sees as essentially historically progressive.[82] If Wendt does project this view of the universe into the past, cultural change is predicated upon a global homogenization of political organization and an important homogenization of state identity emerges from its original Western blueprint.[83] As long as non-Western states are assumed to learn from Western states, there is no room in Wendt's framework for exploring how norms, principles, institutions or values, are diffused multi-directionally.

This last point concerning the essentially unidirectional and progressive diffusion of Western cultural norms is particularly evident in world polity institutionalism approaches to international culture. John Meyer *et al.* set out to determine why the contemporary world is one "whose societies, organized as nation-states, are structurally similar in many unexpected dimensions and change in unexpectedly similar ways."[84] Meyer *et al.* start from the premise that what guides state behavior is not a function of rational or instrumental action, as in neorealist or liberal theories. According to Meyer *et al.* it reflects a universal, modern cultural organization, one that is "not simply built up from local circumstances and history" but reflects an inherently legitimate model of sociopolitical being.[85] The significance of this approach to accounting for state behavior is that it attempts to explain how the homo-genization of nation-states is the result of cultural diffusion by processes of imitation (what they term isomorphism). These processes of imitation are beyond the control of nation-states themselves. That is to say, cultural diffu-sion seeps into the very institutions that make up the nation-state and recon-figures them according to the general proscriptions of world culture. "Social reality," they argue, "is culturally transcendent and causally important" for three reasons: First, nation-states organize themselves according to universal concepts or what they call "models" (i.e. according to "citizenship, socio-economic development and rationalized justice"). Second, the universal acceptance of norms of human rights, scientific research, development and education is unproblematic; and third, the model in question, the Western model embodying all of the above, is universal in scope.[86] Meyer *et al.* ima-gine what they call an island society that becomes part of this world culture by imitating its functionality. Importantly, they add:

> The authority of these general models, legally nonbinding though it may be, goes far in explaining why our hypothetical discovered island society would rapidly adopt "modern" structures and purposes upon incorpora-tion into world society. Alternative models, including whatever traditional structures were in place, have little legitimacy. The correct modern forms are highly developed and articulated, with elaborate rationalized justifi-cations. Particularistic or local models find it difficult to compete with these legitimations.[87]

What world polity institutionalism ultimately argues is that modern rational society at a global level is capable of creating a modern universally legitimate international society by rewiring the domestic institutions of all nation-states. This imitation of bureaucratic forms by different nation-states is not attrib-uted to functional causes: that is to say, the emergence of a specific modern bureaucratic institution cannot simply be attributed to its ability to negotiate the complexities of modern social systems. Bureaucratic homogenization is, as Martha Finnemore explains, rather predicated upon "external cultural legitimation."[88] The natural question is, of course, where does this "modern" world culture originate and why is it considered legitimate on a global scale? Meyer *et al.* are clear on the first point: what is considered the origin of world historical culture is Western Europe, specifically Western Christendom. As they write:

> In this cultural complex, a demystified, lawful, universalistic nature forms the common frame within which social life is embedded, and unitary moral laws and spiritual purposes are clearly differentiated from nature. Spiritual obligations and rights originally devolving from an active and interventionist god are now located in humans and their communities, making individuals the ultimate carriers of responsible purposive action. As legitimated actors having agency for themselves and others, individuals orient their action above all toward the pursuit of rationalized progress.[89]

Western rationality, in the Weberian sense noted in the above passage, of the demystification and universalization of social life, is deemed natural.[90] In addition to demonstrating particularly clearly how the diffusion of Western norms occurs unidirectionally to the non-West, world polity institutionalism completely effaces hierarchical relations of colonial and imperial domination. In effect, world polity approaches depoliticizes the manner in which cultural production occurs. It does so by smoothing out the contradictions that occur in, say justice and equality, that remain in domestic settings let alone in global relations of power. In order to focus on the rational and natural acceptance of a specifically Western modern culture, coercion is entirely absent from their account. Lastly, there is little attention given to cultural diffusion as a function of power.[91]

This discussion of various contemporary IR theories shows how thinking about historical change, cultural and norm diffusion happening at the global level remains within Eurocentric horizons. The various approaches to IR theory mentioned above close off the possibility of mapping transnational norm and cultural diffusions that might originate in imperial zones and return to Europe in intended or unintended ways. They ignore dimensions of state formation contingent upon imperial relations, presenting state formation as an intrinsically self-constituting process. In the next section I argue that the imperial space of experience is much more deeply imbricated or co-constituted with the development of the Western state in ways that remain unaccounted for in international theory.

Planetary modernity: Koselleck and the imperial space of experience

International theory tends to assume a Eurocentric historiography of Western state formation. I take issue with this on the grounds that European modernity is actually a "provincial" component of a constellation of different temporalities and histories that make up planetary history.[92] To elaborate on my position I turn to an important essay by the German conceptual historian Reinhart Koselleck entitled, "'Space of Experience' and 'Horizon of Expectation': Two Historical Concepts."[93] Koselleck is important because he crucially links the moment of planetary colonization beginning in the fifteenth century with the rise of modernity three centuries later.

Koselleck establishes, more generally, a history of modern temporality, showing how time becomes conceived in secular terms over the course of the eighteenth century. Briefly, Christian eschatology conceives of historical time as trending inevitably towards the Last Judgment; modern temporality is open-ended and plural.[94] The significant threshold between Christian eschatology and modernity, for Koselleck, occurred roughly in the early part of the eighteenth century when the term *neue Zeit* (new time) begins to take added significance and over the course of the century, becomes the composite *Neuzeit* (modernity).[95] But according to Koselleck, the crucial feature of modernity and time was the concept of progress as an open-ended possibility. "Progress (*der Fortschritt*)," Koselleck writes:

> a term first employed by Kant, was now a word that neatly and deftly brought the manifold of scientific, technological, and industrial meanings of progress, and finally those meanings involving social morality and even the totality of history, under a common concept.[96]

Progress, as a *"collective singular,"* encapsulated a steady abstraction of the specific historical experience associated originally with technical or scientific advancement that began to refer to the progressive potential of humanity. Nonetheless, a specific chasm opened between what he calls the "space of experience" and the "horizon of expectation." Historical time cannot be taken as an "empty definition, but rather an entity which alters along with history and from whose changing structure it is possible to deduce the shifting classification of experience and expectation."[97] Importantly, Koselleck argues that temporality must be understood and expressed in spatial terms.[98] For Koselleck then the space of experience and the horizon of expectation are two "anthropological givens" that define the conditions of possibility of "real" history.[99] As the space of experience and the horizon of expectation refer to different temporal modalities, the space of experience represents the totality of past recollections, that it has "processed past occurrences, that it can make it present, that it is drenched with reality, and that it binds together fulfilled or missed possibilities with one's own behavior."[100] By contrast, the horizon of expectation is the "future made present; it directs itself to the not-yet, to the nonexperienced, to that which is to be revealed."[101] Koselleck's point, however, is that both these concepts cannot be seen as mirror images of each other, inhabiting different dispositions of time, one towards the recollection of the past to the present and the other of the future returned to the present as expectation. What properly defines modernity and the question of progress then is the perpetual disjunction between both the space of experience and the horizon of expectation:

> My thesis is that during *Neuzeit* the difference between experience and expectation has increasingly expanded; more precisely, that *Neuzeit* is first understood as *neue Zeit* from the time that expectations have distanced themselves evermore from all previous experience.[102]

Here Koselleck contrasts this image of modernity as the progressive difference between experience and expectation with the peasant world inhabiting the cycle of nature. Such a world does not experience the shattering impacts of technological and commercial innovations upon its social organization. Change is conceived as a repetitive cycle of harvests and the designs of nature or God. The very idea that such a medieval world of stasis may appear "restrictive already presupposes the new horizon of expectation of a freer economy."[103]

The chasm between the space of experience and the horizon of expectation that defines modernity and progress has important implications. As Koselleck himself remarks, an important presupposition of the disjunction of past experience from future expectation was a series of technical transformations and discoveries that steadily rendered past experiences anachronistic or incomplete. As Koselleck writes:

> The invention of the printing press; the spread of literacy and reading; the invention of the compass, telescope, and microscope; the development of the experimental sciences; *the discovery of the globe; overseas colonization and the comparison with savages*; the conflict of modern art with the old; the rise of the middle class; the development of capitalism and industry; the unleashing of natural forces through technology – all this belongs to the experience or facts that are always conjured up and tied to the concept of progress and, more than that, to the progression toward something better.[104]

Undoubtedly borrowing from Carl Schmitt, the reference to the discovery of the globe and overseas colonization is key here.[105] For this implied a discovery of plural temporal socio-cultural structures that differentiated the specific European experience and that of non-European peoples. This discovery needed to be fundamentally addressed as a way of legitimizing the Western imperial project: non-European others were deemed to be inhabiting a past (i.e. backward) time period. The "discovery of the globe and its people living at various levels of advancement" crystallized what Koselleck unwieldily calls the "contemporaneity of the noncontemporaneous."[106] That is, the very idea that the encounter with non-European peoples provoked notions of temporal anachronism within a larger constructed universal time and world history:

"The geographical opening up of the globe," Koselleck writes, "brought to light various coexisting cultural levels which were, through the process of synchronous comparison, then ordered diachronically. Looking from civilized Europe to a barbaric America was a glance backward."[107] To put it differently, what modern imperialism hinged on was, as Dipesh Chakrabarty argues, a fundamental historicism in which Europe is continuously placed at the center and origin of modernity and universal progress emanates outward from its own interstices.[108]

However, there is a further important point to be made here. Bliss Cua Lim compellingly shows that the modern notion of universal temporality which sees different peoples or cultures inhabiting anachronistic spaces and times was not confined strictly to the colonial world; it was itself applied to certain sections of European society that were deemed to be anachronistic (see especially Chapter 3). As Lim writes, "The rhetoric of anachronism is consistently employed by proponents of homogeneous time whenever a stubborn heterogeneity is encountered."[109] This heterogeneity can itself be located in the West and was part of a lengthy process of national homogenization, as James Scott has also shown.[110] Or as Michael Perelman argues in *The Invention of Capitalism: Classical Political Economy and the Secret History of Primitive Accumulation*, the transition to a capitalist society in Europe was predicated upon the establishment of a cheap and surplus labor pool that could only occur by forcing (using feudal forms of primitive accumulation) European peasants from their lands.[111] A capitalist society was then predicated upon the development and refinement of continuous methods of eradicating forms of resistance to capital accumulation often experimented and developed in the imperial periphery and later adapted within the West.[112]

The important point, however, is that what Koselleck ultimately accomplishes is to show how a historical colonial and imperial project was constitutive of modernity. Moreover, as Lim argues, Koselleck interestingly echoes Enrique Dussell's thesis locating modernity in a "planetary phenomenon" as the necessary management of the world-historical system beginning with the "discovery" of the Western hemisphere.[113] Dussell conceived of European modernity as not being an "independent, autopoetic, self-referential system, but instead [as] part of a world-system: in fact its center" (but not its origin); rather, modernity, for Dussell is the direct product of an imperial project to "manage" the planet – including the West itself.[114] Modernity, Lim argues following Dussell, "was a specific set of (temporalized and spatialized) management strategies that emerged in the course of Europe's establishing itself as a superhegemonic center to its colonized periphery." But the important point here to stress is that to see modernity as a planetary phenomenon, to "characterize the global nature of this world-historical consciousness," likewise means revealing a set of political, social, economic and cultural flows emanating from the imperial space of experience to the imperial center just as much as the other way around.[115] The imperial space of experience becomes a filter through which planetary modernity, the management of the globe as

Dussell argues, impacts Europe just as much as the periphery – essentially, removing the heterogeneous elements encountered within the West impacting the perpetual drive of progress. To elaborate on the temporal features of this relation between the colonial space of experience and the European space of experience is to conceive of a postcolonial temporality that moves beyond Eurocentric temporal notions of development and progress. As Sandro Mezzadra and Federico Rahola write, "At the very moment when the *dispositifs* of domination, originally forged in the context of the colonial experience, filter into the metropolitan spaces, we find ourselves already, in some way, in a postcolonial time."[116] The question for the next section is to elaborate on this postcolonial temporality as a materialization and normalization of the imperial laboratory.

Bruno Latour and the imperial social laboratories

How are we to understand the relationship between the imperial space of experience and its imperial center? If, as Koselleck argues, modernity is fundamentally coextensive with the planetary project of colonization, how can we understand this interrelationship between imperial metropole and periphery? Alfred McCoy uses the term "imperial mimesis" to describe how practices innovated in the Philippines at the turn of the twentieth century were adapted in the United States and formed the nascent American national security state.[117] Though he never explicitly defines the concept "imperial mimesis" it appears to signify the process by which the metropole over time begins to bear a resemblance to its subordinate periphery. As McCoy writes:

> In this process of imperial mimesis, a state such as the United States that creates a colony with circumscribed civil liberties and pervasive policing soon shows many of those same coercive features in its own society. As the metropole's internal security apparatus starts to resemble the imperial, so its domestic politics begin to exhibit many attributes of the colonial.[118]

It is not exactly clear why we should understand this form of socio-political reverberation and adaptation as a form of mimesis. Mimesis is, for the most part, understood as an aesthetic term used to denote the act of imitating an original work of art (i.e. creating a copy). It can also be used to describe how social relations occurring between various groups emerge because of imitation or mimicry. Mimesis does not capture the necessary distinction between innovation, the coming into being of a novel idea or practice, and its diffusion and adaptation. While the diffusion of governmental practice between metropole and periphery may be, in part, a process of mimesis in which institutions in the metropole progressively adapt social practices from the periphery, mimesis says nothing about the emergence of the practice (or work of art) to begin with. Put differently, we need to be able to understand the relationship between experimentation, innovation and adaptation of imperial practices, norms and knowledge in conjunction with how such practices diffuse back to the metropole. If the imperial space of experience proves to be a certain type of socio-political laboratory, then how does this laboratory of social experimentation tie itself to the metropole?

It is here that I believe that Bruno Latour's theory of the laboratory proves helpful for understanding the relationship between innovation and diffusion. Latour's work problematizes our common understanding of laboratory science as a practice of determining through controlled experimentation whether or not a particular deductive theory is valid. Laboratories are commonly perceived as important spaces of experimentation precisely because they control for variables and constants, determine through statistical inferences processes of causality and correlation, and facilitate the reproduction of experiments. Neopositivist international theory is heavily reliant upon this understanding of the laboratory to the extent that it takes for granted that through the use of statistics and other quantitative methods, it is possible to reconstruct a social "laboratory" that becomes a privileged window into a world "out there."[119] Implied in this viewpoint is that the laboratory space is divorced from the flux of the social world: what happens in the laboratory escapes the social forces governing "out there" so that the laboratory can become a space of cognitive reflection about nature unmatched in the "real" world. As a result, on the basis of a capacity to translate, visualize and map the outside so-called "natural" world through repeatable experimentation, the production of knowledge from laboratory sciences appears valid (or invalid). Reproducing results in various different laboratory settings generates the "force" of scientific conclusions over time.[120]

Latour contests this understanding of how the laboratory functions and how sociologists understand the laboratory as a specially demarcated space from the social world. He argues that we cannot understand how the processes of scientific validation occur without embedding the laboratory into a material ensemble within a social milieu. Epistemologists, for example, are incorrect in searching for cognitive reasons for the historical success of scientific discourse. They, as Latour writes, "ignored the material local setting, that is laboratories [themselves]." Likewise, he claims sociologists are mistaken in searching for sociological relations between scientists or the political and social factors in the "outside" instead of focusing on the material setting and the very instruments that make legible the objects of study.[121] In other words, Latour asserts that "Nothing special is happening in the cognitive and in the social aspect of laboratory practice" to be able to explain how it is that scientific discourse moves from the laboratory to the social world. In fact, what Latour originally contests is the very division between the social world and the scientific laboratory, so that the "'inside' and the 'outside', and the difference of scale between 'micro' and 'macro' levels, is precisely what laboratories are built to destabilize and undo."[122]

On the translation and displacement of the *material* conditions that generate scientific validity Latour presents an altogether different model for understanding the diffusion of scientific knowledge. By way of illustration, Latour turns to the case of Pasteur and what he calls the pasteurization of France. While Pasteur is well known as the founder of microbiology, what, Latour asks, accounts for the seamless acceptance of Pasteur's ideas of the microbe as the vector for understanding disease etiology when during the late nineteenth century there were many rival groups with different "scientific" explanations and evidence? It was, Latour avers, a series of moves or displacements of the material setting of Pasteur's own laboratory that gave him the ability to isolate, grow, and variate the virulence of the anthrax virus under specific conditions. Such techniques permitted the visualization of the microbe within the laboratory, allowing for inoculation and experimentation with epidemiological models of disease propagation. As Latour writes:

> It can now be said that Pasteur has inside his laboratory, on a smaller scale, the "anthrax disease." The big difference is that "outside" it is hard to study because the micro-organism is invisible and strikes in the dark, hidden among many other elements, while "inside" the lab clear figures can be drawn about a cause that is there for all to see, due to translation.[123]

But the true strength of Pasteur's legitimization was precisely the moment when he could demonstrate the "variance of virulence" of his microbes in the outside environment. In other words, he could accomplish this "only by extending the laboratory itself" in a field trial – what Latour interestingly calls a "theatre of the proof", or a staged experiment designed to demonstrate to the public the validity of Pasteur's vaccine.[124] The important point here is what Latour characterizes as a material transformation of the "outside" world, in this case the farm, as a way of assuring that the field trial would be a success: "on condition that you respect a limited set of laboratory practices – disinfection, cleanliness, conservation, inoculation gesture, timing and recording – you can extend to every French farm a laboratory product made at Pasteur's lab."[125] The material transformation of the social world according to laboratory conditions, Latour argues, is certainly not a neutral process; therein lies a form of politics, a way of shaping and modifying social relations through a material reconfiguration, a metamorphoses in social behavior (the establishment and respect for protocols of human and animal hygiene, for example) that strikes at the deadly virulent contagion originally revealed in the Pasteurian lab, and of which Pasteur possessed the legitimate authority to reveal. This subterranean Pasteurian politics of material transformation is one that is necessarily hidden behind the scenes of a political order built on law, rule or sovereignty, but nonetheless historically forms the heart of various developmental projects. For Latour:

> [I]t is clear that in political terms the influence of Pasteurian laboratories reached further, deeper, and more irreversibly since they could intervene in the daily details of life – rebuilding sewage systems, *colonizing*

countries, rebuilding hospitals – without ever being clearly seen as a stated political power.[126]

Identifying and mastering microbial enemies in the tropics was an important element the colonization of the interior, particularly in Africa.[127]

The colonies, moreover, represented ideal spaces of experimentation for the perpetuation of a Pasteurian politics of reform outside institutional and local restraints imposed within metropolitan states. Latour himself points to three reasons why colonies proved to be important spaces of experimentation and experience for these scientists: first, because tropical disease was connected to a whole host of macroscopic objects (parasites and insects), Pasteurian physicians needed to rediscover "the route by which a parasite, an insect, and a man were linked"; second, Pasteurians were usually the ones on the ground without competition from rival teams to contest their theories. Moreover, public imperial authorities allowed them to (re)construct the physical space according to their own specifications, something more difficult to accomplish in the metropole; third, and most importantly, because the objects of disease etiology, parasites and insects, were distinct from microbes, and because examining the connection between man and parasites or insects could not be replicated under original laboratory conditions, Latour argues that:

> [Pasteurians] had to obtain plenary powers and always act on a large scale. Since they could not reduce their contribution to one stage and leave others to apply it, the Pasteurians had to be allowed to *legislate* for the entire social body.[128]

Put differently, the conjunction between disease etiology and social transformation in colonial spaces required unparalleled power to experiment, test and forcibly change social habits and traditions of the local population all in the name of progress. As Margaret Lock and Nguyen Vinh-Kim argue:

> The Pastorian [sic] shift toward a microbial theory of disease causation structured a powerful imaginary of the colonies as vast laboratories where the enactment of hygienic measures could be tested, and the results compared across space and time. On the colonial stage, the proofs of efficacy that gradually accumulated confirmed the underlying doctrine of biological commensurability, allowing colonial lessons to be repatriated to Europe as tried-and-true practice rather than simply as theory ... the social and political conditions in the colonies where colonial powers were not constrained in the implementation of new policies made them a testing ground from which policies could be repatriated.[129]

This idea of how innovation and experimentation with governmental practices becomes "tried-and-true practice[s]" constitutes an important link between innovations in the imperial periphery and their diffusion and impacts upon metropolitan institutions. To be sure, the very process of legitimizing imperial innovations and experiments involves formidable moments of violence against a resistant local population. Imperial laboratories were spaces in which socio-political innovations were largely designed for the subjugation of recalcitrant populations who did not heed imperial authority. Latour tellingly begins his study of the pasteurization of France by calling the first part: "War and Peace of Microbes." His point being that the innovations that propelled microbiology were not due to the particular genius of Pasteur, but rather that they reflect a constellation of actors and actants (i.e. nonhuman actors such as microbes) interacting according to relations of force (geopolitical, social, between scientists, etc.).[130]

Three significant points bear mentioning. First, what Latour's framework allows us to understand are the processes whereby colonial experimentation – by way of a set of material and social environmental transformations – becomes normalized over time. In practice, such processes of normalization happen when a concatenation of alliances between various agents, specific material conditions or requirements and, often times, sheer happenstance all conspire to create propitious conditions for the adaptation of imperial innovations. It should be emphasized, however, that the colonial laboratory was not one in which Western powers possessed absolute power to necessarily socially engineer outcomes to their benefit, though there are cases of that; the practice of imperialism was a *learned* practice that necessitated social experimentation and innovation, novel techniques of discipline and social control to map out who was being governed, who might become a threat and what the colonial powers were, in fact, in possession of. In other words, the colonial laboratory like the Latourian laboratory with its acts of translation, transcription, measurement and calibration – i.e. "places where facts ... can be created out of whole cloths" – is one in which a multiplicity of active agents (human and non-human) operates by way of making and reifying new objects and networks.[131] For example, as Timothy Mitchell shows in *Rule of Experts: Egypt, Techno-Politics, Modernity*, the formation of something called "*the* national economy" in the early part of the twentieth century was "made out of processes that were as much 'material' as they were 'cultural,' and that were as 'real' as they were 'abstract.'"[132] Such material and cultural processes flowed through colonial spaces to emerge as a "new object of knowledge."[133] "Colonialism," Mitchell writes:

> opened up a distance, a space of separation, a relationship of curiosity, that made it possible to see something as "a case," a self-contained object whose "problems" could be measured, analyzed, and addressed by a form of knowledge that appears to stand outside the object and grasp it in its entirety.[134]

The formation of a private property regime, cadastral maps, national statistics, etc., all formed part of a colonial process that objectified what was long perceived to be various elements of a market as opposed to what we now take for granted as the national economy.

Second, the process of imperial innovations emerging from colonial crucibles by no means implies that such incontrovertible innovations remain a permanent feature of metropolitan institutions or state practice. Their applicability, effectivity, or very *raison d'être* may be entirely called into question. Thus, as I show in Chapter 2, the materialization of the concentration camp across the global periphery and its arrival in Europe during the First World War would evidently no longer be conceived as a "normal" feature of governance in a post-Second World War world. Nonetheless, it bears emphasizing that the delegitimation of something like the concentration camp in Europe after the catastrophes of the Second World War doesn't negate the fact that camps become, in essence, part of a colonial archive that under different circumstances may become applicable again (i.e. the Omarska camp in Bosnia, 1992). By way of example, Mathieu Rigouste has recently shown how the French security establishment adapts colonial policing techniques originally developed in the Algerian War of Independence as tools for the metropolitan police.[135] Such techniques restructure policing practice especially within *les banlieues*, or the peripheral ghettos made up of new immigrants and French of North African background.[136] Rigouste's work is particularly interesting because he traces genealogically how the fear of a subversive internal enemy reemerged at the end of the Cold War when the external enemy (the Soviet Union) collapsed. What French defense officials called the *doctrine de la guerre révolutionnaire* (doctrine of revolutionary warfare or DGR) were a set of military and policing techniques designed to act against a wide range of insurrectionist movements. DGR, or better known as counterinsurgency, techniques evolved out of the laboratory of the Algerian War of Independence, were delegitimized after France's defeat and yet reemerge at a time when state officials are primarily concerned with the potential for mass disturbances in French inner cities among a largely North African immigrant class. The result, Rigouste argues, is the recreation of "an intense military policing grid [*quadrillage militaro-policier*] over the territory."[137] The establishment of this type of neo-colonial grid, the retrieval of legal rationalizations from colonial periods and the perception that immigrant populations formed an incessant security threat revitalized a colonial archive that was originally perceived to be discredited.[138]

Third, as I alluded to above, the colonial laboratory is one in which there are a multiplicity of actants at work. As Latour defined it in *The Politics of Nature*, an actant "is any entity that modifies another entity."[139] The key here is this idea of modification which does not imply an intrinsic notion of intentionality. Thus non-human actants become actors insofar as they modify assemblages of relations thereby giving rise to something novel in the world. This understanding action in terms of human/nonhuman *effects* thus calls into question the very distinction between activity and passivity in thinking about something like a colonial laboratory. The colonial laboratory is not one in which there is a singular European "actor" or agent that acts upon an essentially passive colonial space. The colonial laboratory is one in which a multiplicity of actants operate to create new objects of knowledge or novel technologies that become part of the *dispositifs* of governance. For example, in the following chapter, my examination of barbed wire as a spatial segregation tool that migrated from the American West throughout the imperial periphery should itself be considered an actant that has had profound effects on space, human beings, military strategies and ultimately the European concentration camps. Barbed wire, through the imperial crucibles of the late nineteenth century, becomes part of a reorganized network of governance with evidently catastrophic effects.

To be sure, the applicability of Latour's actor-network theory is not without its tensions within the broader goal of developing a postcolonial framework for mapping the imbrications between colony and metropole. As some postcolonial and feminist writers have argued, "Latour's networks often have followed uncritically some of the older colonial contours."[140] Although, as Warwick Anderson continues, Latour initially saw the significance of European colonies as zones of significant transformation by scientific processes, "Latour's engaging story ['Circulating Reference: Sampling the Soil in the Amazon Forest' in *Pandora's Hope*] manages to omit local agents and context, thus turning the network into a sort of iron cage through which no native can break."[141] Sandra Harding's criticism of Latour likewise centers on his aloofness towards the relevance of gender and identity questions for science studies. Latour, as Harding avers,

> [F]orge[s] ahead as if the backs of feminists and other "excluded" have been glimpsed retreating over the horizon of modernity into their natural world of "tradition," but leaving no traces behind in conceptions of modernity or its ideal social relations ... [For Latour, such perspectives are seen as] largely obstacles to scientific and social progress ... Mostly invisible [to him], but not to feminists and postcolonial theorists and researchers, are the long histories of and present projects of male supremacy and imperialism/colonialism, hulking like two proverbial 800-pound gorillas in the parlors, parliaments, board rooms and *laboratories of modernity and its sciences.*[142]

For Harding, Latour's philosophy of science and its implications for such "laboratories of modernity" that interests us here, remains wedded to a specific Eurocentric account of science and the Enlightenment. Nonetheless, while Latour's epistemology may remain in some ways problematic in terms of elucidating the specific feminist or postcolonial actants involved within the specific histories of scientific objects, the metaphor of the laboratory remains productive insofar as it reveals – within Latour's own framework, namely the pasteurization of France – a set of relational conjunctions that are materially constitutive of transnational hierarchies. In other words, nothing epistemologically precludes the type of research projects that Harding advocates from an actor-network theory (ANT) perspective. Furthermore, the concept of the laboratory taken here is meant to illustrate a particular manner in which a new object comes to be in the world and to possess effects. The epistemological advantage of ANT then is to mitigate the essentialization of specific anthropocentric identities, which Donna Haraway originally recognized the limits of in her classic "Situated Knowledges: The Science Question in Feminism and the Privilege of the Partial Perspective."[143]

The following three chapters expand upon this linkage between imperial laboratories, violence and subjugation, the innovations produced historically within such imperial laboratories and the processes of diffusion in Western state formation. During the closing decade of the nineteenth century, a central imperial innovation was the concentration camp. As I show in Chapter 2, the camp represents an apparatus of control, a way of delineating space in order to effectively govern a population deemed a threat to imperial authority. What is unique about the relationship between camp and population is that this notion of threat is no longer simply tied to an objective threat (i.e. the potential that someone or some group of individuals could carry out an act) but the mere fact of being a member of a population signifies being a threat. The camp becomes the apparatus for tying issues of race, degeneracy and pathology within what Foucault has famously called biopower, but one filtered through an imperial context. This connection between subjugation, violence and imperial experimentation also fed into a wider discourse of what kinds of threats local populations pose (in actuality or potentially) for imperial powers. As Lock and Vinh-Kim also note, the management and perception of these populations within various imperial zones becomes laced with the very language of microbiology.[144] And this, in fact, constitutes a wider discursive regime throughout the late nineteenth century, which sees issues of contagion, race, and degeneracy (and the ways in which metropolitan populations become conceived according to an emergent imperial knowledge, see Chapter 3) at the heart of the nexus between empire and metropole. The rise of the modern surveillance state is then intimately tied to this idea that there are populations within the metropole akin to colonial populations that perpetually threaten the established order.

Notes

1   For a notion of the colonial archive see for example, Sebastian Conrad, *German Colonialism: A Short History* (Cambridge: Cambridge University Press, 2012), 162.
2   See especially Kenneth. N. Waltz, *Theory of International Politics* (Reading, MA: Addison-Wesley, 1979), 96.
3   Ibid., 79.
4   See in particular G. J. Ruggie, "Continuity and Transformation in the World Polity: Toward a Neorealist Synthesis," *World Politics* 35, no. 2 (1983).
5   Richard K. Ashley, "The Poverty of Neorealism," in *Neorealism and Its Critics*, ed. Robert O. Keohane (New York: Columbia University Press, 1986).

6   Ibid., 66.
7   Naeem Inayatullah and David L. Blaney, *International Relations and the Problem of Difference* (New York: Routledge, 2004). See especially Chapter 1; Turan Kayaoglu, "Westphalian Eurocentrism in International Relations Theory," *International Studies Review* 12, no. 2 (2010).
8   J. David Singer, "The Level-of-Analysis Problem in International Relations," *World Politics* 1, no. 14 (1961). Barry Buzan, Ole Wæver, and Jaap de Wilde argue, however, that the "levels of analysis" problem cannot be treated as simply a typology, but that "the scheme presents a specific ontology that privileges the state, and obscures and discriminates against those transnational unites that do not clearly fit into the scheme." Barry Buzan, Ole Wæver, and Jaap de Wilde, *Security: A New Framework for Analysis* (Boulder, CO: Lynne Rienner, 1998), 7.
9   Andreas Osiander, *Before the State: Systemic Political Change in the West from the Greeks to the French Revolution* (Oxford: Oxford University Press, 2007), 12; Or, for example, Richard Handler argues that:

> our notions of "nation" and "state" imply similar senses of boundedness, continuity and homogeneity encompassing diversity. The state is viewed as rational, instrumental, power-concentrating organization. The nation is imagined to represent less calculating, more sentimental aspects of collective reality. Yet, both are, in principle, integrated: well-organized and precisely delimited social organisms.
> (Richard Handler, *Nationalism and the Politics of Culture in Quebec* [Madison: University of Wisconsin Press, 1988], 7)

10   R. B. J. Walker, *Inside/Outside: International Relations as Political Theory* (Cambridge: Cambridge University Press, 1993), 168.
11   Here I am referring to John A. Hobson (1858–1940).
12   Waltz, *Theory of International Politics*, 25, 26.
13   Ibid., 26–7; Or as he further extrapolates to the present, "Surely the major reasons for the material well-being of rich states are found within their own borders – in their use of technology and in their ability to organize their economies on a national scale," 33.
14   As Waltz argues, "the absence of imperialism in the face of unbalanced power would sorely require explanation." Ibid., 27.
15   Jane Burbank and Frederick Cooper, *Empires in World History: Power and the Politics of Difference* (Princeton, NJ: Princeton University Press, 2010), 8; my emphasis.
16   See especially Barry Buzan and Richard Little, "Reconceptualizing Anarchy: Structural Realism Meets World History," *European Journal of International Relations* 2, no. 4 (1996).
17   R. O. Keohane and J. S. Nye, *Power and Interdependence* (Glenview, IL: Scott Foresman, 1989).
18   See for example Benno Teschke, *The Myth of 1648: Class, Geopolitics, and the Making of Modern International Relations* (New York: Verso, 2003).
19   Osiander, *Before the State: Systemic Political Change in the West from the Greeks to the French Revolution*, 13. Indeed the reference in the above quote to "western civilization" also, as we shall see, posses another conceptual problem for understanding state-formation in that it typically assumes a Eurocentric starting point by looking primarily at so-called "western civilization."
20   David A. Lake, *Hierarchy in International Relations* (Ithaca, NY: Cornell University Press, 2009), 4.

21 G. John Ikenberry, *Liberal Leviathan: The Origins, Crisis, and the Transforma-tion of the American World Order* (Princeton, NJ: Princeton University Press, 2011). See especially Chapter 4 in the present book for my discussion of Ikenberry.
22 Lake, *Hierarchy in International Relations*, 8–9.
23 Ibid., 8.
24 Ikenberry, *Liberal Leviathan: The Origins, Crisis, and the Transformation of the American World Order*, 107.
25 Lake, *Hierarchy in International Relations*, 40.
26 Ibid., 57.
27 Ikenberry, *Liberal Leviathan*, 67.
28 Ibid., 68.
29 Ibid.
30 Robert Cox, "Social Forces, States and World Orders: Beyond International Relations Theory," *Millennium, Journal of International Studies* 10, no. 2 (1981); Andrew Linklater, "Realism, Marxism and Critical International Theory," *Review of International Studies* 12, no. 4 (1986).
31 Steve Smith, "The United States and the Discipline of International Relations: Hegemonic Country, Hegemonic Discipline?" *International Studies Review* 4, no. 2 (2002).
32 David Long and Brian C. Schmidt, eds, *Imperialism and Internationalism in the Discipline of International Relations* (Albany, NY: State University of New York Press, 2006); Brian C. Schmidt, *The Political Discourse of Anarchy: A Dis-ciplinary History of International Relations* (Albany, NY: State University of New York Press, 1997).
33 Robert Vitalis, "The Noble American Science of Imperial Relations and Its Laws of Race Development," *Comparative Studies in Society and History* 52, no. 4 (2010), 929.
34 Ibid., 911.
35 Duncan Bell, "Race and International Relations: Introduction," *Cambridge Review of International Affairs* 26, no. 1, (2013), 1.
36 Robbie Shilliam, "Race and Research Agendas," *Cambridge Review of Interna-tional Affairs* 26, no. 1, (2013), 156.
37 Meera Sabaratnam, "IR in Dialogue … but Can We Change the Subjects? A Typology of Decolonizing Strategies for the Study of World Politics," *Millen-nium, Journal of International Studies* 39, no. 3 (2011), 787.
38 Immanuel Wallerstein, "Eurocentrism and Its Avatars: The Dilemmas of Social Science," *New Left Review* 226 (1997), 106–107, quoted in Gurminder K. Bhambra, *Rethinking Modernity: Postcolonialism and the Sociological Imagina-tion* (New York: Palgrave, 2009), 4.
39 Stanley Hoffmann, "International Relations: The Long Road to Theory," *World Politics* 11, no. 3 (1959), 350.
40 Ibid., 351.
41 Ibid., 352. This point is amply echoed by the anthropologist Eric Wolf, who writes:

> By turning names into things we create false models of realty. By endowing nations, societies, or cultures with the qualities of internally homogeneous and externally distinctive and bounded objects, we create a model of the world as a global pool hall in which the entities spin off each other like so many hard and round billiard balls.
> (Eric R. Wolf, *Europe and the People Without History* [Berkeley: University of California Press, 1982], 6)

42   Hoffmann, "International Relations: The Long Road to Theory," 360.
43   Ibid., 360–361.
44   See for example Tarak Barkawai, *Globalization and War* (Lanham, MD: Rowman & Littlefield, 2005), 42–43.
45   J. Marshall Beier, "Beyond Hegemonic State(ment)s of Nature: Indigenous Knowledge and Non-State Possibilities in International Relations," in *Power, Postcolonialism and International Relations: Reading Race, Gender and Class*, eds Geeta Chowdry and Sheila Nair (London: Routledge, 2002), 83–84. As Philip Darby and A. J. Paolini argue,

> What is absent [in contemporary international theory] is any sustained attempt to explore the workings of nineteenth-century imperialism, which might have led to rethinking the international politics of the Third World or to a recognition of the significance of cultural factors in world politics.

> One may add here that such "cultural factors" cannot be simply the immanent product of a specific European experience but instead reflect transnational processes of hybridity that affect Europe as much as the so-called rest. Phillip Darby and A. J. Paolini, "Bridging International Relations and Postcolonialism," *Alternatives* 19, no. 3 (1994), 379–380; Or as Jim George puts it "'International Relations,' reduces a complex and turbulent world to a patterned and rigidly ordered framework of understanding, derived from a particular representation of post-Renaissance European historical experience, articulated in orthodox Anglo-American philosophical terms." Jim George, *Discourses of Global Politics: A Critical (Re)Introduction to International Relations* (Boulder, CO: Lynne Rienner, 1994), ix.

46   Ibid.
47   Ibid., 84.
48   Samir Amin, *Eurocentrism* (New York: Monthly Review Press, 1989), vii.
49   Ibid.
50   Ella Shohat and Robert Stam argue that "contemporary Eurocentrism is the discursive residue or precipitate of colonialism, the process by which the European powers reached positions of economic, military, political, and cultural hegemony in much of Asia, Africa, and the Americas." Ella Shohat and Robert Stam, *Unthinking Eurocentrism: Multiculturalism and the Media* (London: Routledge, 1994), 15.
51   Bhambra, *Rethinking Modernity: Postcolonialism and the Sociological Imagination*, 5. Emphasis in the original.
52   James M. Blaut, *The Colonizer's Model of the World: Geographical Diffusionism and Eurocentric History* (New York: Guilford Press, 1993), 2.
53   Anibal Quijano, "Coloniality of Power, Eurocentrism and Latin America," *Nepantla: Views from the South* 1, no. 3 (2000), 541; For the moment I want to bracket the question of racial difference until Chapters 2 and 3.
54   Amitav Acharya and Barry Buzan, *Non-Western International Relations Theory: Perspectives on and Beyond Asia* (New York: Routledge, 2009), 7.
55   Ibid., 8.
56   Ibid.
57   For example, Uday Singh Mehta argues for a striking complicity of British liberal justifications of the imperial project in India on the grounds that India remained deeply backward and historically static. Thus Mehta writes:

> The image one gets of India [through liberal writings on the subject] is of a vacant field, already weeded, where history has been brought to a nullity and

where extant social and political practices are narrowly contained, or altogether absent, primed for reform and constructive efforts.

Mehta further adds:

> From the writings on India and the empire more generally, one gets the vivid sense of thought that has found a *project*, with all its grandeur of scale, implicit permanence, purposefulness, and the absence of need to negotiate with what is extant that the Enlightenment associated with the prerogatives of that term.
>
> (Emphasis in the original)

Uday Singh Mehta, *Liberalism and Empire: A Study in Nineteenth-Century British Liberal Thought* (Chicago, IL: University of Chicago Press, 1999), 12; the striking aspect of the above quote is precisely the notion that the imperial project was perceived as a palimpsest upon which to experiment with establishing novel modalities of governance.

58 Kayaoglu, "Westphalian Eurocentrism in International Relations Theory," 194; emphasis in the original.

59 Adam Watson, *The Evolution of International Society: A Comparative Historical Analysis* (London: Routledge, 1992), 4; Or as Bull himself famously writes:

> A society of states (or international society) exists when a group of states, conscious of certain common interests and common values, form a society in the sense that they conceive themselves to be bound by a common set of rules in their relations with one another, and share in the workings of one another.
> (Hedley Bull, *The Anarchical Society: A Study of Order in World Politics* [London: Macmillan, 1977], 13)

60 Martin Wight, for example, cites the German philosopher Arnold Heeren as arguing for "the union of several contiguous states, resembling each other in their manners, religion, and degree of social improvement, and cemented together by a reciprocity of interests." Martin Wight, *Systems of States* (Leicester: Leicester University Press, 1977), 22; quoted in William A. Callahan, "Nationalising International Theory: Race, Class and the English School," *Global Society* 18, no. 4 (2004), 309.

61 Bull, *The Anarchical Society: A Study of Order in World Politics*, 15, 26–7.

62 Kayaoglu, "Westphalian Eurocentrism in International Relations Theory," 205.

63 Ibid., 205–6.

64 Hedley Bull quoted in ibid., 206.

65 Hedley Bull and Adam Watson, eds, *The Expansion of International Society* (Oxford: Oxford University Press, 1984).

66 Bull, for example, argues that "Third World demands for just treatment seem entirely compatible with the moral ideas that now prevail in the West; indeed, all of these demands take Western moral premises as their point of departure." Hedley Bull, "Justice and International Relations," in *Hedley Bull on International Society*, eds Hedley Bull, Kai Alderson, and Andrew Hurrell (New York: Palgrave, 1984), 212; Subsequent English School theorists have been more nuanced on this point. The are many that argue that there were two schools of thought on this question: the pluralists, who believe that state sovereignty should take precedence, while the so-called solidarists emphasize the propagation of norms, values and culture, as essential requirements for constituting a genuine

global society. On the former see Robert H. Jackson, *Quasi-States: Sovereignty, International Relations, and the Third World* (Cambridge: Cambridge University Press, 1990); On the latter see, for example, Ian Clark, *Legitimacy in International Society* (Oxford: Oxford University Press, 2005).

67 Barry Buzan, "The English School: An Underexploited Resource in IR," *Review of International Studies* 27, no. 3 (2001), 482.

68 Ibid., 483.

69 Edward Keene, *Beyond the Anarchical Society: Grotius, Colonialism and Order in World Politics* (Cambridge: Cambridge University Press, 2002). In the same vein, Kayaoglu criticizes Shogo Suzuki for arguing that imperialism represents a "dark side" of international society "without elaborating how this 'dark side' and a presumably 'good side' have been related." Kayaoglu, "Westphalian Eurocentrism in International Relations Theory," 206; Shogo Suzuki, *Civilization and Empire: China and Japan's Encounter with European International Society* (London: Routledge, 2009).

70 Kayaoglu, "Westphalian Eurocentrism in International Relations Theory," 206.

71 Callahan, "Nationalising International Theory: Race, Class and the English School," 311.

72 Alexander Wendt, *Social Theory of International Politics* (Cambridge and New York: Cambridge University Press, 1999), Ch. 6.

73 Ibid., 141–2.

74 As Wendt argues, "Enemies are constituted by representations of the Other as an actor who (1) does not recognize the right of the Self to exist as an autonomous being, and therefore (2) will not willingly limit its violence toward the Self." Ibid., 260.

75 Ibid. This in and of itself is a highly dubious assertion on its own terms given the weight of scholarship which shows the importance of non-European international social interaction, particularly in the realm of trade. See in particular Wolf, *Europe and the People Without History*. And more recently John M. Hobson, *The Eastern Origins of Western Civilization* (Cambridge: Cambridge University Press, 2004).

76 Wendt, *Social Theory of International Politics*, 279; Wendt appears to admit that the Napoleonic Wars and Hitler's Germany are examples of post-Westphalian Hobbesian relations. Kayaoglu, however, argues that Wendt's emphasis on "self-restraint" as embodying an acceptance of the Other is theorized as a specifically European feature. Kayaoglu, "Westphalian Eurocentrism in International Relations Theory," 211.

77 Wendt, *Social Theory of International Politics*, 268.

78 It is striking that while Waltz devotes an entire chapter to theories of imperialism Wendt's *Social Theory of International Politics*, the social constructivist response to neorealism, does not deal with theories of imperialism at all.

79 Ibid., 314.

80 Kayaoglu, "Westphalian Eurocentrism in International Relations Theory," 211.

81 Katalin Sarvary, "No Place for Politics? Truth, Progress and the Neglected Role of Diplomacy in Wendt's Theory of History," in *Constructivism and International Politics: Alexander Wendt and His Critics*, eds Stefano Guzzini and Anna Leander (London: Routledge, 2006), 168.

82 For example, Wendt writes:

> the history of international politics will be unidirectional: if there are any structural changes, they will be historically progressive. Thus, even if there is no guarantee that the future of the international system will be better than the past, at least there is reason to think it will not be worse.
>
> (Wendt, *Social Theory of International Politics*, 312)

83 Kayaoglu, "Westphalian Eurocentrism in International Relations Theory," 211.
84 John W. Meyer, John Boli, George M. Thomas, and Francisco O. Ramirez, "World Society and the Nation-State," *American Journal of Sociology* 103, no. 1 (1997), 145.
85 Ibid., 147–8.
86 Ibid., 148.
87 Ibid., 148–9. As Ann Towns writes:

> As a causal force that is exogenous to virtually all states, world culture serves as a single causal factor that exerts the same force on all states. Given that world polity institutionalism hinges all its explanatory force on world culture, it is a particularly serious problem that the approach has not accounted for what makes Western, rationalized culture such an allegedly successful candidate for diffusion.
>
> (Ann E. Towns, *Women and States: Norms and Hierarchies in International Society* [Cambridge: Cambridge University Press], 25)

88 Martha Finnemore, "Norms, Culture and World Politics: Insights from Sociology's Institutionalism," *International Organization* 50, no. 2 (1996), 330.
89 Meyer et al., "World Society and the Nation-State," 168.
90 As Finnemore writes, "By rationality, institutionalists mean simply the structuring of action in terms of ends and means. Rational action, in Western cultural terms, is not only good, it is natural." Finnemore, "Norms, Culture and World Politics: Insights from Sociology's Institutionalism," 331.
91 Finnemore herself draws attention to this aspect of world polity institutionalism when she writes:

> The lack of case study analysis or on-the-ground investigation of the mechanisms whereby world culture produces isomorphism obscures the roles of politics and power in world history and normative change ... Destroying cultural competitors, both figuratively and literally, is a time-honored way of establishing cultural dominance ... Cultural rules are often established not by persuasion or cognitive processes of institutionalization but by force and fiat.
>
> (Ibid., 340)

Ann Towns aptly notes that a consequence of the world polity approach is that:

> One is left with the suspicion that world polity theorizing relies heavily on modernization theory's notions of 'cultural contact' and natural selection – the mere exposure to rational (modern) scripts leads states to abandon the 'old,' as the anticipated benefits of Western rationality somehow automatically triumph over alternatives.
>
> (Towns, *Women and States: Norms and Hierarchies in International Society*, 22)

92 Dipesh Chakrabarty, *Provincializing Europe: Postcolonial Thought and Historical Difference*, Princeton Studies in Culture/Power/History (Princeton, NJ: Princeton University Press, 2000), 16; and Achille Mbembé, *On the Postcolony* (Berkeley: University of California Press, 2001), Introduction.
93 Reinhart Koselleck, "'Space of Experience' and 'Horizon of Expectation': Two Historical Categories," in *Futures Past: On the Semantics of Historical Time*, ed. Keith Tribe (New York: Columbia University Press, 2004).
94 Reinhart Koselleck, "Neuzeit: Remarks on the Semantics of Modern Concept of Movement," in *Futures Past: On the Semantics of Historical Time*, ed. Keith

Tribe (New York: Columbia University Press, 2006), 232; As Koselleck writes, "It was only when Christian eschatology shed its constant expectation of the imminent arrival of doomsday that a temporality could be revealed that would be open for the new and without limit."

95   Ibid., 224.

96   Reinhart Koselleck, "'Progress' and 'Decline': An Appendix to the History of Two Concepts," in *The Practice of Conceptual History: Timing Concepts, Spacing Concepts*, ed. Todd Samuel Presner (Stanford, CA: Stanford University Press, 2002), 228; also quoted in Bliss Cua Lim, *Translating Time: Cinema, the Fantastic, and Temporal Critique* (Durham, NC: Duke University Press, 2009), 79–80.

97   Koselleck, "'Space of Experience' and 'Horizon of Expectation': Two Historical Categories," 258.

98   Ibid., 260. "When one seeks to form an intuition of time as such, one is referred to spatial indications, to the hand of the clock or the leaves of a calendar that one pulls off every day." Moreover Koselleck adds:

> Historical times can be identified if we direct our view to *where* time itself occurs or is subjectively enacted in humans as historical beings .... Put more concretely, on the one hand, every human being and every human community has a space of experience in which one acts, in which past things are present or can be remembered, and, on the other, one always acts with reference to specific horizons of expectation.
>
> (My emphasis. Reinhart Koselleck, "Time and History," in *The Practice of Conceptual History: Timing Concepts, Spacing Concepts*, ed. Todd Samuel Presner [Stanford, CA: Stanford University Press, 2002], 102, 111)

99   Koselleck, "'Space of Experience' and 'Horizon of Expectation': Two Historical Categories," 258–259.

100   Ibid., 261.

101   Ibid., 259.

102   Ibid., 263.

103   Ibid., 264.

104   Koselleck, "'Progress' and 'Decline': An Appendix to the History of Two Concepts," 225; my emphasis.

105   See especially Carl Schmitt, *The Nomos of the Earth in the International Law of the Jus Publicum Europaeum* (New York: Telos Press, 2003).

106   Koselleck, "'Space of Experience' and 'Horizon of Expectation': Two Historical Categories," 266.

107   Koselleck, "Neuzeit: Remarks on the Semantics of Modern Concept of Movement," 238.

108   Dipesh Chakrabarty, *Provincializing Europe: Postcolonial Thought and Historical Difference*, Ch. 1.

109   Lim, *Translating Time: Cinema, the Fantastic, and Temporal Critique*, 84.

110   James C. Scott, *Seeing Like a State: How Certain Schemes to Improve the Human Condition Have Failed* (New Haven, CT: Yale University Press, 1998). What is missing in Scott's account is an adequate analysis of the implications of colonial knowledge production and its feedback into Europe. Scott assumes that:

> virtually all the initiatives associated with the "civilizing missions" of colonialism were preceded by comparable programs to assimilate and civilize their own lower-class populations, both rural and urban. The difference, perhaps, is that in the colonial setting officials had greater coercive power over an

objectified and alien population, thus allowing for greater feats of social engineering.

(379 n19)

But this perspective is predicated upon an internal developmental model that sees high modernism as being an intrinsically European affair divorced from its imperial relations. Moreover, as Helen Tilley notes, missing in Scott's account is how empire grappled with heterogeneity in novel ways:

> imperial management and control, particularly in the wake of the empire's dramatic expansion in Africa, forced British officials and other interested parties to grapple actively with transnational and inter-territorial trends. Ideas of heterogeneity and diversity, far from being absent, were ever present in their discourse and became integral to the logic of empire building. Thinking like an empire meant drawing attention to competing interests and pointing out the ways in which one issue or problem was nested within another. It also meant avoiding watertight compartments of knowledge and drawing upon burgeoning disciplines, such as ecology and anthropology, that emphasized social and natural interrelations. Indeed, commentators often likened the empire to a "living organism" whose very "complexity" required not only new kinds of institutions but also a new "machine of knowledge."
>
> (Helen Tilley, *Africa As A Living Laboratory: Empire, Development and the Problem of Scientific Knowledge, 1870–1950* [Chicago, IL: University of Chicago Press, 2011], 21)

111 Michael Perelman, *The Invention of Capitalism: Classical Political Economy and the Secret History of Primitive Accumulation* (Raleigh, NC: Duke University Press, 2000).
112 Sidney W. Mintz, *Sweetness and Power: The Place of Sugar in Modern History* (New York: Penguin, 1986), Ch. 2; Ann Laura Stoler, *Capitalism and Confrontation in Sumatra's Plantation Belt, 1870–1979* (New Haven, CT: Yale University Press, 1985).
113 Likewise, Ian Baucom writes that:

> the virtue of Koselleck's model ... is to empty "modernity" of any normative content, to alienate it from the exclusive property claim of any particular cultural formation, to prevent it from functioning as no more than a codeword, variously, for "Europe", "America", of "the West" ... "
>
> (Ian Baucom, "Township Modernism," in *Beyond the Black Atlantic: Relocating Modernization and Technology*, eds Walter Goebel and Saskia Schabio [London: Routledge, 2006], 70)

114 Quoted in Lim, *Translating Time: Cinema, the Fantastic, and Temporal Critique*, 85.
115 Ibid., 86.
116 Sandro Mezzadra and Federico Rahola, "The Postcolonial Condition: A Few Notes on the Quality of Historical Time in the Global Present," *Postcolonial Text* 2, no. 1 (2006).
117 Alfred W. McCoy, *Policing America's Empire: The United States, the Philippines and the Rise of the Surveillance State* (Madison: University of Wisconsin Press, 2009), 36–40.
118 Ibid., 295.
119 Patrick T. Jackson, *The Conduct of Inquiry in International Relations: Philosophy of Science and Its Implications for the Study of World Politics* (New York: Routledge, 2010), 69.

120 As Latour writes, "an important feature of fact construction is the process whereby 'social' factors disappear once a fact is established." Bruno Latour and Steve Woolgar, *Laboratory Life: The Construction of Scientific Facts* (Princeton, NJ: Princeton University Press, 1986), 23.

121 Bruno Latour, "Give me a Laboratory and I Will Raise the World," in *Science Observed: Perspectives on the Study of Science* (London: Sage, 1983), 160–161.

122 Ibid., 143.

123 Ibid., 147.

124 Bruno Latour, *The Pasteurization of France* (Cambridge, MA: Harvard University Press, 1988), 85.

125 Ibid., 152.

126 Ibid., 158; my emphasis; As Latour further writes

> No matter if they are economists, physicists, geographers, epidemiologists, accountants, microbiologists, they make all the other objects on such a scale ... that they can gain strength, reach incontrovertible conclusions, and then extend on a larger scale the conclusions that seem favorable to them. It is a political process. It is not a political process. It is since they gain a source of power. It is not since it is a source of fresh power that escapes the routine and easy definition of a stated power political power.
>
> (167; emphasis in the original)

127 Latour, *The Pasteurization of France*, 141; See also Eric T. Jennings, *Curing the Colonizers: Hydrotherapy, Climatology and French Colonial Spas* (Raleigh, NC: Duke University Press, 2006), 34. Jennings argues that issues relating to climate, nonetheless, remain of prime importance for the French colonial project.

128 Ibid., 143, emphasis in the original; or as Latour further puts it:

> With only whites and blacks, with only miasmic regions and healthy or dangerous climates, that Colonial Leviathan which spread across the globe could never have been built. Nor can the colonial medicine of the Pasteurians be explained in terms of "society" and its "interests", since the Pasteurians were capable, once more, of moving their programs of research sufficiently to obtain a richer definition of society than had all the exploiters or exploited of the period. The Pasteurians reshuffled the cards by daring to change profoundly the list of actors playing a role in the world, by modifying the trials of strength, and by inserting the laboratory into the strangest and least predictable place.
>
> (Ibid., 144–145)

129 Margaret Lock and Nguyen Vinh-Kim, *An Anthropology of Biomedicine* (Malden, MA: Wiley-Blackwell, 2010), 179.

130 Latour, *The Pasteurization of France*, 7. As Latour writes, "I start with the assumption that everything is involved in a relation of forces but that I have no idea at all of precisely what a force is."

131 See for example Zine Magubane, "Simians, Savages, Skulls, and Sex: Science and Colonial Militarism in Nineteenth-Century South Africa," in *Race, Nature, and the Politics of Difference*, eds Donald S. Moore and Anand Pandian (Durham, NC: Duke University Press, 2003), 100.

132 Timothy Mitchell, *Rule of Experts: Egypt, Techno-Politics, Modernity* (Berkeley: University of California Press, 2002), 82.

133 Ibid., 100.

134 Ibid., 100.

135 Mathieu Rigouste, *L'ennemi Intérieur: La généalogie coloniale et militaire de l'ordre sécuritaire dans la France contemporaine* (Paris: La Découverte, 2011).

136 To be sure, the term *banlieu*, strictly speaking, means a neighborhood. However, it is often understood in contemporary France to signify zones of poverty and of potential social unrest.
137 Ibid., 8.
138 Ibid., 279.
139 Bruno Latour, *The Politics of Nature: How to Bring the Sciences into Democracy* (Cambridge, MA: Harvard University Press, 2004), 237.
140 Warwick Anderson, "From Subjugated Knowledge to Conjugated Subjects: Science and Globalization, or Postcolonial Studies of Science," *Postcolonial Studies* 12, no. 4 (2009), 392.
141 Ibid., 392.
142 Sandra Harding, *Sciences from Below: Feminisms, Postcolonialities, and Modernities* (Raleigh, NC: Duke University Press, 2008), 27. My emphasis.
143 Donna Haraway, "Situated Knowledges: The Science Question in Feminism and the Privilege of Partial Perspective," *Feminist Studies* 14, no. 3 (1988). Hence, the importance of Haraway's concept of the "material-semiotic actor" as a way of thinking beyond the anthropocentric reifications of linguistic production.
144 Lock and Nguyen Vinh-Kim, *An Anthropology of Biomedicine*, 179. "The majority of these practices sought to manage space and people in terms of conceptions of hosts, reservoirs and infectious pathogens – key concepts of microbiology."

2 Imperial laboratories of violence

A genealogy of the camp

There was no Nazi atrocity – concentration camps, wholesale maiming and murder, defilement of women or ghastly blasphemy of childhood – which the Christian civilization of Europe had not been practicing against colored folk in all parts of the world in the name of and for the defense of a Superior Race born to rule the world.[1]

And then one fine day the bourgeoisie is awakened by the terrific boomerang effect [*choc en retour*]: the gestapos are busy, the prisons fill up, the torturers standing around the racks invent, refine, discuss.[2]

Not long ago Nazism transformed the whole of Europe into a veritable colony.[3]

Introduction

Crucial for understanding the circulation of norms, practices, knowledge and culture is the idea that imperial spaces were sites of creative experimentation to transform the socio-political environment of both metropole and periphery. As Chris Godsen warns, however, this emphasis on creativity and experimentation:

> takes us away from notions such as fatal impact, domination and resistance or core and periphery, emphasizing that colonial cultures were created by all who participated in them, so that all had agency and social effect, with the colonizer and colonized alike being radically changed by the experience.[4]

We should not be so quick to forget that imperial relations were constituted by structures of domination and that such structures hinged upon ubiquitous forms of material, structural, symbolic and cultural violence. Stressing the co-constitution of identity between colonizer and colonized risks obfuscating the very real and systemic patterns of violence that the maintenance of imperial governance required. "Colonial cultures" were as much constituted by asymmetric processes of racialization and domination that historically constructed the "native" as an object to be molded for specific productive purposes, as by processes of hybridity stressed by many postcolonial scholars.[5] Nonetheless, reemphasizing this aspect of imperialism, that is the inherently violent means to secure imperial domination, does not preclude seeing the practice of empire-building through violence as itself experimental and creative, the product of violent interactions between imperial authorities and a resistant population. On the contrary, the imperial space was particularly well suited for experimenting, testing, and the innovative development of more lethal and efficient means of killing.[6] Imperial spaces did not have the juridical limitations imposed on intra-European warfare, for example. The blurring of combatant and non-combatant was brutally revealed during intense periods of colonial warfare. Because imperial authorities were constantly facing local insurrections that necessitated military means of pacification, new theories and doctrines of colonial warfare and how to forcibly remove and intern local populations were developed and implemented. Historians are subsequently recognizing that certain imperial domains were, in fact, spaces of extreme, if not genocidal, violence.[7] Historians, in particular, have investigated the connections between such genocidal violence in the imperial periphery and the intensification of violence within Europe, especially, during the Second World War.[8]

Sebastian Conrad, for example, argues that a more fruitful way of understanding the imbrications between imperialism and European warfare would also be "to think in terms of a shared colonial archive involving ways of behaving, rituals, forms of knowledge and imagination."[9] This colonial archive is constituted by "common knowledge on the treatment, exploitation, and the extermination of 'sub-humans' accumulated by the western powers over the course of colonial history."[10] The Nazi totalitarian goal of world conquest and its stepping stone of colonization in Eastern Europe was not simply the direct product of past German colonial experiences; it was rather the coagulation of a diverse set of European imperial histories in which violence against the "colonized" was normalized.

My own goal in this chapter is to look more specifically at how the camp, as an aspect of this colonial archive, materially coalesced into a novel apparatus of social control and ultimately the death machine that underpinned Nazi Germany's totalitarianism. First, I examine how the late nineteenth century was central moment in global politics. It was characterized by an imperial realignment with the rise of the United States, the collapse of the Spanish Empire and the extended dominance of Anglo–French imperial authority throughout the African continent. This imperial realignment, which has typically escaped the attention of international theorists, had important consequences within the imperial periphery by creating conditions of systematic rebellion and insurgency. Imperial warfare was largely premised on disaggregating a local population in ways that would reduce local support for enemy insurgents. Camps, bounded by the material innovation of barbed wire pioneered in the American West, proved to be enormously useful in managing and controlling populations during such imperial counterinsurgency campaigns.

The crucial question here is then how did an apparatus of militarized control become applicable within Europe itself over the subsequent decades?

Second, I believe that Hannah Arendt's insights on imperialism and totalitarianism prove important. For Arendt, Nazi continental imperialism emerged out of the wreckage of the European nation-state system in the aftermath of the First World War. She famously argues in *The Origins of Totalitarianism* that a genealogy of Nazi totalitarianism must return to the experience of nineteenth-century imperialism in order to trace a constellation of elements that crystallize into totalitarianism.[11] Late imperialism and the scramble for Africa, for Arendt, "appear so close to totalitarian phenomena of the twentieth century that it may be justifiable to consider the whole period a preparatory stage for coming catastrophes."[12] But while many have focused on Arendt's claim about imperial "boomerang effects," the emergence of racism and bureaucracy for example, I argue that Arendt gives us a more convincing account of the collapse of the European nation-state system as a result of imperialism. Imperialism revealed and exacerbated latent contradictions at the heart of the modern nation-state between self-determination, human rights, assimilation and eventually denaturalization. At the crucial moment in the aftermath of the First World War, the European nation-state system was unable to address the growing and novel problem of statelessness resulting from these system-wide contradictions. As a result, the camp, that imperial innovation designed to manage populations in the imperial periphery, becomes uniquely suited for application within Europe itself.[13]

Late nineteenth-century imperialism and its geopolitical changes

In his recent book *Bloodlands: Europe Between Hitler and Stalin*, the historian Timothy Snyder argues that what underpins the intensification of mid-twentieth century mass killings, from the mass starvation of the Ukrainian peasants in 1933 by Stalin to the killing fields of Eastern Europe during the Second World War, "has less to do with the intellectual heritage of the Enlightenment and more to do with the possibilities of imperialism."[14] With respect to Germany, extermination was understood to be part of a larger project to create a racially pure and economically profitable living space (*Lebensraum*).[15] The key to establishing this viable living space was the direct colonization of Germany's eastern frontier. The Soviet Union was seen by Hitler as a source of natural resources (especially foodstuffs) within a larger project of imperial competition with Britain and, to an extent, the United States. "Hitler," Snyder writes, "confronted the two chief inheritances of the British nineteenth century: *imperialism as an organizing principle of world politics*, and the unbroken power of the British Empire at sea."[16] Because Germany could not (yet) compete militarily with Britain's naval power to challenge its imperial position across the planet the only option left for it to pursue was to expand eastwards, taking over the western part of the Soviet Union to the Ural Mountains. *Lebensraum*, in Hitler's thinking, would prove to be the answer to Germany's ability to sustain itself indefinitely in its future imperial wars against Britain and the United States.[17]

As Snyder implies and as many international theorists recognize, Hitler's Germany undoubtedly was a revisionist power bent upon upsetting the status quo.[18] While such processes of systemic revisionism have been studied at length by international theorists in terms of great power conflicts, how such great power conflicts translate into ubiquitous violence against entire populations, including the creation of a vast network of concentration and extermination camps, remains largely unexamined.[19] The violence unleashed because of empire-building and imperial transitions was not circumscribed within clear categories of interstate violence; the Second World War was not primarily a war between states and their respective military apparatuses. This undoubtedly was the first global conflict in which the forced relocation, internment and/or extermination of entire populations was deemed to constitute a significant aspect of the war effort. Put differently, to understand the link between global total war and the concentration and extermination of populations requires going back to the imperial crucibles that set in motion a set of experiments of violence and internment.

Germany's attempt at tilting the global scales of power in its favor was obviously not without precedent. The late nineteenth century marked a period in which the international system began to fundamentally shift.[20] We may note, for example, the decline of the Spanish Empire throughout this time as a result of various independence movements in Latin America; the slow-motion decay of the Ottoman and Hapsburg empires; the consolidation of Franco–British imperial dominion in Africa, especially in South Africa by the British against Dutch/Boer interests; and quite surprisingly at the time, the Japanese victory in 1905 against the Russian Empire, ushering in Japanese imperial dominance of the Far East. As we shall see in greater detail, the rise of the United States as a global power would have certain unintended consequences that would impact developments across the imperial periphery and later within Europe itself. As Eric Hobsbawm notes, the period from about 1880 to 1914 was characterized by a constant revolutionary instability throughout the global periphery in conjunction with the continuous imperial expansion by new powers. Imperial transitions not only ushered in colonial conflicts that required novel means of suppression, but as Hobsbawm writes, "The bourgeois century destabilized its periphery in two main ways: by undermining the old structures of its economies and the balance of its societies, and by destroying the viability of its established political regimes and institutions."[21]

Snyder's characterization that "imperialism was the organizing principle of world politics" echoes with Hannah Arendt's original arguments about the destruction wrought by European imperialism throughout the global periphery. In the preface to the section on imperialism in *The Origins of Totalitarianism*, Arendt draws attention to the unique attributes of modern (i.e. nineteenth-century) imperialism and its reverberating effects on Europe. First, she argues, a central characteristic of its novel form of "power politics" was:

[a] shift from localized, limited and therefore predictable goals of national interest to the limitless pursuit of power after power that could roam and lay waste the whole globe with no certain nationally and territorially prescribed purpose and hence no predictable direction.[22]

More generally, Arendt claims that before the nineteenth century it was essentially an anachronism to even speak of "world politics." In essence, the emergence of a genuinely "world politics" contained a deeper contradiction that would unravel the very foundations of the European state system:

Before the imperialist era, there was no such thing as world politics, and without it, the totalitarian claim to global rule would not have made sense. During this period, the nation-state system proved incapable of either devising new rules for the handling of foreign affairs that had become global affairs or enforcing a Pax Romana on the rest of the world.[23]

To be sure, this perspective is somewhat idiosyncratic. International theorists typically do not demarcate the nineteenth century as the moment when there emerged a genuine conception of "world politics" as opposed to regional interstate relations. Nor is the late nineteenth century usually highlighted for special attention by international theorists, who primarily look at this time period as part of the European "long peace" before the deluge of the First World War.[24] For Arendt, however, nineteenth-century imperialism, in contrast to antecedent practices of European colonization dating from at least the Spanish conquest of the Americas, expressed an unlimited desire for global domination that was unique in history. It resulted in the conquest of peoples who would or could never be integrated into the metropolitan nation-state out of fear that to do so would upset the delicate balance between internal homogeneity and the limitations imposed by domestic institutions. Modern imperialism was predicated upon concepts derived from capitalist "business speculation" and the economic necessity of continuous capital accumulation. This notion of business speculation provided the basis for a unique political principle in the modern era: "Expansion as a permanent and supreme aim of politics is the central political idea of imperialism."[25] This focus of modern imperialism could only be put into motion by an "unlimited accumulation of power."[26] This continuous expansion of power had devastating consequences; continuous capital accumulation unleashed a fever-pitch desire to transcend the confines of nation-state boundaries in order to remain perpetually in motion throughout the globe. Tellingly, Arendt argues:

The concept of unlimited expansion that alone can fulfill the hope for unlimited accumulation of capital, and brings about the aimless accumulation of power, makes the foundation of new political bodies – which up to the era of imperialism always had been the upshot of conquest – well-nigh impossible. In fact, its logical consequence is the destruction of all living communities, those of the conquered peoples as well as of the people at home. For every political structure, new or old, left to itself develops stabilizing forces which stand in the way of constant transformation and expansion. Therefore all political bodies appear to be temporary obstacles when they are seen as part of an external stream of growing power.[27]

As a result of this continuous imperial expansion, European imperial powers were faced with a set of colonial wars in which the population could not be segregated so easily, if at all, from the insurgents. We see around this time period, the beginning of imperial counterinsurgency methods that targeted the entirety of the population as a whole as a central mechanism of imperial domination. The rebellions in Cuba during the early part of the 1890s forced Spanish authorities to innovate counterinsurgency methods, especially forcible detentions; the British realized that only by separating the Boer civilian population from the insurgents could it hope to win the war. The United States adopted Spanish methods that it originally used as a justification for humanitarian intervention, including especially the policies of reconcentrating local populations in its own quest to master the Philippines. As a result, the camp, designed to radically reconfigure the relationship between a population of bodies and imperial authority, is characterized by Joël Kotek and Pierre Rigoulot, as "one of the responses concerning the question of how to manage the masses in the democratic, national and colonial age."[28] In the next section, I explore historically how the materialization of the camp emerged throughout the various imperial crucibles of the nineteenth century.

The imperial laboratory and the emergence of the camp

Giorgio Agamben's work explores the nexus between the state of exception as a sovereign/juridical instrument designed to exclude human life from the juridical order and the working of the camp as a zone that lies "outside" the law. For Agamben, the camp represents the moment in modern history which conflates the legal exception and the rule: where the state of exception is no longer considered an exceptional act of sovereign decision in the face of factual danger, but rather becomes the norm or rule: *"The state of exception thus ceases to be referred to as an external and provisional state of factual danger and comes to be confused with juridical rule itself."*[29] For Agamben, the camp becomes the "permanent spatial arrangement" of this attempt to completely exclude human life from the juridical order. As Agamben writes:

The paradoxical status of the camp as a space of exception must be considered. The camp is a piece of land placed outside the normal juridical order, but it is nevertheless not simply an external space. What is excluded in the camp is, according to the etymological sense of the term "exception" (*ex-capere*), *taken outside*, included through its own exclusion. But what is first of all taken into the juridical order is the state of exception itself. Insofar as the state of exception is "willed," it inaugurates a new juridico-political paradigm in which the norm becomes indistinguishable from the exception. The camp is thus the structure in which the state of exception – the possibility of deciding on which founds sovereign power – is realized *normally*. The sovereign no longer limits himself, as he did in the spirit of the Weimar constitution, to deciding on the exception on the basis of recognizing a given factual situation (danger to public safety): laying bare the inner structure of the ban that characterizes his power, he now de facto produces the situation as a consequence of his decision on the exception. This is why in the camp the *quaestio iuris* is, if we look carefully, no longer strictly distinguishable from the *quaestio facti*, and in this sense every question concerning the legality or illegality of what happened there simply makes no sense. *The camp is a hybrid of law and fact in which the two terms have become indistinguishable.*[30]

While Agamben presents a forceful and logical analysis of the ontological structure of the camp as the space which conflates norm and exception, what ultimately allows the designation of a type of biological life not worth living, his *history* of how this structure materially came into being remains largely unexplored. Agamben departs from the Aristotelian distinction between *zoē*, the fact of life that all beings have in common, and *bios*, the uniquely human characteristic of living in common, and argues that an essentially ahistorical sovereign power through the state of exception constitutes "the politicization of bare life … the decisive event of modernity." Yet this "decisive event" is overdetermined by this ontological original moment, the division of the concept of life, and makes his account appear teleological.[31] It remains fundamentally unclear throughout Agamben's text what the historical events are that constitute the "thresholds" that drive this politicization of bare life: how exactly does this "decisive event of modernity" occur and reveal itself as the camp? Coupled with this is that Agamben's theorization of the camp remains firmly within Europe and European political thought. "Agamben builds an artificial discursive wall around 'the West,'" as Michael Rothberg rightly notes, "that prevents him both from seeing forces outside Europe as constitutive of modernity … Agamben's 'West' is a 'pure, absolute … space' that cannot be productively transformed from within or without because its rise and fall are sealed off from the heterogeneous global history."[32]

Agamben does, however, cursorily point to the fact that actual camps emerged within imperial domains beginning with the Spanish in Cuba in 1896 and the British during the Boer War. "What matters here," Agamben writes, "is that in both cases, a state of emergency linked to a colonial war is extended to an entire civil population."[33] This fact becomes, as he continues, "clearer in the Nazi *Lager*."[34] Yet Agamben never adequately explains the relationship between these two events: the colonial normalization of the state of emergency/exception and this particular ontological structure of the Nazi camp. What remains missing from Agamben's theorization of the camp is precisely *how* this materialization and normalization of the camp emerged in the imperial periphery and how, especially, it later (re)appears within Europe as something entirely novel.

As Achille Mbembé recognizes, exploring the relationship between the sovereign state of exception and its effects on bodies necessitates a detour through the colonial experience. As he writes,

A fact remains, though: in modern philosophical thought and European political practice and imaginary, the colony represents the site where sovereignty consists fundamentally in the exercise of a power outside the law (*ab legibus solutus*) and where "peace" is more likely to take on the face of a "war without end."[35]

Because the colonial space was conceived as a "frontier" zone inhabited by "savages," Mbembé argues, the intra-European rules that defined notions of sovereignty, territoriality and civilization were deemed to be in abeyance. The inherently hierarchical relationship between the European colonizer and the non-European colonized precluded the possibilities of implementing intra-European juridical foundations of mutual coexistence that structured for example the *Jus Publicum Europaeum*. "Beyond the line," as Carl Schmitt would characterize the juridical relationship between Europe and its colonial territories, Europeans could create new forms of property relations, new ways of classifying people, and new "cultural imaginaries" that would solidify socio-political stratification within colonized populations: all of which, of course, was designed to enforce European supremacy within a newly constructed, colonized space.[36] Moreover, as Mbembé argues:

> [C]olonies are zones in which war and disorder, internal and external figures of the political, stand side by side or alternate with each other. As such, the colonies are the location par excellence where the controls and guarantees of judicial order can be suspended – the zone where the violence of the state of exception is deemed to operate in the service of "civilization."[37]

The state of exception that allows for the continuous suspension of a local juridical order was in fact the central building-block of the colonial state. Given that imperial authorities were faced with continued armed resistance by native inhabitants, who were largely deemed to constitute an inferior race, the triumph of European civilization was predicated upon the deployment of continuous military power outside the boundaries set by domestic and international law.

To be sure, Mbembé does not focus on the fact that something unique happened in the last decade of the nineteenth century with this emergence of the camp in Cuba and South Africa that would have a significant impact on the relationship between the practice of juridical sovereignty and its effect on a population. While the ideas were in place to justify a perpetual colonial state of siege, to differentiate between savage and civilized, etc., the *materialization* of the permanent state of exception in a space of internment was historically contingent – subject to a wider global political context in which imperial powers were faced with the necessity of controlling, surveilling and relocating populations. As Emmanuelle Saada argues, "empires have historically been characterized by their outer frontiers and by acute attention to the control of movements from the periphery towards the center."[38] However, one may add that empires were as much concerned with internal movement within the periphery as with monitoring the movement of peoples between center and periphery. Why, the question begs, did camps proliferate in the last decade of the nineteenth century in Cuba and South Africa, and subsequently, throughout the imperial periphery? What was so special about this particular time period and not others? Precisely because of a set of global and peripheral set of changes and upheavals occurred such that the camp presented itself as a "solution" to the predicament of how to properly control a population.

As I alluded to above, the late nineteenth century was a crucial period in history when new imperial powers were exerting themselves in various places. In particular, the rise of the United States throughout the nineteenth century represents a substantial shift in global economic and political power away from Europe. This last decade of the nineteenth century was the time when the United States took over the last Spanish possessions in the Caribbean and East Asia during the Spanish–American War, and when the United States began seeing itself as a rising economic power. Yet this American imperial overseas expansion was nonetheless preceded by decades of westward continental expansion and consolidation. The significance of this expansion for understanding the history of the camp is twofold. First, as Reviel Netz shows, it would inadvertently usher in the central innovation of barbed wire as one of the most important material tools for controlling space, and ultimately a population, while integrating it within a wider American capitalist economy.[39] Second, because American practices of Indian warfare and the relocation of Indian tribes into reservations anticipated more generally patterns of population control that would be adapted in other imperial settings.

Barbed wire

American expansionism and consolidation of the West was made possible by the crucial invention of barbed wire. Invented in the late 1860s by Joseph K. Glidden, barbed wire consisted of multiple barbs of coil with a sharp edge tied together with wire. It was, as Netz shows, especially cheap to produce, better resistant to the natural elements and well-suited to the purpose of cattle herding and controlling space in the American West.[40] Barbed wire achieved the important goal of herding cattle by inflicting a form of static "violence, so that it more effectively protected the space it enclosed."[41] "The key," Netz continues, "to the entire success of this technology was, of course, its ability to stop cows."[42] And this was of primary importance because it permitted controlling the production of beef from herding cattle on the plains of Texas and the Midwest and driving them to the factory slaughterhouses based in Chicago. Barbed wire thus managed to fundamentally integrate the West into the Eastern capitalist economy through the control of the cattle and the production of beef. As we shall see in the case of the British in South Africa, the use of barbed wire would not only be applicable to the husbandry of animals but also of individuals. It proved enormously helpful in controlling the movement inside a space, but also outside, by essentially reducing human beings to the status of animals. More generally, as Netz argues, understanding the historical evolution of the camp forces us to grapple with the environmental history of how animals were subjected to novel mechanisms of control that connect colonization, capitalism and warfare: "For animals are always part of the social picture ... the history of animals is part and parcel of history – that reality where all is inextricably tied together, humans, animals, and their shared material world."[43]

Accompanying the consolidation of the American West was a long-term process of forcing Indian tribes onto specifically demarcated reservations. The policy began in earnest during the 1830s, before the invention of barbed wire, with the Indian Removal Act passed by Congress, and culminated in the creation of Indian reservations in Oklahoma in the 1860s. Nonetheless, the notion of a reservation can be traced to the very beginning of English colonization of North America with the Quinnipiacs' Connecticut reservation of 1638. "The basic intent of a 'reservation,'" as Paula M. Marks argues, "has always been to segregate natives within defined geographical boundaries." Such boundaries, however, were "incompatible with [Indians'] own understanding of the land's contours, uses and meaning."[44] This very incompatibility between, on the one hand, a sedentary and largely agricultural way of life versus, on the other, a nomadic existence in which the concept of property was unknown, framed European distinctions between "civilized" and "savage" ways of being. Hence, it became a long-term goal of the English, and subsequently American officials, to force Native Americans to settle into a particular locale where they would be more easily controlled, and "where they would be 'civilized' with missions and schools."[45]

By the 1830s this attempt at civilizing Native Americans through forced relocation was coming into full swing. The Cherokee nation, for example, was systematically displaced into internment camps in Georgia, only to be further pushed West for the sake of opening up land for white settlers. As one soldier recounted, the harshness of the treatment meted out to Native Americans was akin to treating them not unlike the herding of animals:

> [I] witnessed the execution of the most brutal order in the history of American warfare. I saw helpless Cherokee arrested and dragged from their homes, and driven at the bayonet point into the stockades. And in the chill of a drizzling rain on an October morning. *I saw them loaded like cattle or sheep* [into] *six hundred and forty-five wagons and headed for the West.*[46]

While the forcible removal of Indian tribes onto reservations was usually perceived as a humanitarian act, it obviously did not preclude instances of extreme violence between white settlers and Native Americans over the course of the Indian Wars. In the Texas territories, for example, during the mid-1820s, Samuel Austin, the "father of Texas" railed against the native tribes: "The Indians ... may be called universal enemies to man ... There will be no way of subduing them but extermination."[47] In fact the history of the Texas Rangers as a policing group originates, as Robert Perkinson shows, in this attempted displacement and killing of the Native tribes on the Texas frontier. Nonetheless, the wider project of pushing Native Americans into reservations in the Western frontier, managed by the newly created Office of Indian Affairs, was later centered on implementing policies designed to assimilate Native Americans to "Western civilization" – of essentially "eradicating Indian cultural practices" and forcibly controlling the movement of Native American populations.[48] Part of this policy was the destruction of the bison population, which was accomplished not only by direct extermination, but especially by controlling the free manner in which bison roamed the American West through the explosive use of barbed wire. "In short," Bill Yenne writes, "the postwar [i.e. the Civil War] strategic doctrine of the US Army would be geared toward the Herculean task of forcing the West's entire indigenous population onto reservations."[49]

Population control and colonial warfare

In 1895 the Spanish Empire was faced with an intractable insurgency on the island of Cuba. There, General Valeriano Weyler, in an attempt to put down the local insurgency that was being fed by popular support in the countryside, ordered the forcible removal of the eastern population of the island to fortified towns and villages in the West in a policy that was called at the time *reconcentracion*.[50] The goal of this policy was primarily to preclude the local population from aiding and abetting the insurgents. Weyler also hoped that it would remove the possibility that locals would see and report Spanish movements, while reducing the effects of rebel propaganda and demoralizing the insurgents by essentially holding hostage their family members.[51] Weyler's policies certainly lacked any concern for the welfare of the population placed in these zones (which were as Donald Schmidt argues, "nothing more than frontier stockades used by Americans in the American West").[52] The brutality of this policy of *reconcentracion* was not lost on the rest of the world. President McKinley, in his messages to Congress in 1898, justifying American intervention during the Spanish–American war, characterized Spanish policy as "not civilized warfare; it was extermination."[53] In other words, Weyler's policies revolved around an inherently military logic to suppress the rebellion by concentrating and controlling a mass of people, irrespective of whether or not they constituted a threat. However, the unintended consequence of a complete lack of adequate planning for those people who were forced to move resulted in anywhere from 300,000 to 400,000 deaths as result of disease, hunger and unsanitary conditions.[54]

Turning to Asia, after the United States defeated the Spanish Empire during the Spanish–American War it was also faced with a hostile population, especially in the Philippines. What American officials learned during the Indian Wars would prove crucial for the pacification of the Philippines. As Iain R. Smith and Andreas Stucki argue:

> US Officers regarded the Filipinos as [quoting the then Secretary of War] "by no means civilized" and in "identically the same position as the Indians of our country have been for many years" [so that] the Filipino insurgency "must be subdued in much the same way."[55]

In 1905, for example, Colonel David Baker led a constabulary force to put down a rebellion in the Batangas. "In an area suspected of harboring rebels," as Alfred McCoy writes, "constabulary troops herded residents into concentration camps and unleashed terror to discourage contact with the guerillas."[56] Or as one general recounted, "We executed a 'Weyler' campaign but did it according to military law."[57] Civilian concentration in the Philippines was influenced not only by the preceding events in Cuba and South Africa but especially by the example of Indian reservations and the possibilities of educating and assimilating the local population, even if it meant forcibly removing people into specially constructed camps.

General Valeriano Weyler's implementation of the forced *reconcentracion* would have lasting implications for how other colonial powers would manage their civilian populations during such times of irregular war. Emily Hobhouse, the wife of a British parliamentarian, wrote about the practices adopted by the British during the second Boer War between 1899 and 1902. There, Hobhouse observes, the British "by the care of Lord Roberts and Lord Kitchener, adopted the politics of Spain, while ameliorating its methods."[58] Indeed, as Kotek and Rigoulot show, the British press was actively using the example of General Weyler as a positive method of suppressing the Boer rebellion; referring directly to Weyler's "politics of reconcentration," one newspaper in particular made the argument that any woman or child who aided the Boer insurgency was deemed an active participant and subject to internment, while adding "We [the British] have undertaken to conquer the Transvaal, and if we cannot ensure this but for the displacement of the Dutch inhabitants, they must be displaced – men, women and children."[59] Now what is also remarkable about the British case is that, in contrast to the Spanish in Cuba, the British made full use of barbed wire as a tool to master space in the Transvaal and, especially, to enclose the camps that the British created. The British strategic command realized that barbed wire allowed them to address the fundamental "problem of motion": "Which side would have the ability to concentrate its power at the place and time to suit its purposes?"[60] The problem during the Boer War was that the British reliance upon train transportation made it vulnerable to Boer sabotage. While the Boers were essentially free to move on horseback over large connected spaces, the British could not easily engage Boer insurgents beyond their rail point. As a result, Netz argues, the British high command stumbled upon the idea of setting up a series of "blockhouses," essentially rectangular huts made out of sheet iron, all along the rail line and connected by telegraph.[61] However, while the initial impetus for using barbed wire along with these blockhouses was the protection of the railway, the British realized that such a system worked to striate space in a remarkable way: "it was a pure space-controlling mechanism."[62] As Netz shows, the British innovation of using barbed wire and blockhouses meant that:

> the way was now open for imperial powers to extend their control over space across the entire land governed. The modern form of control over space, first tried on the Great Plains over the bodies of cows, now entered human history itself.[63]

Barbed wire proved enormously important in the construction of "refugee" or concentration camps for Boer noncombatants. However, determining who was a combatant and who was not was often difficult to do. In this manner, the segregated apparatus that was the British camps was structured around making sure, as in Cuba, that the local population would not come to the aid of the Boer insurgents. While the Spanish did not take seriously the needs of those interned in its camps, "the British were determined to treat civilians humanely."[64] Hobhouse's point about ameliorating Spanish methods is important. Initially, these camps were poorly managed; they did not provide adequate food, access to water and medical supplies, as this was not a priority for the British high command under Lord Kitchener. It is estimated in the initial years, beginning in 1902, approximately 116,000 people were in various camps across South Africa. Of which until the end of the war approximately 28,000 White Boers died and 14,000 Black Africans, who were generally interned in far more miserable conditions.[65] Elizabeth van Heyningen has, however, recently made the point that what is interesting about the concentration camps established by the British is that they became special experimental zones in emergency public health.[66] Beginning with Lord Milner, who replaced Lord Kitchener who was responsible for vastly expanding Weyler's methods, the British "began to see the camps as a means of demonstrating the virtues of British rule to their new Boer subjects."[67] Welfare replaced violence as a tactic of social control, which included the so-called virtues of British rule, mainly centered on inculcating in Boer women techniques for the better nursing of infants, emphasizing the importance of clean water, providing better rations, etc. In other words, the British concentration camp became a sort of micro-imperial laboratory for what may be understood as a positive form of biopolitics that would restructure Afrikaner society as a whole.[68] Naturally, while the British concentration camp attempted to instill in its social experimentation the modernization and urbanization of the Boer population, it left to the side the Black African population who saw little benefit to the British run order.

Across the northwest and northeast border of South Africa, German imperial authorities put into practice new forms of internment against the rebellious native Nama and Herero population, beginning in 1904. German officials also learned the lessons of the Spanish and British experience, of interning a significant portion of a population (particularly Nama women and children) under rebellion and the use of barbed wire to demarcate a spatial enclosure. But Germany's first camp (*konzentrationslager*) proved to be novel in that it forced its inhabitants to engage in hard labor under extremely harsh conditions. What was "discovered" in these German camps – especially in the case of Shark Island (*Haifischinsel*) – was that one could eliminate a significant proportion of the population through the attrition of hard labor, lack of food and poor sanitary conditions. This attrition was something that imperial authorities on the ground desired.[69] What is striking in the German case of internment is that it fused the plan of eradicating a certain population from a given territory with that of the internment of men, women and children in order to suppress a revolt. Recall, for example, Lothar von Trotha's infamous order of 1904, which stated:

> I the great General of the German troops send this letter to the Herero people. The Herero are no longer German subjects ... The Herero people must leave the country. If the nation does not do this I will force them with the *Groot Rohr* [cannon]. Within the German border, every Herero, with or without gun, with or without cattle will be shot. I will no longer accept women and children, I will drive them back to their people or I will let them be shot.[70]

This order captures a set of important precursors that would become extremely important thirty years later in Germany: the idea that a certain group no longer belong to a polity, that its juridical status becomes essentially stateless, and that therefore it becomes entirely possible that "shooting" Herero (including "shooting" women and children) becomes legitimate. The German case reveals a certain concatenation between practices of modern military pacification campaigns and the desire to remove a group from a certain territory.

In brief, colonial warfare proved to be, as Paul Gilroy argues, a central crucible for the "creative deployment of killing technology in their different confrontations with the world's uncivilized hordes."[71] If anything, the lesson of the Boer War, for example, was the seamless conjunction between violence – the burning of Boer farms – and the forcible transfer of women and children to concentration camps. Camps were essential to the maintenance of spatial control of colonial populations. Nonetheless, imperial authorities placed special emphasis on military technology for the violent suppression of local insurgents. The classic example of superior technology was on display during the battle of Omdurman in Sudan, where with the latest modern weapons including machine guns and artillery, Lord Kitchener (the same Lord Kitchener responsible for the propagation of concentration camps in South Africa) inflicted 23,000 casualties on the rebels, with only 47 British killed and 382 wounded. It was possible with advanced technologies of violence to inflict massive casualties against combatants and noncombatants alike. Moreover, as Gilroy himself notes, there was an altogether implicit assumption in many texts published at the time on colonial warfare that prisoners need not be taken; what was of even graver concern, however, was the possibility of being taken prisoner. As Gilroy quotes Colonel C. E. Callwell: "in conflict with savages and semi-civilized opponents, *and even with guerillas in a civilized country*, there is no such thing as surrender. The fate of the force which sacrifices itself in a small war is in most cases actual destruction."[72] The conjunction between the innovations and applicability of internment and the application of wholesale massacres for the sake of maintaining European hegemony, what constituted important aspects of what is part of the "colonial archive," created a novel arrangement or apparatus that would form the basis of Nazi empire-building in Eastern Europe and the Soviet Union. What needs to be better understood is how such a colonial archive happened to become so easily applicable within Europe itself.

The collapse of the European system of states and "problem" of statelessness

Imperial spaces were important areas for experimenting with novel technologies of violence and, as I have shown, apparatuses of material control of space and populations. But how are we to understand the links between the importance of the camp for imperial management and its applicability in a European context? The experimental results derived from the prosecution of the Boer War, as Netz argues, needed a substantial intra-European crisis in order become relevant:

> To move from experiment to established practice – to make barbed wire settlement a routine phenomenon – barbed wire had to first be replicated many times over. For this settlement to become standard, there would have to be a major crisis, calling for the mass-scale control over populations. Then came World War I.[73]

As both Netz and Kotek and Rigoulot note, the First World War was crucial in that it resulted in the problem of controlling masses of enemy soldiers or civilians under occupation. Not until the American Civil War had there been a military situation which required the accommodation of enemy prisoners of war.[74] The extraordinary length of industrialized warfare would create not only the mass concentration of armed forces, but also as a consequence the possibilities of masses of long-term prisoners of war. Accommodations beyond military barracks had to be implemented to control and surveil such a large number of individuals. The cost-effectiveness and simplicity of barbed wire camps proved enormously appealing: "Surround a school with barbed wire – and you have a camp." Or as Netz quotes a text from 1919 by C. P. Dennett entitled *Prisoners of the Great War* describing the emerging camp form:

> enclosures surrounded by a barbed wire fence about ten feet high; in some camps a single fence, in others an extra fence about fifty to seventy-five feet outside the first fence. To be caught in the space between the two fences meant death.[75]

But it was not only prisoners of war who could be subjected to interment in temporary camps. Anyone deemed to potentially represent a threat during this period of quasi-total war needed to be accounted for and subject to state control. In the case of France at the beginning of hostilities, the state declared that all "foreign nationals of enemy powers, along with prostitutes and ex-convicts [*repris de justice*] of all countries are liable to be interned starting the first of September 1914."[76] Internment camps cropped up throughout the French countryside. Fifty or so camps were created for the purposes of interning approximately 60,000 individuals. To be sure, as Kotek and Rogoulot note, camp surveillance was often lax and "It was more the case of a concern to save money that certain camps were surrounded by barbed wire."[77] By the end of the First World War, the very idea of enclosing human beings by barbed wire for extended periods of time had begun to be considered a normal practice.

While the specific crisis of the First World War gave the impetus to adopt the imperial innovation of the camp as a way of controlling enemy troops and potential civilian threats, a new category of individuals for whom camp internment would prove particularly useful was the new mass of stateless persons. It is Arendt's important contribution to note the connection between this rise in statelessness and the collapse of the European system of states as a long-term consequence of imperial expansion. Arendt argues that this continued push for greater imperial expansion over the course of the nineteenth century completely destabilized the European continent itself in that it amplified a set of paradoxes at the heart of the European system of nation-states. Because imperialism compelled the creation of novel forms of external rule, new forms of bureaucratic structures and racial categories of separation, the destruction of this European system paved the way for the adaptation of various imperial technologies, particularly the camp, to be applied in Europe. For Arendt, the contradiction at the heart of Europe revolved around four main issues: the right of self-determination, the problem of denaturalization, the lack of international enforcement of human rights, and the ability to be outside any juridical order.[78] The explosion of these contradictions after the

First World War, Arendt argues, left an immense juridical and political void that would have repercussions for a large set of "minority" populations set adrift after the breakup of continental empires.[79] The newly independent states in Eastern Europe were by no means analogous to the French or British nation-state; they were comprised of a mixture of religions and ethnicities that sought ethnic homogeneity beyond state boundaries and who conceived of the state as conjoined with a form of ethnic nationalism.[80] This unstable situation provoked the forced dislocations of minorities outside these newly established states. Such minorities would as a result become effectively denaturalized and stateless, living on the margins of other nation-states in legal purgatory. It also led to the collapse of one of the central norms in European public law: that of asylum.

The surge of statelessness reveals the complete failure of European inter-state law to develop solutions to the juridical status of individuals in what was nominally public *inter*-state law. Neither assimilation or naturalization, nor repatriation en masse proved to be an answer to the growing mass of stateless people. The mainly Western European nation-states, faced with masses of stateless or denaturalized people, abdicated their responsibilities to protect these people's *human* rights in favor of maintaining *national* coherence. The nation-state, Arendt argues, "transferred the whole matter to the police."[81] This led to the paradoxical situation where the deportation of stateless individuals, itself a sovereign right, was deemed illegal should no other state legally accept them. Western states were unable to significantly repatriate the stateless populations within their territorial borders, resulting in the proliferation of internment camps. The contradictory status of minority populations throughout Europe composed of sovereign nation-states revealed, as Arendt argues, a fateful logic in the minds of state officials: "The representatives of the great nations knew only too well that minorities within nation-states must sooner or later be either assimilated or liquidated."[82]

This specific logic would underpin Germany's actions during the 1930s leading to the destruction of European Jews. To be sure, in Nazi policies, there was no question about the potential for the assimilation of the displaced Jewish population. The Nazis proceeded in steps to render its own Jewish population internally stateless, devoid of civil or political rights, and forcibly deported to other parts of Europe; only to subsequently implement a policy of forced concentration in various camps inside Germany and Eastern Europe. This policy would subsequently be applied throughout the territories that Germany occupied.[83]

This specific practice, of constructing an array of camps, constituted the building blocks of Nazi Germany's totalitarian empire, especially in the East. Prior to the implementation of Operation Barbarossa, the German invasion of the Soviet Union that began in June 1941, Hitler's general staff and the SS conjured up *Generalplan Ost*, which stipulated that the Eastern frontier would become in effect a colonial possession of Germany.[84] "General Plan East" involved the radical Germanization of the Eastern frontier through population transfers of Germanic Northern Europeans (*volksdeutsche*). General Plan East, while calling for the "removal" of a significant portion of the local population, also involved very detailed plans for recreating idealized, Germanized farming communities. At numerous levels, from the bureaucratic management of entire regions to the formation of agricultural communes, the "East" proved to be in the minds of the SS planners at the time "a tremendous opportunity to put their theories [of 'agricultural settlement, racial science and economic geography'] into practice."[85] In other words, German planners conceived of the "East" as a palimpsest, a special form of laboratory, for establishing the radical vision of a pure, seamless, self-sufficient and racially pure community. This plan initially called for the elimination of between 31 and 45 million people. As Snyder describes it:

> After the corrupt Soviet cities were razed, German farmers would establish, in Himmler's words, "pearls of settlement," utopian farming communities that would produce a bounty of food for Europe. German settlements of fifteen to twenty thousand people each would be surrounded by German villages within a radius of ten kilometers ... Colonization would make Germany a continental empire fit to rival the United States, another hardy frontier state based upon exterminatory colonialism and slave labor. The East was the Nazi Manifest Destiny. In Hitler's view, "in the East a similar process will repeat itself for a second time as the conquest of America." As Hitler imagined the future, Germany would deal with the Slavs much as the North Americans had dealt with the Indians. The Volga River, he once proclaimed, will be Germany's Mississippi.[86]

The reference here to the genocide of Native Americans in North America is quite revealing. It demonstrates a certain awareness and knowledge about how certain populations represent threats or roadblocks to the construction of an empire. Indeed, as I argued, the process of colonization of the American West during the nineteenth century had significant consequences for the materialization of the camp that would figure so prominently in Nazi totalitarian rule.

At the same time, during the war with the Soviet Union, Nazi planners conceived of the pacification campaign in the rear of the frontline in terms of a traditional form of colonial subjugation. As Bloxham argues, the "Barbarossa jurisdiction decree" allowed groups of German soldiers or SS to liquidate men, women and children in the attempt to pacify a region. For Bloxham:

> The Barbarossa jurisdiction decree was an order straight from the lawless world of colonial warfare ... there can be no doubting the similarity of ruthless methods and the racist, dehumanized vision of the enemy in colonial "anti-insurgency" warfare outside Europe.[87]

Nonetheless, given that German forces were unable to defeat Stalin's armies completely on the battlefield, such dystopian visions of "transform[ing] eastern Europe into an exterminatory agrarian colony" would have to wait.[88] It is here, in the failures of transforming the East into Germany's own continental colonial possession, that Snyder locates the genesis of Hitler's Final Solution. Unable to deport Jews to the Ural Mountains, nor to such places as Madagascar because of the British navy, Himmler improvised German colonization plans by merging Germany's war effort with what Alfred Rosenberg called the "biological eradication of Jewry in Europe."[89]

The unsystematic murder of Jews in German occupied zones in the East was reorganized into a set of death factories that essentially took over all German war aims. To be sure, the German concentration camp first emerged in November 1933 when in the aftermath of the Reichstag fire of February 27 the German government under Hitler ordered political enemies to be arrested and interned. However, the vast array of camps under SS reorganization in 1936 began in 1938 to host a new category – "the *Volksschädling* (pest harmful to the people)" – of those who could be political enemies of the Reich.[90] Later on, stateless peoples would also find themselves interned in camps not only in Germany, but throughout Europe. However, as Wolfgang Sofsky notes, "the outbreak of the war led to a radical caesura."[91] The result of the war was the dramatic expansion of the camp system to include nine major concentration and extermination camps located in Eastern Europe, beginning in 1941.

Conclusion

By the time the Second World War ended with the Third Reich's defeat in 1945, well over 60 million people had perished in the inferno set in motion 6 years earlier. Not only was the war the most bloody in terms of military casualties, as an estimated 24 million military personnel were killed or wounded, and not only did it result in unparalleled devastation of the European continent, especially of the western Soviet Union, but it was the first war in which the civilian toll far outstripped military losses. That civilian losses in the maelstrom of war proved to be so high was undoubtedly a function of the total mobilization of each state's capacity to wage mass industrial warfare; but what the Second World War also revealed was a systemic desire on the part of the main belligerent in the conflict, Nazi Germany, to target certain populations for extermination. In no previous military conflict had a great power gone to such lengths, even to the point of undermining its own military efforts against its enemies, to develop an entire infrastructure for the mass internment and killing of a civilian population deemed to be racially impure.[92]

Auschwitz came to symbolize this industrial fabrication of corpses on a scale previously unimaginable. Wolfgang Sofsky describes the uniqueness of Nazi Germany's death machine as "a climactic high point in the negative history of social and modern organization."[93] For Hannah Arendt, this commitment to extermination embodied in the death-factories in the East represents "an attack upon human diversity as such, that is, upon a characteristic of the 'human status' without which the very words 'mankind' or 'humanity' would be devoid of meaning."[94] For her, this attack on human diversity was something entirely original in the history of Western politics, which until this time had accorded the "enemy" a place in remembrance. To be sure, the Nazi infrastructure for mass killing was by no means encapsulated in what historian Timothy Snyder calls the "rapid industrial killing" of individuals; this image represents an "all too clean and simple" perspective on what constituted the many facets of the Nazi states' ability to kill.[95] The people who perished in the Nazi inferno also did so through a vast network of concentration and labor camps as well as a result of the mass shooting of civilians (Jews especially) on the Eastern Front.[96]

Even if Nazi Germany's widespread network of death was much more extensive than the camp, the extermination camp nonetheless remains etched in the historical memory of the Second World War as marking a fateful turn in the history of so-called modern Western civilization. While mass murder has been a recurring practice in human history, Sofsky argues, the camp as an apparatus of control represents a different and unique moment in the organizational capacity and implementation of absolute and indiscriminate violence. Its twentieth-century uniqueness in turn reveals a capacity for experimentation in tormenting its victims under conditions of permanent violence, of sealing victims into a "closed universe" of terror and "break[ing] their resistance, herd[ing] them together, shred[ing] social ties; it dissolves action; it devastates life."[97] Or, as Primo Levi captures this facet of Nazi violence:

> One is truly led to think that, in the Third Reich, the best choice, the choice imposed from above, was the one that entailed the greatest affliction, the greatest waste, the greatest physical and moral suffering. The "enemy" must not only die, he must die in torment.[98]

In essence, as Sofsky argues, the "camp was a laboratory of violence" in which "its models are terror punishment, excess, and massacre."[99] This metaphor of the camp as a "laboratory" of violence strikingly echoes with Hannah Arendt's original claim that the Nazi camps represent "special laboratories to carry through its experiment in total domination."[100] By total domination Arendt meant the liquidation of "all spontaneity" in order to reduce the human to "the most elementary reactions, the bundle of reactions that can always be liquidated."[101] Camp experimentations were an exercise in "the transformation of human nature itself" – for example, the creation of the *Muselmänner* – in order to create a "system in which men are superfluous."[102] Nazi scientists, for example, experimented with new forms of mass sterilization in Auschwitz in order to later apply these techniques against Slavic peoples.[103] As much as the camp was a means of killing or working to death its victims, it also proved to be an experimental crucible for testing radically new methods of governance and would confirm their mantra that "everything was possible."[104] In essence, Nazi imperial state-formation was predicated upon this entire infrastructure of death-making.

To conclude, international theorists have largely circumvented the issues surrounding why Nazi Germany perpetrated the Holocaust. Focusing instead on systemic factors that led to the Second World War, there is little attention paid to Germany's attempt to carve out its own continental empire and how it constructed this vast array of camps as a way of maintaining its supremacy. There is little recognition among international theorists regarding the historical links between the imperial shifts during the latter part of the nineteenth century, the violence and internment imposed on populations across imperially dominated spaces, and the repatriation of these experimental techniques back into Europe during the Second World War. Instead, what I have shown in this chapter is that technological and sociopolitical changes throughout the imperial periphery came to impact how European imperial states managed their own populations

Notes

1   W. E. B. Du Bois, *The World and Africa: An Inquiry into the Parts Which Africa Has Played in World History* (New York: International Publishers, 1965), 23.
2   Aimé Césaire, *Discourse on Colonialism* (New York: Monthly Review Press, 2001), 36.
3   Frantz Fanon, *The Wretched of the Earth* (New York: Grove Press, 2004), 101.
4   Chris Godsen, *Archaeology and Colonialism: Cultural Contact from 5000 BC to the Present* (Cambridge: Cambridge University Press, 2004), 25.
5   As Achille Mbembé writes, "the colonized, like the animal, was an object of experimentation in a game that the colonizer played with himself/herself, conscious that between him/her and the colonized there hardly existed a community of essence." Achille Mbembé, *On the Postcolony* (Berkeley: University of California Press, 2001), 27.
6   Isabel V. Hull, *Absolute Destruction: Military Culture and the Practices of War in Imperial Germany* (Ithaca, NY: Cornell University Press, 2005).
7   See especially A. Dirk Moses, ed., *Empire, Colony, Genocide: Conquest, Occupation and Subaltern World History* (New York: Berghahn Books, 2008).
8   Enzo Traverso, *The Origins of Nazi Violence* (New York: New Press, 2003).
9   Ibid., 165.
10   Robert Gerwarth and Stephan Malinowski, "Hannah Arendt's Ghosts: Reflections on the Disputable Path from Windhoek to Auschwitz," *Central European History* 42, no. 2 (2009), 287.
11   Hannah Arendt, "A Reply to Eric Voegelin," in *Essays in Understanding: 1930–1954 Formation, Exile and Totalitarianism*, ed. Jerome Kohn (New York: Schocken Press, 1994).
12   Hannah Arendt, *The Origins of Totalitarianism* (New York: Harcourt, 1994), 123; see also Karuna Mantena, "Genealogies of Catastrophies: Arendt on the Logic and Legacy of Imperialism," in *Politics in Dark Times: Encounters with Hannah Arendt*, ed. Seyla Benhabib (Cambridge: Cambridge University Press, 2010).

13 To be sure, my argument is not, as recent historians have debated, whether or not there are direct causal relationships between the specific experiences of German colonization before the First World War and Nazi imperial conquest during the 1940s. It is true that many aspects of German colonial history, from the development of racial science by Eugene Fischer and the genocide perpetuated against the Herero and Nama in Namibia and against the Maji-Maji in what is now Tanzania reflect broad patterns of experiences, knowledge and violence that would reemerge in Nazi colonization plans on the Eastern Front. However, I believe that the causal links are more tenuous and need to take into account changes in global politics during late European imperialism, the consequences of the First World War and the explosion of statelessness during the interwar years. More generally, as Sebastian Conrad writes:

> There cannot be a direct link between the Herero war and the Nazi atrocities that does not recognize the important and transformative character of the ordeals of the First World War. The First World War was not the radical rupture it is often described as, but must itself be placed within the larger imperial context of the epoch. This implies that it is necessary to register, for example, the "reimportation" of strategies of colonial warfare – the use of machine guns, gas attacks, air raids, the deployment of colonial army units – to Europe.
> (Sebastian Conrad, *German Colonialism: A Short History* [Cambridge: Cambridge University Press, 2012], 164)

14 Timothy Snyder, *Bloodlands: Europe between Hitler and Stalin* (New York: Basic Books, 2010), 156. This is not to say there weren't significant ways justifying empire-building among Enlightenment thinkers. For example, Louis Sala-Molins argues that many French Enlightenment thinkers, in particular Condorcet and Rousseau, were complicit in justifying European slavery in the colonial West Indies. Louis Sala-Molins, *Dark Side of the Light: Slavery and the French Enlightenment* (Minneapolis: University of Minnesota Press, 2006). For a look at the tensions between empire and Enlightenment, see also Russell A. Berman, *Enlightenment or Empire: Colonial Discourse in German Culture* (Lincoln, NE: University of Nebraska Press, 1998).

15 The term itself was coined by the geopolitical theorist Friedrich Ratzel at the turn of century and originally referred to the acquisition of overseas colonial territories by imperial Germany "in the context of his biological theories." As Woodruff D. Smith explains, the concept of *Lebensraum* originated out of the confluence of late nineteenth-century "migrationist colonialism" and external romanticized agrarianism. However, *Lebensraum* imperialism, as opposed to *Weltpolitik* economic imperialism, stressed the survival and regeneration of the *Deutschum* – the cultural/racial entity that needed to be protected through imperial expansion. Woodruff D. Smith, *The Ideological Origins of Nazi Imperialism* (New York: Oxford University Press, 1986), Ch. 5.

16 Snyder, *Bloodlands: Europe between Hitler and Stalin*, 156. In the case of Stalin, Snyder argues, his "challenge ... was to defend the homeland of socialism, the Soviet Union, against a world where both imperialism and capitalism persisted," 157. My emphasis.

17 Shelley Baranowski argues that a central aspect of Nazi Germany's imperialism was autarky. As she writes:

> Lebensraum was intended to solve contemporary obsessions, the perceived overpopulation of Slavs who jeopardized the German food supply, the chronic

weakness of agriculture in the "Old Reich," the renovation of Germany's historically determined right to rule through settlement, and the final decisive triumph over the threat of annihilation by Germany's enemies, both internal and external.

(Shelley Baranowski, *Nazi Empire: German Colonialism and Imperialism from Bismarck to Hitler* [Cambridge: Cambridge University Press, 2010], 268)

Consider also Himmler's characterization of global politics:

We are living in an age of economic empires in which the primitive urge to colonization was again manifesting itself ... The boom in world economy caused by the economic effects of rearmament could never form the basis of a sound economy over a long period, and the latter was obstructed above all by the economic disturbances resulting from Bolshevism.

(Quoted in Donald Bloxham, *The Final Solution: A Genocide* [Oxford: Oxford University Press, 2009], 184)

18 See especially Randall Schweller, *Deadly Imbalances: Tripolarity and Hitler's Strategy of World Conquest* (New York: Columbia University Press, 1998); John J. Mearsheimer, *The Tragedy of Great Power Politics* (New York: Norton, 2001).
19 See especially Robert Gilpin, *War and Change in World Politics* (New York: Cambridge University Press, 1981).
20 Reviel Netz, *Barbed Wire: An Ecology of Modernity* (Middletown, CT: Wesleyan University Press, 2009), 131.
21 Eric Hobsbawm, *The Age of Empire: 1875–1914* (New York: Vintage, 1989 [1987]), 277.
22 Arendt, *The Origins of Totalitarianism*, xviii.
23 Ibid., xxi.
24 Paul W. Schroeder, "Necessary Conditions and World War I as an Unavoidable War," in *Explaining War and Peace: Case Studies and Necessary Condition Counterfactuals*, eds Gary Goertz and Jack S. Levy (New York: Routledge, 2007), 147.
25 Ibid., 125.
26 Arendt, *The Origins of Totalitarianism*, 137.
27 Ibid., 137–138.
28 Joël Kotek and Pierre Rigoulot, *Le siècle des camps: emprisonnement, détention, extermination, cent ans de mal absolu* (Paris: Jean-Claude Lattès, 2000), 25.
29 Giorgio Agamben, *Homo Sacer: Sovereign Power and Bare Life* (Stanford, CA: Stanford University Press, 1998), 168; emphasis in original.
30 Ibid., 170.
31 Ian Baucom, *Specters of the Atlantic: Finance Capital, Slavery, and the Philosophy of History* (Raleigh, NC: Duke University Press, 2005), 185.
32 Michael Rothberg, *Multidirectional Memory: Remembering the Holocaust in the Age of Decolonization* (Stanford, CA: Stanford University Press, 2009), 63.
33 Agamben, *Homo Sacer: Sovereign Power and Bare Life*, 166.
34 Ibid., 167.
35 Ibid., 23.
36 Ibid., 25–26. As Schmitt writes, "Beyond the line was an 'overseas' zone in which, for want of any legal limits to war, only the law of the stronger applied." Carl Schmitt, *The Nomos of the Earth in the International Law of the Jus Publicum Europaeum* (New York: Telos Press, 2003), 93–94.
37 A. Mbembe, "Necropolitics," *Public Culture* 15, no. 1 (2003), 11–40, 24.

38 Emannuelle Saada, "The History of Lessons: Power and Rule in Imperial Formations," *Items and Issues: Social Science Research Council* 4, no. 4 (2003), 17.
39 Netz, *Barbed Wire: An Ecology of Modernity*, 21–23.
40 Ibid., 27.
41 Ibid., 28.
42 Ibid., 30.
43 Ibid., 17.
44 Paula M. Marks, *In a Barren Land: American Indian Dispossession and Survival* (New York: William Murrow & Company, Inc., 1998), 14–15.
45 Ibid., 15.
46 Quoted in John L. Dickerson, *Inside America's Concentration Camps: Two Centuries of Internment and Torture* (Chicago, IL: Lawrence Hill Books, 2010), 30; my emphasis.
47 Quoted in Robert Perkinson, *Texas Tough: The Rise of America's Prison Empire* (New York: Picador, 2010), 53.
48 Bruce Elliott Johansen and Barry Pritzker, eds, *Encyclopedia of American Indian History, Volume 1* (Santa Barbara, CA: ABC-CLIO, 2008), 501.
49 Bill Yenne, *Indian Wars: The Campaign for the American West* (Yardley, PA: Westholme Publishing, 2005), 112.
50 Hence the term that would enter widespread use beginning with the British: concentration.
51 Kotek and Rigoulot, *Le siècle des camps: emprisonnement, détention, extermination*, 52.
52 Donald E. Schmidt, *The Folly of War: American Foreign Policy, 1898–2005* (New York: Algora Publishing, 2005), 34.
53 www.h-net.org/~hst203/documents/mckinley.html; To be sure, it should come as no surprise that while using the rhetoric of a "humanitarian" intervention in Cuba, the United States would itself employ the same techniques of concentration and colonial warfare, as I mentioned above. It seems as though the line between humanitarian intervention and imperial subjugation in many cases is quite thin.
54 Klaus Muhlhahn, "The Concentration Camp in Global Historical Perspective," *History Compass* 8, no. 6 (2010), 545.
55 Iain R. Smith and Andreas Stucki, "The Colonial Development of Concentration Camps (1868–1902)," *Journal of Imperial and Commonwealth History* 39, no. 3 (2011), 419.
56 Alfred W. McCoy, *Policing America's Empire: The United States, the Philippines, and the Rise of the Surveillance State* (Madison: University of Wisconsin Press, 2009), 135.
57 Netz, *Barbed Wire: An Ecology of Modernity*, 193.
58 Quoted in Kotek and Rigoulot, *Le siècle des camps*, 67.
59 Netz, *Barbed Wire: An Ecology of Modernity*, 68.
60 Ibid., 99.
61 Ibid., 101.
62 Ibid., 103.
63 Ibid., 106.
64 Ibid., 195.
65 Kotek and Rigoulot, *Le siècle des camps*, 70.
66 Elizabeth van Heyningen, "A Tool for Modernisation? The Boer Concentration Camps of the South African War, 1900–1902," *South African Journal of Science* 106, no. 5/6 (2010).
67 Ibid., 1.
68 Ibid., 10. Here I understand the term biopolitics in the Foucauldian sense, as it:

"derive[s] its knowledge from, and define its power's field of intervention in terms of the, birth rate, the mortality rate, various biological disabilities, and the effects of the environment." Or as Foucault further describes, "Biopolitics deals with the population, with the population as a political problem, as a problem that is at once scientific and political, as a biological problem and as a power's problem."

Foucault, "Society Must Be Defended," 245.

69   Casper Wolf Erichsen, "Forced Labor in the Concentration Camp on Shark Island," in *Genocide in German South-West Africa: The Colonial War of 1904– 1908 and Its Aftermath*, eds Jürgen Zimmerer, Joachim Zeller and E. J. Neather (London: Merlin Press, 2007).

70   Quoted in Dominik J. Schaller, "From Conquest to Genocide: Colonial Rule in German Southwest Africa and German East Africa," in *Empire, Colony, Genocide: Conquest, Occupation, and Subaltern Resistance in World History*, ed. A. Dirk Moses (New York: Berghahn Press, 2008), 304.

71   Paul Gilroy, *Postcolonial Melancholia* (New York: Columbia University Press, 2005), 20. The emblematic of text in the English language of colonial warfare remains that of Colonel C. E. Callwell, *Small Wars: Their Principles and Practice*, published in 1896. As Gilroy aptly characterizes Callwell's text: "The deadly combination of indigeneity and insurgency meant that they were only awaiting the carrying out of that suspended sentence. Their extinction supplies timely proof that the modern laws of nature and history are acting as one," 22; Indeed, Gilroy's idea that colonial warfare reflects the a war against the already "socially dead" is analogous to Arendt's emphasis on the role played by the so-called Laws of History or Nature against objective enemies of totalitarian states. Arendt, *The Origins of Totalitarianism*, 465.

72   Gilroy, *Postcolonial Melancholia*, 22.

73   Netz, *Barbed Wire: An Ecology of Modernity*, 207.

74   Ibid., 210.

75   Ibid., 213.

76   Kotek and Rigoulot, *Le siècle des camps*, 100.

77   Ibid., 103.

78   For an significant analysis of Arendt's thought on these issues, see especially Christian Volk, "The Decline of Order: Hannah Arendt and the Paradoxes of the Nation-State," in *Politics in Dark Times: Encounters with Hannah Arendt*, ed. Seyla Benhabib (Cambridge: Cambridge University Press, 2010).

79   Arendt, *The Origins of Totalitarianism*, 270.

80   Ibid., 231. As Arendt writes, "National sovereignty ... lost its original connotation of freedom of the people and was being surrounded by a pseudomystical aura of lawless arbitrariness."

81   Ibid., 287.

82   Ibid., 273.

83   Arendt captures this when she writes:

None of the statesmen was aware that Hitler's solution of the Jewish problem, first to reduce the German Jews to a nonrecognized minority in Germany, then to drive them as stateless people across borders, and finally to gather them back from everywhere in order to ship them to extermination camps, was an eloquent demonstration to the rest of the world how really to 'liquidate' all problems concerning minorities and stateless.

(Ibid., 290)

84 Himmler is quoted as saying "It [General Plan East] is the greatest piece of colonization which the world has ever seen." Quoted in Mark Mazower, *Hitler's Empire: How the Nazis Ruled Europe* (New York: Penguin Press, 2008), 205.
85 Mazower, *Hitler's Empire: How the Nazis Ruled Europe*, 206. Or as Baranowski puts it:

> Its super-highways would link countless villages of settlement, allowing not only expanded possibilities for tourism, especially Croatia and the Crimea, but also permit a high standard of living for the master race, 'material amenities' through the benefits of mass production and labor of colonized peoples.
> (Baranowski, *Nazi Empire*, 277)

86 Snyder, *Bloodlands: Europe Between Hitler and Stalin*, 160.
87 Bloxham, *The Final Solution: A Genocide*, 201.
88 Snyder, *Bloodlands*, 163.
89 Quoted in Snyder, *Bloodlands*, 188.
90 Wolfgang Sofsky, *The Order of Terror: The Concentration Camp* (Princeton, NJ: Princeton University Press, 1993), 33.
91 Ibid., 34.
92 For example, Omer Bartov writes:

> The 'ethnocrats' of the SS may have come up with ingenious arguments to justify killing as an economically sound means to prevent overpopulation and to bring about a modernization of the economy and a Germanization of the Reich's Lebensraum in the East, but there can be no doubt that, from the standpoint of the German war effort, this was a disastrous decision.
> (Omer Bartov, *Germany's War and the Holocaust: Disputed Histories* [Ithaca, NY: Cornell University Press, 2003], 93)

93 Wolfgang Sofsky, *The Order of Terror: The Concentration Camp*, 12.
94 Hannah Arendt, *Eichmann in Jerusalem: A Report on the Banality of Evil* (New York: Penguin Books, 1994), 268–269.
95 Timothy Snyder, *Bloodlands*, xiv.
96 As Snyder argues, more people died from starvation and shooting than from carbon monoxide. Ibid., xv.
97 Ibid., 14.
98 Primo Levi, *The Drowned and the Saved* (New York: Vintage, 1989), 120.
99 Sofsky, *The Order of Terror: The Concentration Camp*, 14, 23.
100 Hannah Arendt, *The Origins of Totalitarianism*, 392.
101 Ibid., 456.
102 Ibid., 457–458.
103 Donald Bloxham, *The Final Solution: A Genocide*, 181.
104 Ibid., 459.

3 Imperial subjects at home and the rise of the modern surveillance state

Four kinds of social pollution seem worth distinguishing. The first is danger pressing on external boundaries; the second, danger from transgressing the internal lines of the system; the third, danger in the margins of the lines. The fourth is danger from internal contradictions, when some of the basic postulates are denied by other basic postulates, so that at points the system seems to be at war with itself.[1]

Introduction

As I discussed in the previous chapter, the materialization of the camp was, in part, predicated upon the segregation of what were perceived to be internal threats against either imperial or state authority. Whether foreigners living within a state during times of war, prostitutes, vagrants, the insane, the poor, criminals, etc., a certain segment of the domestic population was conceived by state officials as an objective threat that needed to be accounted for and, ideally, placed under constant surveillance. More generally, in this chapter I wish to show that the operationalization of modern state power lies not simply, as commonly asserted by international theorists, in its capacity to deploy the means of "legitimate" violence to protect a specifically demarcated territory – what many claim to have its origins in seventeenth-century Europe; it also, and especially, is predicated upon the establishment of an entire machinery of information-gathering apparatuses to allow state officials to construct and map an evolving constellation of internal and external threats.

The story of the rise of the modern surveillance state is often told in European or Western terms. Beginning in the nineteenth century, Karl Marx noted in *Capital*: "The work of directing, superintending and adjusting becomes one of the functions of capital, from the moment that the labour under capital's control becomes cooperative. As a specific function of capital, the directing function acquires its own specific characteristics."[2] Max Weber also theorized surveillance as being part of the *rationalization* of modern European life through bureaucratic organizations based on hierarchy and regimentation.[3] Almost a century later, Michel Foucault would greatly expand the theorization of surveillance as a function of relations of discipline that circulate throughout different institutions such as the hospital, workshop, school and, especially, prison.[4] Implicit in Marx and Weber, and more explicit in Foucault, surveillance is a way of reinforcing a norm and by implication of constituting the abnormal. Surveillance entails not the rejection of the abnormal but a constant expansion of knowledge about what constitutes it and how to master it. What I wish to show in this chapter is that the relationship between surveillance as a set of techniques of state practice and the constitution of abnormality or deviancy historically was substantially impacted by European and American imperial experiences. More specifically, the categories, the classification schemes, the racial and gendered typologies, the ways of detecting criminal abnormality and deviancy at home and throughout the imperial periphery were historically imbricated by the specific experiences of managing populations that were largely opaque to the imperial gaze. The lack of detailed knowledge about the local population forced imperial authorities to develop information-gathering techniques along with ways of mastering local languages and sources: the use of spies, innovations such as fingerprinting or the experimentation with new technologies to categorize differences in peoples (whether with biometric data or other physical features, for example) were ubiquitous throughout the imperial periphery and the metropole.[5]

I am not arguing in this chapter that the modern European/American surveillance state *originated* in the imperial periphery. My argument is that the imperial crucible provided over the course of the nineteenth and early twentieth centuries a space of experimentation in social control and surveillance to the extent that imperial surveillance helped constitute a specific discursive formation.[6] This discursive formation impacted how the emergent Western imperial nation-states perceived their own populations and how they categorized and drew divisions within them. The nineteenth century was a time when concerns over race and degeneracy came to the fore; concerns about internal threats to the "health" of a population appear paramount and the development of ways to detect such opaque threats became imperative.[7] Moreover, as I will argue, this discursive formation worked on the basis of a metaphor that linked colonial and Western peoples. In other words, certain European groups were deemed to be *similar* to colonial peoples and hence subjected to ever-increasing forms of state surveillance. Metaphors, here, work not simply as a descriptive means but as way of creating new objects of inquiry that propel new forms and justifications of social control. As Nancy Stepan argues, "Metaphors ... through their capacity to construct similarities, create new knowledge."[8] She continues:

> The analogy [between colonized and European peoples] helped constitute the objects of inquiry into human variation – races of all kinds (Slavic, Mediterranean, Scottish, Irish, yellow, black, white, and red), as well as other social groups, such as "the child" and "the madman." The analogy helped define what was problematic about these social groups, what

aspects of them needed further investigation, and which kinds of measurements and what data would be significant for scientific inquiry.[9]

Stepan's metaphors here work in ways to create new objects with agency such as the microbes described in Pasteur's laboratory. This chapter looks at how the imperial laboratory contributed to the formation of apparatuses of social control targeting newly defined social groups on the basis of metaphors derived from imperial knowledge.

The colonized at home: the construction of internal "others"

The analogy between colonized peoples and certain social groups within Europe occurs long before the nineteenth century. In *The Fall of Natural Man*, Anthony Pagden makes the interesting observation that Spanish aristocrats and theologians at the time of the colonization of the Americas during the sixteenth century drew analogies between native Indians and peasants back in Spain. Both Indians and Spanish peasants were said to be no different than the very "animals among which they worked." And, Pagden adds, "Peasants, like Indians, were thought to be proverbially stupid and thus easily overcome by their passions."[10] The very term "Indies" came to signify "any environment in which men lived in ignorance of the Christian faith and of the proper modes of human life."[11] For the Spanish theologians at the time, native Indians were not intrinsically inferior to Europeans; rather, the difference between them and European aristocracy was in their environment, much like the local peasants in the Spanish countryside. Mark Netzloff shows how discourses of internal colonialism in the British Isles over the course of the seventeenth century worked by representing the underclass in colonial terms. For example, he cites the *Hireling Ministry None of Christs* by Roger Williams of 1652: "We have Indians at home – Indians in Cornwall, Indians in Wales, Indians in Ireland."[12] Indeed, Netzloff's main argument is that:

> In the early modern period, England's underclass was increasingly represented and legislatively codified as a distinct and unruly culture, a seemingly alien group whose status necessitated more intensified mechanisms of social control in the form of anti-vagrancy statutes, the creation of work houses, and recommendations for overseas transportation.[13]

Early modern industrialized and imperial expansion accentuated social mobility at the same time that it perpetuated class divisions. "The potential disruptive avenues of social mobility," Netzloff writes, "enabled through travel, commerce, and colonial migration necessitated intensified forms of surveillance and control over subaltern class groups."[14]

Social anxieties that resulted from violent dislocations due to rapid industrialization in England and France became much more acute during the middle of the nineteenth century. In France for example, Olivier Le Cours

Grandmaison makes the connection between the violent suppression of the insurgency in Algeria and the workers' revolt in Paris in 1848. During this crucial event, the French working classes were racialized and bestialized. Eugene Buret, a prominent liberal writer at the time, characterized the French working neighborhoods as:

> a cursed neighborhood, a true ghetto ... Here, if you dare to enter, you will see at every step men and women wither because of misery; semi-nude children that are decaying with filth. Here, in the house of civilization, you will meet thousands of fallen men, because of brutalization, into a life of savagery.[15]

In another place he writes: "Extreme misery forces populations into a savage life ... Pauperism is equivalent to a social interdiction: the paupers are men outside society, they are *outlaws*."[16] Two things are interesting in Buret's discussion. First, is this juxtaposition of a condition of savagery as a result of industrial capitalism and the condition of the overseas colonial populations. Second is that the emergence of an internal population at the heart of the "civilized" European metropole deemed to be akin to colonized peoples – which as Buret was keen on arguing – creates a veritable condition of internal civil war.[17]

Buret's fears of outright civil war became apparent during the events of the 1848 revolution. In June of 1848, thousands of workers rebelled in the streets of Paris, setting up barricades to protest the closing of the National Workshops.[18] The response of the provisional government was swift: it recalled the Army of Africa from Algeria to put down the rebellion by the workers. Friedrich Engels himself sarcastically called the victims of this suppression the "bedouins of the metropole" because the army employed the same techniques of brutal repression it developed in Algeria against them in the very heart of Paris.[19] Indeed, Engels characterized the army's onslaught against the Parisians, which included artillery strikes against masses of workers, women and children and cavalry pursuits that took no prisoners as, "a war of extermination." As Engels writes, "the bourgeoisie proclaimed the workers as not being ordinary enemies that are vanquished, but enemies of society that are [to be] exterminated."[20] As the newly appointed defense minister General Cavaignac stated at the time, "Now that I learned how to discipline the men of Africa, I leave for France to apply my system on these good Parisians who say they are in a Republic."[21] The implication of "my system" was clear to all, as Le Cours Grandmaison notes, and meant in practice an equivalence relation between French subaltern workers and Algerian peasants.

The analogy between colonial populations and certain European groups also operated across relations of race and gender. The working-class poor throughout the nineteenth century were often categorized in racial terms derived from colonial experiences. As Stepans writes, "the urban poor and the insane were in one way or another constructed as biological 'races apart' whose differences from the white male, and likeness to each other, 'explained' their different and lower position in the social hierarchy."[22] Racial identity was in fact determined "scientifically" with complex instruments of measurement such as "the callipers, cephalometers, craniometers, craniophores, craniostats, and parietal goniometers."[23] Such instruments measured, for example, the protrusion of the jaw or various facial angles. The idea was that such biometric data would confirm the "cultural expectations" that White males were innately (i.e. biologically) superior to White women who were, it was claimed, biologically more similar to African males. As Stepan argues, the dominant perception of nineteenth-century anthropologists was that "Caucasian women were indeed more prognathous or apelike in their jaws than White men, and even the largest women's brains, from the 'English or Scotch' race, made them like the African male."[24] Stepan's point is that an analogy was drawn between African men and White women and that such an analogy worked to maintain the status quo:

> The analogies were used by scientists to justify resistance to efforts at social change on the part of women and "lower races," on the grounds that inequality was a "fact" of nature and not a function of the power relations in a society.[25]

When the status quo comes into crisis, as was the case during the French rebellions in 1848, such "scientific" analogies and rationalization can take on such a lethal role. The violence perpetuated by imperial authorities to pacify their respective imperial dominions was then justified and applied against those "internal" groups deemed to be like certain colonial populations. Such domestic crises or internal rebellions also provoked state officials to enact preventative measures to track, observe, and limit the movement of members of society that might pose a future threat. Thus we have in the aftermath of the 1848 revolt in Paris the installation of points of observation along major avenues to surveil the movement of workers; twenty years later, Baron Haussmann would radically change urban Paris, destroying much of its dense medieval part, creating much more open spaces in order for the state to better monitor and account for what happens in certain neighborhoods.[26] We have, as well, the proliferation of institutions designed to constantly monitor criminals, vagrants and the insane. What I will show in the next section, however, is that the experiences and innovations of governing populations under certain imperial powers helped contribute to the emergence of the modern surveillance state.

The colonial laboratory: a closer look at the imperial surveillance

The year 1857 proved to be an earth-shattering year in the history of colonial India. On May 10th of that year Indian Sepoy soldiers of the British East Indian army rebelled against British officers. The ostensible reason for the mutiny was that the cartridges used for firearms by the army were laced with grease derived from pig and beef fat. In fact the rebellion reflected resistance to the fact that "British officials were nursing plans to finally abolish the

Mughal court, and to impose not just British laws and technology on India, but also Christianity."[27] With Delhi in open rebellion and the British presence in India in peril, the British realized that more direct governance of the sub-continent was imperative to maintain their imperial hegemony. The rebellion itself was ruthlessly crushed in ways reminiscent of the colonial pacification campaigns discussed in the previous chapter.[28] In the wake of the Sepoy rebellion direct administrative structures were established and managed by the British state, essentially displacing the quasi-private East India Company. Here the emphasis was on implementing a series of reforms designed to bureau-cratize Indian governance. As John Darwin argues, "Their [the civilians] authority was enhanced by the new emphasis on administrative and financial stability rather than the forceable annexation of princely states – a practice that had given the Company rule its aggressive, militaristic character."[29]

One of the important consequences of the Indian rebellion of 1857 and the emergence of direct British imperial rule was the opportunity to govern using "scientific" knowledge of the local population. The establishment of the civi-lian "British Raj" (i.e. formal British governance of the subcontinent until independence in 1947) through the Indian Civil Service emphasized the eth-nographic production of knowledge as a way of understanding and governing the great diversity but also of uncovering and cementing certain hierarchies among the Indian population. As Ann Stoler and Fredrick Cooper explain, "'Caste' in India and 'tribe' in Africa were in part colonial constructs, efforts to render fluid and confusing social and political relationships into categories sufficiently static and reified and thereby useful to colonial understanding and control."[30] Chandak Sengoopta argues that this turn toward scientific/administrative management was directly predicated upon an "anthropological interest in charting the physical and cultural characteristics – all of them lumped together as *racial* characteristics – of the population."[31] The nexus between the emergence of racial science and the necessity of classifying, categorizing and managing the extremely diverse Indian population was a ubiquitous aspect of imperial governance. James Scott shows more generally that nineteenth-century high modernist ideals of simplifying and making legible the urban and social space was significantly tied to establishing effi-cient state control.[32] However, the colonial context of implementing such a program was particularly challenging given the barriers of language and cul-ture, especially in colonial India. The British were forced to be far more innovative in their administrative techniques as a result. As Nicholas Dirks argues in his forward to Bernard Cohn's classic *Colonialism and Its Forms of Knowledge*: "The [Indian] colonial state is seen as a theatre for state experi-mentation, where historiography, documentation, certification, and repre-sentation were all state modalities that transformed knowledge into power."[33] During this time (1881) the civilian British Raj completed the first census in India, *The Imperial Gazetteer of India*, along with the Statistical Survey which was comprised of "114 volumes and 54,000 pages, the ethnographic studies of 'tribes and castes,' and the distinct 'histories' compiled by energetic officials, the Civilian Raj extended and codified its administrative knowledge and imposed its categories on an untidy social reality."[34]

Nonetheless, while the knowledge gained as a result of ethnographic field-work increased the ability of the Raj to exert authority over the various populations, it still posed the sharp problem of identifying individual Indians for civil or criminal matters. For one of the most perplexing facets of British colonial rule, as Chandak Sengoopta shows, was the complete lack of ability of British civil servants to correctly ascertain the identity of specific individuals. "Establishing the identities of individual Indians," Sengoopta argues:

> however, was important not only to avert conceptual chaos or to improve administrative efficiency in a largely illiterate environment – the prime motive was to counter what virtually every British official considered intrinsic to Indians: the propensity to lie, deceive, cheat and defraud.[35]

The lack of ability to identify individuals resulted, for example, in the pro-blematic disbursement of state pensions, as impersonators succeeded in making multiple claims.[36] It cast doubt on the fairness of criminal judicial proceedings and the ability to identify and punish habitual offenders. In short, for the sake of bringing British administrative rule to the level of the indivi-dual body and identity, a new technology of individual identification was needed to individualize people divided according to tribe and caste.[37]

Around the mid-nineteenth century William Herschel, an official with the Indian Civil Service in Bengal, experimented with taking individual hand-prints. He initially developed the technique as a way of making sure that a local contractor would not renege on a contract, perhaps even adapting it from Bengali practices. Several years later, Herschel experimented with taking prints of individual fingers and speculated that the markings and grooves were unique to each individual and thus could represent an important means of individual identification. Thus both Cole and Sengoopta show that finger-printing in the Indian context began essentially as a "technique for civil, not criminal, identification" as a way of determining the validity of contracts.[38] If, as Cole argues, fingerprinting emerged in the specific colonial context in which "inferiority of the ruled and their attendant deceptions and frauds provoked the search for greater and more efficient social control and identifi-cation" it should come as no surprise that fingerprints as a technology of marking individual identity took on such importance in late nineteenth-century colonial India.[39] Fingerprints gradually replaced the Bertillonage system that rested upon making a series of anthropometric measurements of the entire body. This technique had been developed in Europe and proved to be unwieldy in India because of not only the absence of a standard operating procedure for measuring and comparing results, but also because in colonial spaces administrators could not differentiate eye color or skin pigmentation.[40] Moreover, the Bertillonage system suffered from a lack of an adequate classifica-tion scheme that would also impact initial attempts at standardizing fingerprinting technology. Indeed, what finally permitted fingerprinting to become a standard procedure for identification was the specific colonial innovation developed by Edward Henry. Henry, who in 1891 became inspector general of the Bengal Police, invented a system to classify fingerprints so that it was possible to search for matches in an efficient manner.[41] The efficiency of Henry's system over the Bertillon anthropometric system ensured that fingerprinting would become a routinized tool for individual identification by state authorities.

The legitimization of fingerprinting in the imperial space of experience and its repatriation back into Europe occurred at the nexus of racial science, Darwinian evolutionary theory and criminal anthropology that was critically influenced by established anthropological theories devised in the colonies. The Henry system was eventually adopted by Scotland Yard and over time institutionalized by policing departments across the world. In the Western imperial metropole, however, fingerprinting was not as broadly used as it was in the imperial settings. While British administrators conceived of fingerprinting as a means to identify individuals in their interactions with the colonial state, the adoption of fingerprinting in the Britain, as Sengoopta argues, became a "purely forensic procedure" for determining criminal recidivism.[42] Furthermore, during the latter part of the nineteenth century, the innovation of fingerprinting reinforced the connection between habitual recidivism and theories of hereditary criminality devised on the basis of evolutionary physical attributes. "Criminals," as Stephen J. Gould describes Cesare Lombroso's nineteenth-century theory of criminality, "are evolutionary throwbacks in our midsts."[43] This idea of "evolutionary throwback" coincides with what imperial authorities perceived to be native peoples. The colonial conceptions of caste or tribe and European ideas of race that were used to represent subjected peoples gained purchase in European criminology of the late nineteenth century. Cole shows through an article written by J. Bruce Thompson in 1870 that "Caste served as a way of applying a fine-grained racial typology even to the native population of Europe," who were often conceived as racial or foreign "others." Notions of hereditary criminality in Lombroso's theories proved enormously influential in defining certain European groups as being physically prone to criminal behavior so that fingerprinting was legitimized as a technique to enhance state surveillance.[44] Ronald R. Thomas shows that:

> the theory and practice of criminology and the history of imperialism consistently intersected one another in the latter part of the nineteenth century. *The empire served as a laboratory in which criminological theories and techniques were discovered, developed, and tested for eventual application on the common criminal back home.*[45]

The application of these criminal theories resulted in the formation of state surveillance apparatuses designed to enhance knowledge about various criminally prone groups. The process of differentiating "'ordinary' citizens from the criminal kind," which was rooted in the colonialist racial typologies and representations of foreign bodies, helps us understand, for example, the adoption of fingerprinting in the United States.[46] Christian Parenti explains that:

> white administrators and police who saw (or imagined) Asians, Africans, and Native Americans as bafflingly homogeneous began to fall back on the infinite uniqueness of fingerprints. Thus, fingerprinting literally migrated from the colonial periphery to the economic core. In the United States the first populations to be fingerprinted en masse were convicts, petty criminals, soldiers, and Native peoples.[47]

In this case, fingerprinting became part of a discursive formation that legitimized social or class stratification. It proved to be an important component of the nascent modern surveillance state always on the lookout for internal dangerous populations or classes.

While fingerprinting has proved crucial, up to this day, for the functioning of the modern surveillance state, it is in fact only one part of a larger development and transformation in the apparatus of modern surveillance *qua* power. Michel Foucault's work on disciplinary and security mechanisms elaborates the striking transformation from the extreme sovereign rituals of violence to the everyday micro-physics of disciplinary mechanisms that began to take hold in Europe at the cusp of the nineteenth century. What is not apparent in Foucault's discussion of the panopticon is that as a mechanism of power and a means of gaining knowledge the imperial space of experience proved to be a crucial testing ground for what became the modern disciplinary strategies. The model of the panopticon as a generalizable model of modern disciplinary power was innovated, experimented, and actualized to a far greater degree in imperial spaces over the course of the nineteenth and twentieth centuries than in Northern Europe

Foucault's illustration of the novel mechanisms of power – wherein power is conceived as a force or relation of forces operating and circulating for the productive affectation of individual bodies, rather than a Hobbesian model of sovereign power – and how it constitutes societal control operates because of three central practices: hierarchical observation, normalizing judgment and the examination.[48] The architectural innovations that permit a seamless observation of individuals, the establishment of standards to measure "normal" behavior, and the knowledge associated with both observation and self-examination constitute the political rationality of modern disciplinary power. For Foucault, Jeremy Bentham's conception of the panopticon is the nexus of these three mechanisms embodied in an architectural form. Indeed, Foucault bases his genealogy of the modern prison and, more generally, modern disciplinary power, on Bentham's idea of being able to surveil a large group of people or prisoners with a small set of managers or guards.

The key to the panopticon was its unique architecture that allowed the observed to internalize the gaze of the observer without *actually* knowing whether the observer was in the act of observing. As Foucault puts it:

[T]he major effect of the Panopticon: to induce in the inmate a state of conscious and permanent visibility that assures the automatic functioning of power. So to arrange things that the surveillance is permanent in its effects, even if it is discontinuous in its actions; that this architectural apparatus should be a machine for creating and sustaining a power relation independent of the person who exercises it; in short, that the inmates should be caught up in a power mechanism of which they are themselves the bearers.[49]

For Foucault, the panopticon proves to be the crucial schematic for modern disciplinary power insofar as it "automizes and disindividualizes power." It results in the "homogeneous effects of power" that make it a much more efficient mechanism for wielding power than the rituals of sovereign power.[50]

Revealingly, Foucault asserts that the panopticon "was also a laboratory." It was a laboratory insofar as "it could be used as a machine to carry out experiments, to alter behavior, to train or correct individuals."[51] "The Panopticon," Foucault continues, "is a privileged place for experiments on men, and for analyzing with complete certainty the transformations that may be obtained from them ... [so that it] functions as a kind of laboratory of power."[52] The metaphor of the laboratory is important for two reasons. First, Foucault stresses that the panopticon is not simply an ideal type of prison architecture, but a "generalizable model of functioning; a way of defining power relations in terms of the everyday life of men." As a result, the panopticon is "polyvalent in its applications" and can be used in multiple settings such as "hospitals, workshops, schools, prisons."[53] It redefines such diverse spaces under a specific economy of power that experiments with training or disciplining individual bodies passing through these spaces. It therefore allows not only the state apparatus itself to surveil individual bodies, but it also allows experimentation with a multiplicity of societal assemblages on a much wider social scale. Second, and more crucially, Foucault never connects this modality of power and experimentation to the imperial setting. For Foucault, the emergence of the panopticon as the modern embodiment of surveillance is embedded in a sociopolitical history of the present that is the West, or more precisely, Northern Europe. As Peter Redfield shows, Bentham's original idea of the panopticon emerged out of the specific experience that his brother Samuel had in imperial Russia. Samuel Bentham was charged by Prince Potemkin to "improve naval production" and as a result conceived of an "'inspection house,' a structure that would, by its very structure, mediate problems of skill and discipline between imported English experts and local Russian peasants."[54] This crucial experience and influence on Jeremy Bentham, who would abstract his brother's innovation, reveals that the panoptic model in fact emerges from *the margins of Europe, and in this sense a potentially colonial genealogy.*[55]

This colonial genealogy at the heart of the transformation of modern disciplinary power and the centrality of surveillance is a missing component of

Foucault's Eurocentric genealogy in *Discipline and Punish*. Theorists and historians show that the panoptic model of power was actualized to a far greater degree in various imperial laboratories. Timothy Mitchell goes so far as to argue that:

> [T]he panopticon, the model institution whose geometric order and generalised surveillance serve as a motif for this kind of power, was a colonial invention. The panoptic principle was devised on Europe's colonial frontier with the Ottoman Empire, and examples of the panopticon were built for the most part not in northern Europe but in places like colonial India. The same can be said of for the monitoring method of schooling, also discussed by Foucault, whose mode of improving and disciplining a population … came to be considered the model political process to accompany the capitalist transformation of Egypt.[56]

Or as Michael Salman argues concerning the American occupation of the Philippines in the late nineteenth century:

> it is in the colonies of the late nineteenth and early twentieth centuries that we find the most complete examples of the "carceral continuum," the concept Foucault introduced to represent the circulation of disciplinary techniques throughout societal institutions and the human sciences.[57]

While Mitchell and Salman point to the actualization of panoptic laboratories of social control, the metaphor of the imperial panoptic gaze has proved crucial for many postcolonial theorists for understanding colonial subjectivity. David Spurr, for example, shows the extent to which travel writing and the rhetorics of imperial discourse more generally operate within a visual representation of command of landscapes or bodies. "The writer is placed," as Spurr writes, "either above or at the center of things, yet apart from them, so that the organization and classification of things takes place according to the writer's own system of value."[58] What is referred to here as the "system of value" is the civilizing mission. What has been less apparent is the reversal of the imperial gaze as a constituting mechanism for understanding the imperial metropole.[59] Mary Louise Pratt, looking at the travel writing literature of the sixteenth and seventeenth centuries, shows the lack of attention to reversing this imperial gaze:

> While the imperial metropole tends to imagine itself as determining the periphery (in the emanating glow of the civilizing mission or the cash flow of development, for example), it habitually blinds itself to the reverse dynamic, the power of colonies have over their "mother" countries … empires create in the imperial center of power an obsessive need to present and re-present its peripheries and its others continually to itself.[60]

To be sure, taking for granted the panopticon as a colonial apparatus needs to be taken with care when examining the specificities of colonial institutions and the state. As Ann Stoler rightly remarks:

> there was no panoptic imperial state but only a partially realized range of efforts to specify uses of and access to public space and to dictate which cultural affinities and styles, and what distribution of affections, would prevail in the street and in the home.[61]

The danger of using Bentham's model, and Foucault's insights on disciplinary and biopolitical security mechanisms, in the colony is that the colonial space was, one the one hand, much more striated with heterogeneous elements that were missed by the imperial gaze. Implied is a "coexistence of modern and premodern orientations with different segments of the imperial project" which calls into question the direct applicability of Foucauldian methodological studies of colonial disciplinary regimes.[62] The was a great chasm between penal theory (for example) and actual conditions in colonial settings for the implementation of reform programs. David Arnold shows in the case of colonial prisons in India, "Administrative and convict resistance were more likely causes of this failure to maintain Benthamite institutions than was the weight of prison numbers."[63] Nonetheless, while Arnold argues that Foucault's disciplinary model does not take into account the various facets of internal resistance to colonial reform programs, that even colonial officials were, on pragmatic grounds, reticent to implement modern reforms, "the prison was ... a critical site for the acquisition of colonial knowledge and for the exercise – or negotiation – of colonial power." Furthermore, Arnold writes, "like Foucault, I see the prison not as an isolated institution, but as something representative of the ways in which colonial knowledge was constructed and developed."[64]

There are two crucial examples that I want to use to illustrate more precisely how this colonial knowledge of surveillance and disciplinary technologies shaped the imperial center.

Ann Stoler's work pushes Foucauldian insights on discipline and biopolitics in the imperial context. In her original study of the Sumatra's east coast plantations she argues that such sites "were virtual laboratories for technical and social experimentation."[65] They were so because Dutch colonial authorities grappled with mastering local resistance to capitalist exploitation. However, it is in her subsequent study on race and desire that she takes head-on Foucault's genealogies of modern disciplinary power and sexuality. Here Stoler questions the representation of concepts such as citizenship, liberalism, race, state welfare and culture as being distinctly "European" and embodying something like an identity of bourgeois "European-ness." For Stoler, rather than departing from the premise that categories of colonizer and colonized were reified and clear, she detects in the historical record of imperial governance "precarious vulnerabilities" revolving around questions of sexuality and morality that would impact the discourse of bourgeois norms. The European imperial project was not a monolithic implementation of European nineteenth-century racial and sexual mores in the imperial context; it was not, simply, the attempt to render, in concrete clarity, the colonized as racially distinct from the European: "Colonialism was not a secure bourgeois project. It was not only the importation of middle-class sensibilities to the colonies, but about the *making* of them."[66] It was about the *making* of such sensibilities in the imperial context because administrators were faced with crucial questions concerning the position of poor Whites in the colonies, about the social status of offspring from mixed unions, about the effects of the upbringing of children of colonists by local nursemaids with their different "blood." In other words, the imperial space of experience provoked anxieties "that even for European-born, the Indies was transformative of cultural essence, social disposition, and personhood itself." It resulted in the perception that "'Europeanness', and by implication the racialized 'Other,' was not a fixed attribute, but one altered by environment, class contingent, and not secured by both."[67]

Imperial administrators also were fearful of miscegenation that would result in the degeneration of the White colonial population, potentially unraveling the imperial order. Imperial administrators were therefore keen on instituting methods of surveillance that targeted sexual relations between European and native inhabitants, of defining the role of nursemaids in the house, for example, as a way of enacting the "intensified surveillance of native servants and European children [and] mark[ing] out the cultural borders of the European community."[68] The imperial surveillance state, Stoler argues, was not simply centered on the colonized, but crucially marked the colonizer's behavior as well, instituting new norms of social behavior for European women especially.[69] Thus Stoler argues that a large part of the civilizing mission during the nineteenth century was centered on "recalcitrant and ambiguous participants in imperial culture at home and abroad."[70] Surveillance in this case was not only visual, as in Foucault's model of the panopticon, but was also meant to reveal the "invisible bonds, those 'attachments that unite us without one being able to say what they are' that might distinguish 'real Frenchmen' and the 'truly Dutch' from their suspect false compatriots."[71] Stoler shows that the *inlandish kinderen*, or children of mixed parentage, were not perceived to be European precisely because they did not possess the "self-discipline, sexual morals, and economic independence that would count them among a citizenry fit for rule."[72] Such children highlighted the blurred racial and social categories that imperial administrators sought to clarify and redefine. Imperial administrators worked to make intelligible ways of demarcating what it means to be a European and the attributes a European purportedly possesses. Racial discourses emanating from imperial laboratories, Stoler argues, were then crucial in defining and structuring a bourgeois disciplinary and biopolitical order that racialized certain internal classes and marginalized groups – viz. criminals, paupers, prostitutes, the insane, etc., but also constituted the meaning of what was the proper identity of the European liberal citizen.[73]

Moving away from European imperial practice, I turn to America's own historical experience in late nineteenth-century imperialism and how that experience impacted the development of its national security state. Alfred McCoy argues that an examination of policing and surveillance innovations produced during the American occupation of the Philippines explains the internal surveillance capacity of the federal government during the early part of the twentieth century. Prior to American imperial expansion the federal government possessed dramatically limited means of coercion over its citizens. As McCoy describes it, "At the dawn of the twentieth century, the federal government, unlike its European counterparts, did not tax, conscript, investigate, regulate, arrest, hospitalize, or otherwise control its citizenry."[74] Such practices were delegated to the individual states without the capacity for centralized bureaucratic administration across the United States. Nonetheless, by the second decade of the twentieth century, under the Wilson administration, McCoy asserts that the contours of the national security began to take shape. The First World War and the corresponding hysteria over which groups might be disloyal to the American war effort required governmental (and as McCoy argues) private apparatuses, such as the American Protective League, to surveil large groups of people within the United States. This was beyond the original capacity of the federal government to enact:

> In prewar decades the federal government had limited intelligence, less operational capacity, and no covert capability. Indeed, before the founding of the Bureau of Investigation in 1908 Washington had no domestic security agency worthy of the name, leaving policing to the cities and surveillance to private agencies such the Pinkertons.[75]

During the First World War, veterans of America's colonial administration began to make their presence felt in the transformation of domestic security services. In 1917, Ralph Van Deman, a colonial officer in the American Army, worked to establish the Military Intelligence Division (MID), whose responsibility was counterintelligence and surveillance. In its operational practices, the MID adopted the same data gathering and mining techniques established in the Philippines. It also profiled sections of the American public according to racial and ethnic characteristics, "seeing certain ethnic communities almost as domestic colonies."[76] Indeed, according to McCoy, a substantial feature of what he calls "imperial mimesis" (see Chapter 1) was not only the translation and adaptation of technological experimentation developed in the Philippines within the federal state apparatus, but the ways in which official governmental and non-governmental discourse translated difference through an imperial filter. As McCoy writes, "colonial veterans came home to turn the same lens on America, seeing its ethnic communities not as fellow citizens but as internal colonies requiring coercive control."[77] In fact,

as C. Vann Woodward notes, the American imperial adventure, which resulted in bringing millions of "non-white" peoples from the Caribbean and
Pacific under American jurisdiction, reinvigorated racial policies and discourses of segregation throughout the South, especially given – quoting an
editorial from the *Atlantic Monthly*, at the time – "If the stronger and cleverer
race is free to impose its will upon 'new-caught, sullen peoples' on the other side
of the globe, why not in South Carolina and Mississippi?"[78] As Woodward
writes:

> At the very time that imperialism was sweeping the country, the doctrine
> of racism reached a crest of acceptability and popularity among respect-
> able scholarly and intellectual circles. At home and abroad biologists,
> sociologists, anthropologists, and historians, as well as journalists and
> novelists, gave support to the doctrine that races were discrete entities and
> that the "Anglo-Saxon" or "Caucasian" was the superior of them all. It
> was not that Southern politicians needed any support from learned circles
> to sustain their own doctrines, but they found that such intellectual
> endorsement of their racist theories facilitated acceptance of their views
> and policies.[79]

While the motivation for establishing new security and surveillance apparatuses was transient – Wilson himself did not seek to establish permanent
institutions and hence the emphasis on private partnerships – McCoy writes,
"this domestic security apparatus would persist for the next half century as a
defining feature of American life."[80] It would persist through the red scare,
through the armed uprising of miners in 1921 and throughout the Cold War
with the strengthening of domestic federal bureaucracies for domestic security
and surveillance. It would maintain a persistent vigilance against those
deemed to be a threat to the strength and vitality of the American way of life.
To put it differently, the moment of crystallization of the modern American
security state occurred roughly around the time of the First World War,
"when Washington was adopting powerful instruments, many of them forged
at the periphery of empire, for actively shaping American society: immigration controls, intelligence testing, drug prohibition, mandatory public health
measures, and internal security."[81]

What was it about the American experience in the Philippines that provoked such an important transformation of the American federal state?
McCoy claims that the significance of the American experience was that it
marked a leap forward in terms of integrating technological innovations for
the purposes of social control. Such technological innovations, encompassing
what McCoy calls an "information revolution" in the latter part of the nineteenth century, included the "quadruplex telegraph (1874), Philo Remington's
commercial typewriter (1874), and Alexander Graham Bell's telephone
(1876)."[82] These domestic information generating innovations were imported
and adapted in the Philippines to create an unprecedented surveillance

machine uniquely adapted for social control. In fact, what the US accomplished in the Philippines was much more far-reaching than what even the French and British were capable of in their respective imperial possessions.[83] In effect, "freed of the constrains of constitution, courts, and civil society, the US regime deployed its information technologies to form what was arguably the world's first surveillance state." It was the world's first surveillance state because none of the European powers "could match the synthesis of legal repression, incessant patrolling, and suffocating surveillance found in the colonial Philippines."[84] Coupled with the rise of the imperial surveillance state was the moralization of governance, the enactment of strict laws against drug use and gambling that would all the more require a stringent imperial presence.

McCoy argues that the result of the Philippine rebellion compelled American authorities on the islands to adapt these technological innovations for the sake of maintaining its grip. In contrast to the European empires, McCoy asserts that US imperial management was not formalized domestically through institutions to train imperial administrators; it did not capture in an orientalist vein the intellectual curiosity of American officials with the local languages, customs, history, archaeology, etc., as it did French and British imperial officials. The American presence in the Philippines was as much utilitarian as it was concerned with pragmatic questions of governance and control. "American colonialism," McCoy argues, "employed a decentralized market model, responding to problems by mobilizing a cadre of contractors for quick, cost-effective solutions."[85] As McCoy continues:

> Armed with authority unimagined in America, these colonial officials conducted an ad hoc experiment in police-state controls, fostering innovations in both data management and shoe-leather surveillance whose sum was a modern police panopticon … America's invention of the surveillance state was an accidental, almost coincidental confluence of long-term trends and ephemeral events.[86]

One of the important tools created by the American authorities was the Philippine Constabulary (PC). Composed of native soldiers and policemen, it engaged in vast counterinsurgency campaigns against rebellious Filipinos by disarming the countryside, apprehending those responsible and by "secur[ing] the capital using intelligence operatives to round up subversives and monitor radical nationalists."[87] The Philippine Constabulary's monitoring activities aided the colonial regime in subverting local resistance by publishing scandalous material while protecting its own allies, a practice that would be applied within the United States.[88] As McCoy writes:

> Using the rich US records, study of the Philippines can take us beyond the view of the colonial police as a blunt instrument for physical coercion to a more nuanced understanding of its role as a panopticon, sweeping the shadows for sensitive information with spies or surveillance and then

selectively releasing, threatening to release, scandal to shape the course of Filipino political careers. Though long ignored, the deft control of information was a key facet of colonial control over elites beyond coercion or manipulation. Just as the threat of fusillades from repeating rifles restrained striking workers or rebellious peasants, or the possibility of public humiliation constrained political elites within the colonial state's tight bounds.[89]

The case of American imperial governance in the Philippines is interesting as well because of the myriad experiments conducted in the realm of social and health policies. A significant part of American imperial governance involved governing public and private behavior and morality. The United States established regulations against the use of drugs such as opium, which resulted in the Harrison Narcotics Act of 1914 controlling the sale and distribution of opiates in the United States.[90] Warwick Anderson's work helps explain the extent to which the American imperial project revolved around establishing spaces of control and discipline over individual bodies. As Anderson argues, "one of the more resonant aspects of the American colonial project was to produce a space for somatic disciplining of supposedly refractory Filipinos."[91] What Anderson means is that American officials believed that Filipinos were incubators of pathogens that would potentially render vulnerable American bodies in such an imperial space because of their purported inherent evolutionary inferiority. The Filipino body, it was commonly imagined by American officials, was one that lacked the discipline to exuviate its waste products in a hygienic manner. "Filipinos," Anderson argues, "then, were cast along with other local fauna as disease dealers, and even apparently healthy Filipinos might secretly carry invisible pathogens from which supposedly pure bourgeois Americans were typically exempt and to which they were more vulnerable."[92]

Anderson sketches the contours of an emerging notion of biomedical citizenship which was predicated on the "Strict enforcement of the rules of personal and domestic hygiene" with the result that:

> Health authorities targeted toilet practices, food handling, dietary customs, and housing designs; they rebuilt the markets, using more hygienic concrete, and suppressed the unsanitary fiestas; and they assumed power to examine Filipinos at random and to disinfect, fumigate, and medicate at will.[93]

In order to establish this biomedical/biopolitical regime Anderson argues that American officials initially rethought the spatial environment of the Philippines to make it more amenable to calculative reason.[94] This step allowed a comparison between a "clean" or ascetic space of the American medical laboratory and the indigenous tropical environment which was blamed for the medical and social ills of the population. It was then a question of "replicat[ing] the controlled conditions of the Bureau of Science" in order to ensure the disinfection of the colonial space from visible and invisible local pathogens.[95]

Surveillance, here, takes on a wider meaning, necessitating not only the visible mechanism associated with the panoptic gaze, but with a larger transformation of the socio-cultural environment as a whole. Indeed, as Anderson quotes James A. Le Roy in 1906 as writing, "The Philippines may be considered today as a laboratory where an experiment with important bearings on the 'race problem' is being conducted."[96]

Anderson draws implications for how public health in the United States was aligned with innovations and discoveries in the colonial periphery. Much like the case of fingerprinting, innovations did not translate automatically and seamlessly into the United States. "In general," Anderson writes:

> the medical experience of empire served to amplify existing features of domestic public health and to reshape structures and policies already in place rather than introducing wholly new procedures and goals. In particular, it tended to focus more attention on the fault lines of race and force recognition of the need to intervene more vigorously to reform the personal and domestic hygiene on the margins of society.[97]

But what is important here is the central place accorded to the transformation of society, whether the imperial space of experience or the metropole, to the requirements of laboratory conditions. Indeed, Anderson briefly turns to Bruno Latour's work on laboratory science to make sense of this process of translation and transformation from the space of the laboratory to society as a whole, resulting in the inability to demarcate the boundaries of both.[98]

Conclusion

International theorists tend to forget the fact that European powers were, historically speaking, imperial powers. Nineteenth-century empire-building occurred within an entirely different spatial cartography than the usually assumed Westphalian model; borders were not clearly demarcated, imperial authority was exerted with various degrees of concentration and populations ebbed and flowed without constant monitoring. At the same time, a "discourse of barbarism" was created to rigidify the boundaries between imperial subjects and those who needed to be "civilized."[99] "The discourse of barbarism," Herfried Münkler writes, "therefore repeatedly assists in the semantic drawing of a boundary that would otherwise be blurred or invisible; it produces an imaginary dividing line to make up for the actual lack of imperial contours."[100] What we have seen, is that the dividing line that Münkler speaks of actually reaches into the very core of the imperial nation-state: in their potential threat to the status quo, working-class neighborhoods of Paris become equivalent to insurrections in Algeria. The constant need for surveillance comes out of the fundamental limitations of imperial authority over the identities of subjected populations. Using categories and classification schemes borne out of various imperial laboratories, the attempt to demarcate the "internal barbarians" became a ubiquitous feature of how Western nation-states organized their security apparatuses.

Notes

1 Mary Douglas, *Purity and Danger: An Analysis of Concept of Pollution and Taboo* (New York: Routledge, 2005 [1966]), 151–152; quoted in Daniel Pick, *Faces of Degeneration: A European Disorder, c. 1848–1918* (Cambridge: Cambridge University Press, 1993), 39.
2 Quoted in Christian Fuchs, "Political Economy and Surveillance Theory," *Critical Sociology* (2012), 4.
3 See for example David Lyons, *The Electronic Eye: The Rise of the Surveillance Society* (Minneapolis: University of Minnesota Press, 1994), 25–26.
4 Michel Foucault, *Discipline and Punish: The Birth of the Prison* (New York: Vintage Books, 1995).
5 C. A. Bayly, *Empire and Information* (Cambridge: Cambridge University Press, 1996).
6 Michel Foucault, *The Archaeology of Knowledge* (New York: Routledge, 2002 [1969]), 130. Foucault understands a discursive formation as an amalgamation of statements that define validity or not of socio-political action.
7 Michel Foucault, *Society Must Be Defended* (New York: Picador, 2003).
8 Nancy Leys Stepans, "Race and Gender: The Role of Analogy in Science," *Isis* 77, no. 2 (1986), 271.
9 Ibid., 272.
10 Anthony Pagden, *The Fall of Natural Man: The American Indian and the Origins of Comparative Ethnology* (Cambridge: Cambridge University Press, 1986), 97.
11 Ibid., 97–98.
12 Mark Netzloff, *England's Internal Colonies: Class, Capital, and the Literature of Early Modern English Colonialism* (New York: Palgrave, 2003), 1.
13 Ibid., 2.
14 Ibid., 3.
15 Quoted in Olivier Le Cour Grandmaison, *Colonizer, exterminer: sur la guerre et l'état colonial* (Paris: Fayard, 2005), 278.
16 Quoted in Pierre Rosanvallon, *La société des égaux* (Paris: Seuil, 2011), 116.
17 Eugene Buret, *De la misère des classes laborieuses en Angleterre et en France*, vol. 2 (Paris: Jules Renouard et Compagnie, 1841), 51.
18 The national workshops were designed to hire at state expense unemployed workers to work in construction projects for a minimum wage. This was (at the time) the only institution, aside from enlisting in the army, that acted as a safety net for the poorest worker. By closing it down, the newly elected conservative government was signaling that the worker's grievances of unemployment and penury were not going to be taken seriously. See, for example, William Fortescu, *France and 1848: The End of Monarchy* (New York: Routledge, 2005), 110–112.
19 For the Engels citation see ibid., 20.
20 Olivier Le Cour Grandmaison, *Colonizer, exterminer: sur la guerre et l'état colonial*, 323.
21 Quoted in ibid., 309.
22 Stepans, "Race and Gender: The Role of Analogy in Science," 264; Edward Said also notes that such analogies worked in the case of Oriental discourses:

> Along with all other peoples variously designated as backward, degenerate, uncivilized, retarded, the Orientals were viewed in a framework constructed out of biological determinism and moral-political admonishment. The Oriental was linked thus to elements in Western society (delinquents, the insane,

women, the poor) having in common an identity best described as lamentably alien. Orientals were rarely seen or looked at; they were see through, analyzed not as citizens, or even people, but as problems to be solved or confined or – as the colonial powers openly coveted their territory – taken over.

(Edward Said, *Orientalism* [New York: Vintage, 1979], 207)

23 Stepan, "Race and Gender: The Role of Analogy in Science," 266.
24 Ibid., 267.
25 Stepans, "Race and Gender: The Role of Analogy in Science," 275.
26 Le Cour Grandmaison, *Colonizer, exterminer*, 332–333.
27 William Dalrymple, *The Last Mughal: The Fall of a Dynasty, Delhi, 1857* (New York: Knopf, 2006), 13.
28 Dalrymple quotes a British soldier as describing the violence in Delhi as:

> a war of extermination, in which no prisoners were taken and no mercy shown – in short one of the most cruel and vindictive wars this world has seen ... Dead bodies lay thick in the streets and open spaces, and numbers were killed in their houses ... Many non-combatants lost their lives, our men, mad and excited, making no distinction. There is no more terrible spectacle than a city taken by storm.
>
> (Ibid., 336)

29 John Darwin, *The Empire Project: The Rise and Fall of The British World-System, 1830–1970* (Cambridge: Cambridge University Press, 2009), 187.
30 Ann Laura Stoler and Frederick Cooper. "Between Metropole and Colony: Rethinking a Research Agenda," in *Tensions Of Empire: Colonial Cultures in a Bourgeois World* (Berkeley: University of California Press, 2014), 11.
31 Chandak Sengoopta, *Imprint of the Raj: How Fingerprinting Was Born in Colonial India* (London: Macmillan, 2003), 42.
32 James C. Scott, *Seeing Like a State: How Certain Schemes to Improve the Human Condition Have Failed* (New Haven, CT: Yale University Press, 1998).
33 Nicholas B. Dirks, "Foreword," in *Colonialism and Its Forms of Knowledge*, ed. Bernard S.Cohn (Princeton, NJ: Princeton University Press, 1996), xi.
34 Darwin, *The Empire Project: The Rise and Fall of The British World-System, 1830–1970*, 187.
35 Sengoopta, *Imprint of the Raj: How Fingerprinting Was Born in Colonial India*, 47–48.
36 Simon A. Cole, *Suspect Identities: A History of Fingerprinting and Criminal Identification* (Cambridge, MA: Harvard University Press, 2002), 64.
37 Christian Parenti, *The Soft Cage: Surveillance in America from Slavery to the War on Terror* (New York: Basic Books, 2003), 49. As Parenti writes, "Among dactyloscopy's chief advantages – or so believed white colonial administrators, police, and bureaucrats – was its ability to compensate for the homogenizing effects of racist perceptions."
38 Cole, *Suspect Identities: A History of Fingerprinting and Criminal Identification*, 65.
39 Ibid., 65. To be sure, as Sengoopta shows in his discussion of the indigo disturbances the adoption of fingerprinting in India did not proceed automatically. In fact the government proved initially reticent in adopting the technique in this context because "the introduction of fingerprinting might well trigger a new controversy just when the indigo situation was improving." Sengoopta, *Imprint of the Raj*, 73.
40 Ibid., 36.

41 Ibid., 138–139.
42 Sengoopta, "'The Colonial Laboratory': Re-Examining the Metaphor," 24.
43 Stephen J. Gould, *The Mismeasure of Man* (New York: W. W. Norton, 1996), 153.
44 Cole, *Suspect Identities*, 94.
45 Quoted in ibid., 96. Ronald R. Thomas, *Detective Fiction and the Rise of Forensic Science* (Cambridge: Cambridge University Press, 2004), 217; my emphasis.
46 Ibid.
47 Parenti, *The Soft Cage: Surveillance in America from Slavery to the War on Terror*, 49. As Parenti further shows, the first uses of fingerprinting as a prophylaxis against fraud was by the New York Police Department at the turn of the twentieth century to combat cheating on civil service entrance exams. Later on, fingerprinting was adopted by the Bureau of Indian affairs as a way of individualizing Native Americans and their land holdings and as a way of facilitating land appropriation, 50–51.
48 Michel Foucault, *Discipline and Punish: The Birth of the Prison*, 170–194.
49 Ibid., 201.
50 Ibid., 202.
51 Ibid., 203.
52 Ibid., 204.
53 Ibid., 205.
54 Peter Redfield, "Foucault in the Tropics: Displacing the Panopticon," in *Anthropologies of Modernity: Foucault, Governmentality and Life Politics*, ed. Jonathan Xavier Inda (Malden, MA: Blackwell Publishing, 2005), 53.
55 Ibid., 54, my emphasis.
56 Timothy Mitchell, *Colonising Egypt* (Berkeley: University of California Press, 1988), 35. For examples of panoptic structures in colonial India see for example Martha Kaplan, "Panopticon in Poona: An Essay on Foucault and Colonialism," *Cultural Anthropology* 10, no. 1 (1995).
57 Quoted in Peter Zinoman, "The History of the Modern Prison and the Case of Indochina," in *Figures of Criminality in Indonesia, the Philippines, and Colonial Vietnam*, ed. Vicente L. Rafael (Ithaca, NY: Cornell University Southeast Asia Program Publications, 1999), 160; Michael Salman, "Nothing without Labor: Penology, Discipline, and Independence in the Philippines under United States Rule," in *Discrepant Histories: Translocal Essays on Filipino Cultures*, ed. Vicente L. Rafael (Philadelphia, PA: Temple University Press, 1995), 115.
58 David Spurr, *The Rhetoric of Empire: Colonial Discourse in Journalism, Travel Writing, and Imperial Administration* (Raleigh, NC: Duke University Press, 1993), 16. Indeed, Mary Louise Pratt focuses on early European travel writings and the intrinsic gaze of not only peoples but of nature itself. As she writes, "The systematization of nature ... is a European project of a new kind, a new form of what one might call planetary consciousness among Europeans." Thus Pratt continues:

> One by one the planet's life forms were to be drawn out of the tangled threads of the life surroundings and rewoven into European-based patterns of global unity and order. The (lettered, male, European) eye that held the system could familiarize ("naturalize") new sites/sights immediately upon contact, by incorporating them into the language of the system.
> (Mary Louise Pratt, *Imperial Eyes: Travel Writing and Transculturation* [New York: Routledge, 1992], 29, 31)

59 See especially Homi Bhabha, "Of Mimicry and Man: The Ambivalence of Colonial Discourse," in *Tensions of Empire: Colonial Cultures in a Bourgeois World*, eds Fredrick Cooper and Ann Laura Stoler (Berkeley: University of California Press, 1997).

60 Pratt, *Imperial Eyes*, 4.
61 Ann Laura Stoler, *Carnal Knowledge and Imperial Power: Race and the Intimate in Colonial Rule* (Berkeley: University of California Press, 2002), 10.
62 Peter Zinoman, *The Colonial Bastille: A History of Imprisonment in Vietnam, 1862–1940* (Berkeley: University of California Press, 2001), 7. Zinoman then contests Partha Chatterjee's point when Chatterjee writes:

> When one looks at the regimes of power in the so-called backward countries of the world today, not only does the dominance of the characteristically "modern" modes of existence of power seem limited and qualified by the persistence of older modes, but by the fact of their combination in a particular state formation, it seems to open up at the same time an entirely new range of possibilities for the ruling classes to exercise their domination.
> (Partha Chatterjee, "More on Modes of Power and the Peasantry," in *Selected Subaltern Studies*, eds Ranajit Guha and Gayatri Spivak [New York: Oxford University Press, 1988], 390)

However, Chatterjee's point should not be dismissed. While Zinoman sees the colonial Indochinese prison as a disorganized zone that became a focal point of anti-colonial resistance, Chatterjee's point concerning the hybridity of regimes of power should be explored in different colonial contexts. On the other hand, Gayatri Spivak argues that introducing Foucault's analysis contributes to a "symptomatic blank in contemporary Western anti-humanism" given the intrinsic effacement of imperial history and the (re)inscription of Western subjectivity. Gayatri Spivak, "Subaltern Studies: Deconstructing Historiography," in *Selected Subaltern Studies*, eds Ranajit Guha and Gayatri Spivak (New York: Oxford University Press, 1988), 18.
63 David Arnold, "The Colonial Prison: Power, Knowledge, and Penology in Nineteenth-Century India" in *Subaltern Studies Reader, 1986–1995*, ed. Ranajit Guha (Minneapolis: University of Minnesota Press, 1997), 155.
64 Ibid., 148. Or as David Scott puts it: "In the colonial world the problem of modern power turned on the politico-ethical project of producing subjects and governing their conduct." David Scott, "Colonial Governmentality," in *Anthropologies of Modernity: Foucault, Governmentality, and Life Politics*, ed. Jonathan Xavier Inda (Malden, MA: Blackwell, 2005).
65 Ann Laura Stoler, *Capitalism and Confrontation in Sumatra's Plantation Belt, 1870–1979* (New Haven, CT: Yale University Press, 1985), 2.
66 Ann Laura Stoler, *Race and the Education of Desire: Foucault's History of Sexuality and the Colonial Order of Things* (Durham, NC: Duke University Press, 1995), 99; emphasis in the original
67 Ibid., 104. Or as Stoler further adds:

> racisms gained their strategic force, not from the fixity of their essentialisms, but from the internal malleability assigned to the changing features of racial essence. In the nineteenth-century Indies cultivation of the European self was affirmed in proliferating discourses on pedagogy, parenting, and servants – microsites in which bourgeois identify was rooted in notions of European civility, in which designations of racial membership were subject to gendered appraisals, and in which "character," "good breeding," dispassionate reason, and proper rearing were part of the changing cultural and epistemic indexing of race.
> (Stoler, *Carnal Knowledge and Imperial Power*, 144)

68 Ibid., 99.
69 Ibid., 60.
70 Stoler, *Race and the Education of Desire: Foucault's History of Sexuality and the Colonial Order of Things*, 109.
71 Stoler, *Carnal Knowledge and Imperial Power*, 112, 114. Quoting J. A. Nederburgh, *Wet an Adat* (Batavia: Kolff, 1898), 88.
72 Stoler, *Race and the Education of Desire*, 130.
73 As Stoler writes:

> The Froebel kindergarten movement that swept through Germany, England, Holland, and France in the mid-nineteenth century, that quintessential laboratory of liberal experiment, in the Indies was heralded not only as a hothouse for nurturing Dutch middle-class sensibilities of morality, self-discipline, and thrift but as a strategic method of removing [European] children from the immoral clutch of native nursemaids, native playmates, and most importantly native mothers. One might be tempted to argue that reformist gestures in the colonies produced these exclusionary, racialized reactions from a more conservative constituency. But this was not the case. These were proposals crafted by the most ardent social reformers whose visions were racially specific, highly class conscious, exclusionary by definition.
>
> (Stoler, *Race and the Education of Desire*, 122)

74 Alfred W. McCoy and Francisco A. Scarano, *The Colonial Crucible: Empire in the Making of the Modern American State* (Madison: University of Wisconsin Press, 2009), 83.
75 Alfred W. McCoy, *Policing America's Empire: The United States, the Philippines, and the Rise of the Surveillance State* (Madison: University of Wisconsin Press, 2009), 296.
76 Ibid., 299.
77 Ibid., 294.
78 C. Vann Woodward, *The Strange Career of Jim Crow* (Oxford: Oxford University Press, 2002), 72.
79 Ibid., 74.
80 McCoy, *Policing America's Empire: The United States, the Philippines, and the Rise of the Surveillance State*, 294.
81 Ibid.
82 Ibid., 21–22; Among other innovations were the establishment of transcontinental telegraph line in 1861, the transatlantic cable in 1866, the key driven accounting machine in 1885, photoengraving in 1881, etc.
83 As McCoy writes:

> The Americans were forced to develop techniques for which there were no names: psychological profiling before psychology was an academic discipline and disinformation before information warfare was a military doctrine. In an American republic with a tradition of local law enforcement, the creation of a centralized colonial police did not simply influence the nature of metropolitan policing as it had in the United Kingdom. Instead, it transformed Washington's nascent national security apparatus.
>
> (Ibid., 34)

84 Ibid., 16.
85 Ibid., 43.

86 Ibid., 35; or as Frances Gouda puts it in the different context of Dutch coloni-
    zation in Indonesia with respect to the freedom associated with experimentation:

> the history of scientific and technological progress or the accumulation of
> social scientific scholarship in the Netherlands itself since the late nineteenth
> century should be approached as a process that was intimately linked to and
> shaped by experimental activities in colonial Indonesia, which was con-
> verted into an unregulated, unrestricted laboratory. In such an environment,
> intrepid researchers from Europe could engage in risky investigations with
> impunity. While conducting their experiments, doctors and social engineers
> did not have to honor considerations for human and social costs that they
> would have confronted in Europe itself.
> (Frances Gouda, "Mimicry and Projection in the Colonial Encounter: The
>   Dutch East Indies/Indonesia as Experimental Laboratory, 1900–1942,"
>   *Journal of Colonialism and Colonial History* 1, no. 2 [2000], paragraph 40)

87 McCoy, *Policing America's Empire*, 82.
88 Ibid., 46.
89 Ibid., 47.
90 Anne L. Foster, "Prohibiting Opium in the Philippines and the United States:
    The Creation of the Interventionist State," in *Colonial Crucible: Empire in the
    Making of the Modern American State*, eds Alfred W. McCoy and Francisco A.
    Scarano (Madison: University of Wisconsin Press, 2009).
91 Warwick Anderson, "Excremental Colonialism: Public Health and the Poetics of
    Pollution," *Critical Inquiry* 21, no. 3 (1995), 644. More generally, the notion of
    imperial hygiene being a significant factor of colonial management is shown by
    Alison Bashford. Bashford ties in the pursuit of health surveillance and man-
    agement in the imperial context with "nation-formation" at home. As she argues:

> The pursuit of "health" has been central to modern identity formation. It has
> become a way of imagining and embodying integrity and, problematically,
> homogeneity or purity of the self, the community, and especially in the early
> to mid twentieth century, the nation. Nation-forming has found one of its
> primary languages biomedical discourse, partly because of its investment in
> the abstract idea of boundary, identity and difference, but also because of the
> political philosophy that thinks of the population as one body, the social body
> or the body of the polity.
> (Alison Bashford, *Imperial Hygiene: A Critical History of Colonialism,
>   Nationalism and Public Health* [New York: Palgrave, 2004], 4)

92 Warwick Anderson, "Pacific Crossings: Imperial Logics in the United States'
    Public Health Programs," in *Colonial Crucible: Empire in the Making of the
    Modern American State*, eds Alfred W. McCoy and Francisco A. Scarano
    (Madison: University of Wisconsin Press, 2009), 278–279. Indeed, a process
    analogous to what was occurring in imperial India: "bodies were being counted and
    categorized, they were being disciplined, discoursed upon, and dissected, in India
    as much as they were in Britain, France, or the United States." David Arnold,
    *Colonizing the Body: State Medicine and Epidemic Disease in Nineteenth-
    Century India* (Berkeley: University of California Press, 1993), 9.
93 Anderson, "Pacific Crossings: Imperial Logics in the United States' Public
    Health Programs," 280. As Anderson importantly notes:

New doctrines of colonial warfare demanded the intense surveillance and disciplining of local populations: it was supposed that reform of the social and moral terrain, a policy of attraction and transformation, would turn "savages" into docile, disciplined subjects. It was no longer enough to protect a colonial garrison or enclave militarily and medically; the goal was now to occupy and organize a territory and a people, cultivating new forms of life within "protection zones." ... Through the discipline of hygiene, Filipinos might eventually become properly self-governing.

(Ibid., 281)

Indeed, Anderson's point here is coextensive with what David Scott calls colonial governmentality, departing from the Foucauldian notion. Scott writes:

the formation of colonial modernity would have to appear as a discontinuity in the organization of colonial rule characterized by the emergence of a distinctive political rationality – a colonial governmentality – in which power comes to be directed at the destruction and reconstruction of colonial space so as to produce not so much extractive-effects on colonial bodies as governing-effects on colonial conduct.

(Scott, "Colonial Governmentality," 35)

94 Following Henri Lefebvre's insights on abstract space (a space amenable to calculative reason, legible to the tools of governmental practice), Anderson shows that the imperial laboratory in the Philippines worked to produce a "formal body, a body abstracted, fragmented" through the seamless (i.e. coercive) merging of the medical laboratory with a heterogeneous society as a whole. Anderson, "Excremental Colonialism: Public Health and the Poetics of Pollution," 651–652.
95 Ibid., 654.
96 Quoted in ibid., 655.
97 Anderson, "Pacific Crossings," 284.
98 Anderson, "Excremental Colonialism: Public Health and the Poetics of Pollution," 655.
99 Herfried Münkler, *Empires* (New York: Polity, 2007), 96.
100 Ibid., 97.

4 American hegemony and the neoliberal laboratory in the Americas

Who can doubt that there is an American empire? – an "informal empire," not colonial in polity, but still richly equipped with imperial paraphernalia: troops, ships, planes, bases, proconsuls, local collaborators, all spread around the luckless planet.[1]

[P]eople were in prison so prices could be free.[2]

While the previous chapters focused on instances of "formal" imperialism and the laboratory effects that impacted the formation of modern nation-states, in this chapter I turn my attention to informal practices of imperialism in order to show how laboratory-like conditions still emerge that have repercussions for hegemonic states. International theorists typically conceive of informal imperialism as a form of hegemony over peripheral areas. Informal imperialism (as a set of politico-economic practices that underpin international hegemony) operates without direct control over a given territorial space. David Rock argues that informal empire was typically understood "[as] a system in which one nation restricted the sovereignty of another for commercial or financial profit without imposing direct political control."[3] Gregory A. Barton and Brett M. Bennet define it as:

> [A] willing and successful attempt by commercial and political elites to control a foreign region, resource, or people. The means of control included the enforcement of extra-territorial privileges and the threat of economic and political sanctions, often coupled with the attempt to keep other would-be imperial powers at bay.[4]

Various forms of informal empire preceded and coexisted historically with modern forms of direct imperialism, as John A. Gallagher and Ronald E. Robinson have famously shown.[5] Informal and formal imperial governance cannot be so easily disaggregated in British imperial history, and more often than not reflected assemblages of governance that did not (and could not) entirely reflect the will of British politicians and administrators.[6] Indeed, as Karuna Mantena argues in her recent book *Alibis of Empire: Henry Maine and the Liberalism of Empire,* "[*I*]*ndirect rule,* the rule through native institutions, was often championed as both more efficient and more fruitful for stabilizing imperial rule."[7] The informality of empire also varied in kind and degree. George Steinmetz shows that informal empire is constituted by a diverse set of relations between European and indigenous institutions and practices that was "an overarching colonial state."[8] Even so, Ann Stoler argues on methodological grounds that terms such as "'indirect rule' and 'informal empire' are unhelpful euphemisms, not working concepts."[9] By that she implies that such terms mask the concrete realities of sovereignty, power and violence over a given territory in question.

Taking the above into consideration, this chapter explores the conjunction between changes in American hegemony over the course of the 1970s and the subsequent neoliberalization of the United States in the early 1980s. While the story of the emergence of neoliberalism has been told from many different angles, I argue that this "Reagan–Thatcher neoliberal counterrevolution" represents the normalization of a set of economic theories that were initially experimented with in Chile during the mid-to-late 1970s and later adopted within the United States and the United Kingdom.[10] Beginning in the late 1960s with the American defeat in the Vietnam War, and later the collapse of the Bretton Woods agreement, the spike in oil prices and the especially the economic crises of stagflation throughout the industrialized North, American political and economic supremacy was radically challenged. However, as Giovanni Arrighi has shown, this neoliberal counterrevolution was not simply a response to a particular economic crisis condition; it was more importantly a *political* reassertion of American global hegemony by the means of economic structural adjustment. Moreover, this project of restoring American supremacy abroad was fundamentally entwined with a domestic reassertion of governmental authority. As Greg Grandin succinctly puts it, "the restoration of American's global military power and the restoration of laissez-faire capitalism were increasingly understood to be indistinguishable goals."[11] What connects the international dimension of crisis management and hegemonic reassertion with domestic neoliberalization is precisely the manner in which the operationalization of neoliberal reform was experimented with and innovated in various American informal laboratories. The Chilean laboratory in particular permitted under authoritarian conditions the radical transformation of the economy according to principles and theories laid out by the Chicago School of economics. This experience would then become perceived as a necessary developmental model not only across the global South, but also, with varying degrees, across the North.

This chapter proceeds as follows. In the first section I depart from G. John Ikenberry's recent discussion on post-Second World War American liberal hegemony. While Ikenberry importantly draws our attention to the hierarchical components of this *après guerre* international order and its processes of norm diffusion, he crucially misses the profound crisis of American hegemony of the 1970s. In the second section I turn to both Robert Brenner and

Giovanni Arrighi to show, first, the importance of both inter-capitalist competition (Brenner) and the collapse of American international political legitimacy in the wake of the Vietnam War (Arrighi) to account for the erosion of American control over the global South. Lastly, I turn to the specific case of Chile and show how it became an important laboratory setting for the experiment and development of neoliberalism. This socio-political/economic innovation proved to imbricate both a project of reasserting American hegemony abroad and governmental authority at home.

American global hegemony: from the Second World War to the crisis of the 1970s

In his recent book entitled *Liberal Leviathan: The Origins, Crisis, and the Transformation of the American World Order*, G. John Ikenberry importantly reevaluates the post-Second World War international architecture as hierarchical.[12] Though he refers to "American domination" in some of its forms "as crudely imperial," the thrust of his book is meant to show that the post-Second World War environment marked a critical break from this colonial past. Post-1945, the United States established an international order that he characterizes as liberal hegemonic.[13] That is to say, rather than being another form of imperial domination, which as he understands it implies a relation of hierarchy between core states and peripheral dependencies, in which the former compels through the use of force the compliance of the latter, the United States established a consent-driven international order that was rooted in the ideals of Western liberalism.[14] What he characterizes as liberal hegemony is a form of "rule and regime-based order created by a leading state. Like empire, it is a form of hierarchical order – but, in contrast, it is fused with liberal characteristics."[15] The merit of turning to Ikenberry's text is that it rightly problematizes the canonical image of international relations theory and its theoretical assumptions about the relation between anarchy and international order. Ikenberry argues that anarchy as such cannot explain the historical evolution of international orders and the way states interact in such a way that constitutes and preserves a social milieux. As realists see it, international order emanates from periods of geopolitical equilibrium, in which balancing coalitions among various states preclude the possibility of a hegemon from emerging. But such balancing does not and cannot explain the "American led liberal international-order."[16] Hierarchy, as Ikenberry argues, is a much more prevalent condition in defining the contours and architecture of international orders than political realism suggests.[17]

The theoretical core of Ikenberry's text is that international order revolves around three different logics: balance, command, and consent. Balance is the central feature of a realist understanding of international order; command characterizes the condition of imperial governance; and consent, what Ikenberry takes to be the prevalent feature of American liberal hegemonic order, refers to "shared interests and the rule of law" that constitutes its historical novelty.[18] Of course, such "logics" are not mutually exclusive in practice; a consent-driven hegemonic order also relies upon instances of coercive power to assure its maintenance. As Ikenberry importantly admits, liberal-hegemonic powers sometimes need "to *discipline* and coerce weaker states, particularly in Latin America and the Middle East."[19] It also relies on balancing, as the United States did in the context of the Cold War. Nonetheless, this liberal-hegemonic order actualizes three important institutional features. The first is that "the leading state sponsors and operates within a system of negotiated rules and institutions."[20] Such an order circumscribes the potential for the arbitrary use of power by the leading state by "sponsor[ing] rules and institutions *and* acts in accordance with them."[21] Second, the hegemonic state provides a set of public goods for the international system. Ikenberry follows the literature of hegemonic stability theory, which sees in hegemonic ordering a net benefit from economic and political stability. Third, a liberal-hegemonic order allows for the establishment of "channels and networks for reciprocal communication and influence."[22] Whether in the form of direct lobbying or multilateral institutions, weaker powers have the ability to communicate their preferences and influence the decision-making of the hegemonic power. These three features mark the constitution of a liberal-hegemonic order that, Ikenberry asserts, fundamentally distinguishes it from past imperial orders.

What characterizes this American liberal-hegemonic order in practice is the progressive development of various international institutions put in place to guarantee political and economic stability in the Western world. At the political level we have the emergence of NATO and its security agreements to counteract Soviet influence in Europe. The United Nations was organized in 1947 as an international forum for states to negotiate and adjudicate their conflicts. We have, in other words, a set of rules and conventions that constitute and regulate international relations in such a way that benefits American foreign policy. Economically, Ikenberry argues, the contours of American liberal hegemony draw from the internationalization of American New Deal initiatives. As Ikenberry writes:

> Progressive notions of New Deal liberalism became part of America's postwar vision. The industrial democracies would provide a new level of social support – a safety net – under the societies of the Atlantic world. If the citizens of these countries were to live in a more open world economy, their governments would take steps to stabilize and protect market society through the welfare state – through employment insurance, retirement support, and other social protections. In this way, architects of the postwar system sought to build domestic support and construct an encompassing political coalition within countries around the new international order. National security and social security were now closely linked.[23]

Part of linking national security and social security was the construction of an international economic system that would regulate international finance and trade between Western states. American policymakers, Ikenberry argues, were cognizant of the relationship between economic insecurity and crises and the potential for violence. Such an international economic structure was put in place when the memories of the great depression were still fresh and faith in unregulated markets was virtually non-existent. The Bretton Woods system of currency exchange, which created the International Monetary Fund and other international institutions, established the dollar as the main currency of reference by fixing its convertibility in gold. The premise of this financial system was to stabilize the international monetary order while "establish[ing] new techniques of international economic management that gave governments the ability to reconcile movements of trade and capital with policies that promoted stable and full-employment economies."[24] In other words, Ikenberry presents an image of American liberal hegemony as a reflection of its own domestic social arrangements: of circumscribed power through institutions, a focus on securing open markets, a vision of progressive human rights, and the maintenance of law and order derived from the consent of the governed.

To be sure, this liberal hegemonic order that Ikenberry theorizes reflects a set of problematic formulations that derive from its Western-centric liberal assumptions. Ikenberry is clear that the origins of this American order initially pertain to Western liberal democracies and progressively expand outwards, especially with the end of the Cold War.[25] State and societal modernization is a key part of this liberal vision, with its emphasis on science, technology, learning and adaptation.[26] In other words, there is a developmental logic at work in Ikenberry's text – one that is accepted without question – a traditional Western/Eurocentric bias towards what he perceives to be the universality of liberal values: open markets, human rights, democratic governance, free consent towards the international rules established in and by the West, and so forth. And the process of expansion of this order remains the socialization (i.e. through the acceptance of norms and domestic institutions promoting individual human, political and civil rights) of other nation-states within this particular American order, which American progressive liberalism clearly embodies and inculcates in various international institutions.

Ikenberry's vision of this American liberal hegemonic international order, its evolution and transformation, affects how he understands its current crisis. For Ikenberry, this current crisis involves questioning "the merits of living in a world dominated by unipolar America."[27] However, what this crisis shows is not anything intrinsic in the liberal tradition as he understands it, nor its universal validity that he takes for granted. This crisis certainly does not reflect changes in American socio-political organization over the last few decades. Rather it emanates from the central geopolitical shift of the end of the Cold War with the emergence of American unipolarity. For Ikenberry, the crisis at the heart of today's international order is a "crisis of authority *within* the old hegemonic organization of liberal order, *not* a crisis in the deep principles of the order itself. It is a crisis of governance."[28] This crisis of authority or governance within the international order stems from multiple sources: changes in the norm of sovereignty, new sorts of threats, and the rise of illiberal powers such as Russia and China. But Ikenberry's main focus is on the decision-making of the Bush administration and the *choices* it made in reconceptualizing a more militant role for American power (i.e. the Bush doctrine). Bush's obvious imperial posture redefined the unique role of American leadership from the post-Second World War liberal order, making it a more proactive and reflecting what Ikenberry calls a "conservative nationalist" vision of global order.[29] In brief, he does not consider any of the structural features of liberal hegemony as consequential for understanding the contemporary political-economic crises.

But is this the only hegemonic crisis that occurred during the six decades comprising American liberal hegemony till the present? Ikenberry draws a straight line from 1945 to the present. Conspicuously absent from his analysis is the subject of the Vietnam War and the implications that it had for American hegemony internationally and domestically. We should also recall that it was in the early 1970s that the international economic and financial system fell into a deep crisis and ushered in a series of important international structural changes that also impacted domestic economic practices: this was when the Nixon administration took the United States off the gold standard and allowed for a flexible currency trading regime which led to the liberalization of financial capitalism beginning in the early 1980s. The demise of the Bretton Woods system and the larger transition from embedded liberalism to what is now commonly referred to as neoliberalism does not fit into Ikenberry's larger argument about what constitutes the crisis and transformation of world order.[30] In other words, Ikenberry's glossing over the deep-seated economic crises of the 1970s is part and parcel of a framework that sees American hegemony acting in a "more or less" positive manner within its ever-growing orbit of client states.[31] Ikenberry never questions the virtues of American capitalism and its expansion. Ikenberry never asks why the Bretton Woods agreement failed, or why the New Deal domestic framework or embedded liberalism – what underpinned American liberal hegemony in the post-war period – dramatically changed in such a way as to ultimately undermine the institutional frameworks of global capitalism. Put differently, what Ikenberry sees as a contemporary political and economic crisis of American hegemony is anything but novel; the roots of this contemporary crisis can be traced back to a set of structural changes in the 1970s and 1980s. These structural changes occurred in tandem within the United States and throughout the global South as a way of reasserting American hegemony internationally and domestically.

The global turbulence of the 1970s: the crisis of American hegemony

The most significant crisis of American hegemony in the aftermath of the Second World War occurred during the 1970s. This largely appeared to be an economic crisis, where the economic growth rates in the United States slowed dramatically compared to the 1950s and 1960s. A crucial question for political economists is: why did this happen? Robert Brenner's work in *The Boom and the Bubble: The US and the World Economy*, and later in his *The Economics of Global Turbulence*, attempts such an explanation. Brenner focuses on explaining the dramatic change in economic growth in the post-war world economy from the years of expansion to the stagnation of the 1970s. Brenner argues that the economic crisis of the 1970s was rooted in the very conditions of economic expansion of the 1950s and 1960s. That is to say, Brenner's analysis focuses on the rise of Germany and Japan in the post-war world and their ability to use new productive technologies along with cheap rural labor to establish a condition of high profitability. The rise of Germany and Japan did not, at first, affect American economic hegemony. As Brenner writes:

> US multinational corporations and international banks, aiming to expand overseas, needed profitable outlets for their foreign direct investment. Domestically based manufacturers, needing to increase exports, required fast-growing overseas demand for their goods. An imperial US state, bent on "containing communism" and keeping the world safe for free enterprise, sought economic success for its allies and competitors as the foundation for the political consolidation of the post-war capitalist order ... All these forces thus depended upon the economic dynamism of Europe and Japan for the realization of their own goals.[32]

Ikenberry would undoubtedly agree with this assessment that American hegemonic interests were tied to the success of Germany and Japan in rapidly re-industrializing.[33] What Ikenberry misses is that an inevitable by-product of smoothing out the "uneven development" within the industrial North was that certain nation-states became over time economically more competitive than the US. Because of this ability to compete against American products and their significant increases in productivity, both Germany and Japan were able to export more cheaply their products across the world, thereby undermining US manufacturing market shares. "[M]anufacturers," Brenner writes, "were thus able to combine relatively advanced techniques and relatively low wages to sharply reduce relative costs vis-a-vis those required to produce the same goods in the earlier-developing US."[34] Increasing competitive pressures by newly industrialized countries resulted in the "*aggregate* rate of profit in the international manufacturing sector" declining sharply.[35] This expressed itself in a transformation of US trade and current account surpluses to deficits, weakening the value of the US currency. At the same time, the inflexible currency regime of Bretton Woods was premised on pegging the dollar to a standard price of gold which accentuated these balance of payment imbalances. As a result of an increase in demand for marks and yen, inflationary pressures set in domestically in the US, further weakening the prospects for economic growth.

Brenner's argument is that the economic crisis of the 1970s reflected a "decline in the manufacturing rate of profit across the advanced capitalist economies" as a result of "over-capacity and over-production."[36] American firms were placed in a position in which they could not increase prices in order to keep up with increasing domestic labor costs. Moreover, their profitability was being undermined because of the higher productivity of their competitors in Germany and Japan. Brenner acknowledges that this international situation provoked an American domestic political crisis that the Johnson administration initially attempted to address through fiscal and monetary austerity. However, this policy did not halt declining economic growth. As Brenner explains, the Nixon administration realized that the:

> *political costs* of sustaining a serious anti-inflationary policy proved unacceptable ... Well before the defeat of the Republicans in the congressional elections of November 1970, and as high interest rates threatened to choke off the recovery, the government turned once again to fiscal stimulus and the Fed accompanied a policy of easy credit. As Nixon was to put it several months later, "We are all Keynesians now."[37]

The devaluation of the dollar was, as Brenner shows, a way of shifting the burden of declining profits more evenly across the industrialized world (i.e. negating the inherent benefits of a strong dollar for German and Japanese exporters). However, this proved not to be the panacea that state administrators sought in order to reestablish American domestic manufacturing profitability. On the contrary, as Brenner writes, "By the end of the 1970s, the manufacturing sector on an international scale was at an impasse, as was the Keynesian programme of demand management that had been implemented to revitalize the world economy."[38] System-wide manufacturing profitability could not be rescued on the basis of fiscal and monetary policies: the continuation of such policies only furthered a run on the dollar, provoking a threat to the "dollar's position as an international reserve currency."[39] The result was what Brenner calls the "shift to Reaganism/Thatcherism" which reversed fiscal and monetary stimulus in order to "dampen the growth of wages, as well as by directly redistributing income to capital through reduced taxes on corporations and diminished spending on social services."[40] The emergent neoliberalization of economic activity, through the deregulation and liberalization of finance and other business sectors, "aimed ... at bringing about a revitalization of, and thereby a shift into, domestic and international financial sectors ... by means of suppressing inflation."[41] Brenner sees the transformation of the world and domestic (US) economy as fundamentally tied to the crisis of system-wide manufacturing profitability. Neoliberalization was thus meant to address this economic crisis at the very center of American *economic* hegemony.

Giovanni Arrighi contests Brenner's explanation of the world-wide economic crisis of profitability as the main factor in explaining the subsequent long stagnation of the 1970s and the emergence of the neoliberal alternative. To be sure, Brenner's work is helpful in showing that intra-capitalist competition provoked an important crisis that had substantial reverberations for embedded liberalism within the industrialized North. In contrast to

Ikenberry's narrative, Brenner sees the economic tribulations of the 1970s as reflecting internal contradictions in the very financial and economic capitalist architecture that otherwise appears unproblematized within the wider literature on American liberal hegemony. Brenner does not, as Arrighi argues, convincingly explain the set of international geopolitical and domestic conditions that influenced policy choices leading to the Reagan–Thatcher monetarist (counter)revolution.[42] What Brenner misses is that the crisis of profitability located in the first world industrialized North was fundamentally refracted by a crisis of American liberal hegemony beginning in the late 1960s:

> The crisis of profitability that marked the transition from the long boom to the long downturn, as well as the great stagflation of the 1970s, were themselves deeply affected by the parallel crisis of American hegemony which ensued from the Vietnam War and the eventual American defeat. As for the Reagan-Thatcher counterrevolution, it was not just, or even primarily, a response to the unsolved crisis of profitability but also – and especially – a response to the deepening crisis of hegemony.[43]

Brenner, Arrighi argues, misses the "broader political context" underlying this crisis in American liberal hegemony precisely because his analysis is primarily focused on inter-capitalist competitive pressures (i.e. between the United States, Germany and Japan) and not on how the US was concern with maintaining its hegemonic position throughout the global South.[44] By contrast, Arrighi shows that the changes in the US balance of payments (and the corresponding fluctuations in US currency prices that would lead to enormous fluctuations in international and domestic fiscal and monetary policies) were fundamentally part of an ongoing geopolitical project during the 1960s: "the US government sought to contain, through the use of force, the joint challenge of nationalism and communism in the Third World."[45] And, as Arrighi shows, the changes in politico-economic policies beginning with Reagan and Thatcher "came from the unresolved crises of US hegemony in the Third World rather than in the crisis of profitability as such."[46]

The Vietnam War was the main event of this larger US project to dominate the global periphery either through direct military means or the use of proxies. However, the catastrophic engagement in Vietnam proved to have not only enormous economic implications – the increase in defense expenditures resulted in growing budget deficits at the same time that the Johnson administration was busy funding the Great Society initiative – but also resulted in a fundamental crisis of legitimacy. Internationally, "the joint military and legitimacy crises of the US world power were the expression of the failure of the US military-industrial complex to cope with the problems posed by world-wide decolonization."[47] Whereas Ikenberry takes for granted that American liberal hegemony "provides a basis for weaker and secondary states to make decisions to *willingly* join and *comply* with the rules and institutions of this order" the reality was far more complex and conflictual. Newly decolonized states were subject to intense American pressure to satisfy its growing economic and political needs throughout the Cold War.[48] Re-industrialization in many Northern states, along with ever-increasing military demands to keep up with the arms race with the Soviet Union by the United States, was predicated upon the consistent ability to extract primary materials from the global South. What emerged over the course of the 1950s and 1960s was a set of "highly effective and efficient organizational links between Third World primary inputs and First World purchasing power" and resulted in "powerful vested interest[s] ... in preserving maximum present and future flexibility in the use of Third World resources for the benefit of First World states."[49] There was a tension between the demands of continuous capital accumulation by the industrialized North (in the global South) and the progressive demand for the "exercise of full sovereignty" by newly decolonized states. When it became clear that the liberal hegemon could not directly subjugate Vietnam into "complying," as Ikenberry would argue, with its demands "the US government temporarily lost most, if not all of its credibility as the policeman of the free world."[50] The loss of American credibility suffered as a result of its defeat in Vietnam resulted in what Arrighi characterizes as a "power vacuum" that was accentuated throughout the 1970s. Events such as the rise of OPEC, the oil price crises, the Yom Kippur War and the fall of the Shah in 1979, all happened concurrently with "the escalation of inter-capitalist competition," as Brenner has shown, and resulted in a profound economic crisis throughout the North.[51] This political-economic crisis perpetuated the impression among political leaders and public opinion across the world that the United States was incapable of addressing this systemic crisis.

All told, the conjunction between an international political crisis derived from the Vietnam war and the crisis in profitability produced (though aided by extremely lax US monetary policy) the inflationary uptick in the early 1970s and the collapse of the system of fixed exchange rates. "In short," Arrighi writes:

> the interaction between the crisis of profitability and the crisis of hegemony, in combination with the US inflationary strategy of crisis management, resulted in a ten-year increase in world monetary disorder, escalating inflation and steady deterioration in the capacity of the US dollar to function as the world's means of payment.[52]

This finally paved the way for the dramatic shifts in the set of international and domestic policies designed to reassert American hegemony. The monetarist counterrevolution embodied in tight monetary and fiscal policies was designed to reassert faith in the US dollar as the international reserve currency. But what the increase in real interest rates accomplished in a spectacular fashion was the direct reassertion of US control over Third World countries that heavily borrowed US dollars in the open market at a time when there was a massive supply of petrodollars being recycled through Western banks. Such countries faced ruinous repayment rates that necessitated international organizations such as the IMF and World Bank provide them with structural adjustment programs. Significantly, such structural adjustment programs gave primacy to Western corporate interests through deregulation and the ability to repatriate US dollar assets back home. Direct changes in US monetary policy resulted in a series of debt crises that, as David Harvey argues, were in fact "orchestrated, managed and controlled both to rationalize the system and to redistribute assets during the 1980s and 1990s."[53] These debt crises were part of a way of reasserting American hegemony throughout the global South in such a way that was inconceivable merely through military means.

The American-led liberal order, and its reassertion of hegemony in the 1980s, was in fact predicated upon the very need "to *discipline* and coerce weaker states, particularly in Latin America and the Middle East" – as Ikenberry writes – through political and economic means. The debt crises of the 1980s were part of this capacity to discipline. However, these crises, characterized as well by the explosive development of financial securitization and the proliferation of asset bubbles, represent what Arrighi calls a "signal crisis" of the "dominant regime of accumulation" of the American post-Second World War order.[54] A signal crisis signifies a "deeper underlying systemic crisis" when leading capitalist entities begin switching their economic activities away from production and trade to "financial intermediation and speculation."[55] This initial move from investment in material production to the fictitious world of financial speculation and engineering initially forestalls and enhances the capacity for wealth generation for a certain class. Nonetheless, it cannot embody a lasting resolution of the underlying contradictions. "On the contrary," as Arrighi writes, "it has always been the preamble to a deepening of the crisis and to the eventual supersession of the still dominant regime of accumulation by a new one."[56] What Arrighi calls the terminal crisis is then the "end of the long century that encompasses the rise, full expansion, and demise of that regime" – what is potentially occurring today.[57] The signal crisis of American political and economic hegemony provoked a set of policies to enhance capital accumulations beneficial to American business and state to the detriment of the global South. What Ikenberry sees as American behavior being "crudely imperial" in certain contexts was in fact the way of maintaining and reinvigorating international forms of capital accumulation for the benefit of American hegemony and its allies. As I will show in the last section of this chapter, this manifestly neo-imperial economic order was not only meant to be applicable throughout the global South; the Reagan–Thatcher (counter)revolution was also an internal revolution that adapted some of the experiences and practices developed in the global periphery to reinforce American hegemony at home and abroad.

Neoliberalization in the Americas brought home: the Chilean experiment

As I argued above, American liberal hegemony entered a profound crisis in the 1970s as a result of intra-capitalist competition and the consequences of the American defeat in the Vietnam war. Both of these factors are missing in Ikenberry's narrative of American international hegemony, which only focuses on certain aspects of what Arrighi calls America's terminal crisis. What is missing in Ikenberry's work is any sense of the reassertion of American hegemony beginning in the 1970s that culminated in the Reagan–Thatcher monetarist counterrevolution. In Ikenberry's framework, as mentioned above, the New Deal era was internationalized in the aftermath of the Second World War as a way of mitigating the worst excesses of unregulated capitalism to promote social and economic welfare. Liberal hierarchy here works, as I argued above, unidirectionally: from American embedded liberalism and its progressive instantiation in various international organizations and through the socialization of states into this American-led international order.

What remains unexplored are the reverse impacts: how patterns of international hegemony create the conditions for domestic institutional change. What were the domestic consequences of the reassertion of American hegemony in the mid-to-late 1970s for American domestic institutions? How, in other words, did the political-economic discourse go from the Nixonian "We are all Keynesians" to, a decade later, the famous Thatcherite mantra "TINA" (There Is No Alternative) and the radical implementation of monetarist policies and the contraction of the state? Indeed, at a party conference in 1980 Thatcher explicitly called for discipline and fortitude in the face of a grave economic/inflationary crisis. At the same time, she insisted that her policies were to be considered "normal, sound, and honest."[58] In other words, Thatcher promoted the inevitable and natural nature of her program at the same time as she stressed the urgency of its adoption.

The depoliticized and inevitable necessity for the neoliberalization of the United Kingdom was part of what Pierre Bourdieu and Loïc Wacquant have shown to be the manifestation of a vulgate borne out "of a new type of imperialism." As they further add:

> [This vulgate's] effects are all the more powerful and pernicious in that it is promoted not only by the partisans of the neoliberal revolution who, under cover of "modernization," intend to remake the world by sweeping away the social and economic conquests of a century of social struggles, henceforth depicted as so many archaisms and obstacles to the emergent new order, but also by cultural producers (researchers, writers and artists) and left-wing activists, the vast majority of whom still think of themselves as progressives.[59]

Bourdieu and Wacquant point to how the "cultural imperialism" of neoliberal discourse has seeped into the very vocabulary of economic governance, making it appear entirely natural and self-evident. As they observe:

> the automatic effect of the international circulation of ideas ... tends, by its very logic, to conceal their original conditions of production and

signification, the play of preliminary definitions and scholastic deductions replaces the contingency of denegated sociological necessities with the appearance of logical necessity and tends to mask the historical roots of a whole set of questions and notions.[60]

Indeed, the active concealment of the origin of these neoliberal ideas and how they came into practice, I claim, points to how much neoliberal discourse forgets its origins in the authoritarian crucibles of Latin American (neo)imperial experiments.[61] What I wish to show is how these neoliberal ideas, as part of a larger project to reassert American hegemony, were in fact initially deployed in the experimental crucibles of South America before being legitimized and normalized for implementation in the United States.[62]

To see, then, the imbrications between the reassertion of American hegemony in the 1970s and the neoliberalization of the American domestic political economy, it is important to recall that the crisis of legitimacy provoked by America's war of attrition in Southeast Asia coincided with the emergence of novel social movements that challenged the social mores of American society. The Civil Rights Movement, the feminist movement, the sexual revolution, and the student rebellions against the war effort, revealed latent trends of racism, sexism, and other forms of social domination at the heart of American society. These movements, as Harvey notes, "challenged the traditional structure of networked class relations."[63] Domestic emancipatory developments during the 1960s and 1970s proved to be part of what Arrighi describes as the "highly depressing experience for the bourgeoisie of the West" because it fundamentally called into question the authority of the state and the ruling classes throughout the capitalist world.[64] While the 1960s represented an enormous surge in democratic participation across the developed world, in the United States especially with the Voting Rights Act of 1965, Samuel Huntington would argue in 1976, such an expansion, along with an increase in governmental expenditure on social welfare, "*produced a substantial ... decrease in governmental authority.*"[65] This happened because democratic participation, for Huntington, increased ideological polarization, which in turn undermined governmental authority when the results of governmental action did not fulfill expectations. Indeed, the significant changes in fiscal, monetary and social policies in the late 1970s were reflective of this perceived need to reassert domestic governmental authority. The Reagan administration then worked towards directly challenging the central collective compact between labor, management and the state that the New Deal established, in order to recreate a "good business environment" for continuous capital accumulation.[66] As David Harvey argues, unleashing financial power proved to be a convenient way to "discipline working-class movements," essentially reasserting a form of class power over a society riveted by social stratification and the loss of governmental authority.[67] But how was this process legitimized in the first place?

Understanding what Jaime Peck terms the neoliberalization of the state necessitates a detour through Chile during the 1970s.[68] The "crudely imperial" policies of the United States in Latin America during the 1970s proved to be a crucial feature of the neoliberalization of the United States itself. The experimental implementation of economic orthodoxy – the deregulation of state power, financialization or the unrestrained practice of financial and trading markets, privatization and the destruction of forms of social solidarity such as trade unions – established Chile as the first large-scale neoliberal laboratory. Chile subsequently legitimized a neoliberal discourse that would prove to be incredibly malleable in different contexts. "The Chilean case," as Juan Gabriel Valdés argues, "became a model, a unique phenomenon that did not stem from any historical experience. Rather, it originated directly from what the Chicago Boys termed 'economic science': a science to be found mostly in their textbooks."[69] It is the implementation and experience of neo-liberal revolution that proved crucial for its normalization as a valid or "tried and true" theory for subsequent implementation in the United States.

Under conditions of what later became known as shock treatment, Latin America during the 1970s proved to be the crucible for experimenting with the ideas put forward by the Chicago School of economic theory. In Latin America, economic regulatory mechanisms were radically and quickly trans-formed in favor of market-based solutions characteristic of (neo)imperial reassertion.[70] The Chicago School of economic theory, embodied in the writ-ings and teachings of Milton Friedman, who won the Nobel Prize in 1976, advocated the deregulation of markets and the contraction of the state as a way of promoting individual freedom and wealth.[71] Friedman, von Hayek and other neoconservative proponents, believed that markets in general possess an internal rationality that nullifies the potential for state domination. The ideas emanating from the Chicago School of economics depoliticized eco-nomic questions by emphasizing how "markets" were able to address sub-stantive political problems. Neoliberalization, Wendy Brown argues following Michel Foucault, takes for granted that "The political sphere, along with every other dimension of contemporary existence, is submitted to an economic rationality ... [and that] all dimensions of human life are cast in terms of a market rationality."[72] Neoliberalization was then much more than simply the financialization of the international and domestic economies, as Arrighi argues, but the attempt at completely rewiring the political-economic form of American liberal hegemony in a much more authoritarian manner domestically.

The novelty of neoliberalization, as Peck argues, "denotes the repeated (necessity for) renewal and reinvention of a project that could never be fixed as a stable formula, and which has lurched through moments of innovation, overreach, correction, and crisis."[73] This political-economic project was first concretely experimented with in Chile during that country's own internal crises of the 1970s.[74] What was significant in this case was that the neoliberal experiment occurred in the aftermath of the American influenced *coup d'état* by General Augusto Pinochet on September 11, 1973. The election of the leftist Salvador Allende in 1970 was deemed by the Nixon administration a grave threat to American strategic and corporate interests in the Western hemisphere. National security advisor Henry Kissinger argued at a meeting of the NSC that Allende's program "would pose some very serious threats to our interests and position in the hemisphere, and would affect developments and our relations to them elsewhere in the world." Chile, Kissinger continued, could "become part of a Soviet/Socialist world, not only philosophically but in terms of power dynamics; and it might constitute a support base and entry point for expansion of Soviet and Cuban presence and activity in the region."[75]

In this Cold War geopolitical context, what Valdés calls the "ideological transfer" of Chicago School economic ideas through their progenitors, the Chicago Boys, was perceived transnationally by American and Chilean elites as a way of countering the legitimacy of socialist/Marxist ideas. The Chicago Boys – Chilean graduate students at the University of Chicago, whose studies were financed in part by the Ford Foundation and the State Department, and who would later become faculty members in various economics departments in Chile – embarked on the radical transformation of the Chilean economy.[76] As Mario Sznajder writes:

> Chile had become a kind of socio-economic laboratory in which a neo-liberal experiment was being carried out with scant political hinderance. In the second half of the 1970s, the military government gave priority to the economic experiment, relying on its success to legitimise the future political framework of limited democracy, which in turn would provide the required guarantee for the survival and defence of the neoliberal model.[77]

This radical transformation was largely justified as a reaction against everything that Salvador Allende's socialist economic program stood for. What was characterized as *La vía chilena al socialismo*, social spending to alleviate poverty, protection of domestic industries, a moratorium of foreign debt repayment, made the Nixon administration so fearful of its turn towards the Soviet Union.[78] For the purposes of "shocking" the economic system in order to push for dramatic changes that the Chicago Boys would otherwise have been unable to accomplish, authoritarianism and economic reform occurred hand in hand. The result was that what were ostensibly political decisions, the determination of the contours of the socio-economic order, was not determined democratically, but rather by economic experts.[79] The authoritarianism of the Chilean coup was characterized by the arrest of over 13,000 people deemed "Marxist subversives"; grave abuses of human rights occurred over a prolonged period of time, including executions of political dissidents.[80] Nonetheless, with the economy in shambles in the aftermath of the coup, Chile was an ideal place for experimenting with ideas that had been gestating among the Chicago Boys and their teachers for many years.

First and foremost, these economists "radically altered the Chilean economic paradigm, bringing it into line not just with military self-interest in retaining control but also with the *general tendencies of the world economy*."[81] "The goal [of the Chicago Boys' attempt at reform]," as Valdés further adds, "was nothing less than the transformation of the state, of customs, and of culture" but especially, as Pinochet himself remarked, to engender a complete "change in mentality."[82] The explicit purpose of economic transformation was to tame the hyperinflation of the preceding years, but it proved to be an opportunity to implement:

> a radical economic liberalization program based on the indiscriminate use of market mechanisms, the dismantling and reduction of the state, deregulation of the financial sector, and a discourse that ascribed to market forces the ability to solve practically any problem in society.[83]

The Chicago Boys' economic plan was largely spelled out in a document entitled "El Ladrillo" ("The Brick") in the early 1970s drafted in collaboration with the CIA.[84] It followed the economic orthodoxy imbibed by Chicago School theorists, stressing, in principle, the desire to free market forces from the constraints imposed by the state. However a crucial difference was the extent to which it stressed the importance of worker discipline in achieving economic goals. Consider, for example, how Milton Friedman describes the effects of freedom of exchange:

> So long as effective freedom of exchange is maintained, the central fea- ture of the market organization of economic activity is that it prevents one person from interfering with another in respect of most of his activ- ities ... *The employee is protected from coercion by the employers for who he can work, and so on. And the market does this impersonally and without centralized authority.*[85]

Here the role of authority at the level of the corporation presupposes the seamless ability of individual labor to transition from one employer to another. However, in the section aptly entitled "Discipline" the Chilean economists stress that "[Discipline] is a fundamental requirement without which economic development is impossible. The current relaxation of labor discipline is without doubt one of the main causes of the economic meltdown we face." As it importantly adds:

> You can not ignore how any group of people who decide to perform an activity in common should be organized, which means setting functions, procedures, hierarchies and assigning responsibilities to each individual. If an organization is not set, the activity to be performed to achieve a goal is irrelevant or involves a huge waste of resources. These principles are valid for any organization be it sports, political or religious, and have greater importance when economic activity is to be performed. *The sur- vival and success of a company depends on the efficiency of your organi- zation, which involves discipline and obedience to authority hierarchies.* The objectives of participation must be understood within the framework

and the restrictions imposed by efficient organizations livelihood and therefore require a high degree of responsibility in the participants.[86]

Thus what a significant part of "El Ladrillo" concerns itself with is how the implementation this program results in the *"restablecimiento del principio de autoridad a nivel nacional"* and a compliant labor force.[87] Crucially the actualization of this neoliberal political economic project in the Americas is this accentuation of authority and hierarchical relations that are not endogenous to the functioning of the market.

As a result of the privatization of finance and the lowering of tariffs and taxation, Chile became, as one *New York Times* journalist characterized it, "a banker's delight." According to this journalist, the Chicago Boys economically and politically cemented Chile's position in the US imperial orbit.[88] This transformation of the Chilean economy along Chicago School theories, for the purposes of aligning it, as Valdés argues, with the world economy, captured the imagination of a whole host of academic economists, journalists and policymakers in the United States and in various international organizations:

> From the mid-1970s onwards, the country enjoyed privileged treatment by the International Monetary Fund (IMF) and the commercial banks. Chile was doubtless the country most visited and commented upon by journalists from the international conservative press, as well as by a distinguished list of academics headed by the most prominent members of the Chicago School of Economics, including Milton Friedman himself. The reason for this interest is easy to comprehend: Chile had become the first and most famous example of applying the rules of economic orthodoxy to a developing country. Foreign trade was liberalized, prices were freed, state companies were privatized, the financial sector was deregulated, and state functions were drastically reduced.[89]

A *Barron's* editorial in 1980 quoted Arnold Harberger, a professor at the time at the University of Chicago who was perhaps even more influential than Milton Friedman with the Chicago Boys, as arguing that the Chilean reforms were "the most important reforms made in the underdeveloped world in recent history." As the editorial further adds, quoting an anonymous colleague of Harberger's: "The economics textbooks say that's the way the world should work, but where else do they practice it?"[90] Implied here is that the economic program of the Chicago Boys is suitable for implementation throughout the developing world as a way of generating economic growth and efficiency.[91] But there is also a certain implication for what needs to be done within the United States itself that was at the time faced with a growing crisis of stagflation. Of course, the obvious authoritarianism of the Pinochet government and its breaches of international human rights conventions was a significant source of contention and even opprobrium; Friedman himself would be tagged as complicit in legitimizing the Pinochet regime through his own trip to Chile in 1975 and his meeting with Pinochet. His receipt of the Nobel Prize in 1976 was accompanied by protests. But as Corey Robin has recently uncovered, in 1981 American academics including Friedman, Hayek, James M. Buchanan and Arnold Harberger, along with their counterparts from many other countries, met in Viña del Mar under the auspices of the Mont Pelerin Society, to demonstrate the effectiveness of Chilean market reforms and the need to learn its lessons for the US itself. The inherent authoritarian setting in Chile should not be seen as anything detrimental to the neoliberal project, according to participants. On the contrary, as Robin cites Eric Brodin's original commentary on the Viña del Mar conference, "what is politically possible in authoritarian Chile, may not be possible in a republic with a congress filled with 'gypsy moths' for whom political expediency often takes precedence over economic realities, especially in an election year."[92] Again, implied here is a certain perception that a reassertion of governmental authority within the US is necessary to address domestic and international political-economic questions.

The Chilean example represented a success story for a reinvigorated conservative movement in the United States and the United Kingdom during the mid-to-late 1970s. In 1981 Hayek himself would speak of Chile as "as great success," and predicted "The world shall come to regard the recovery the recovery of Chile as one of the great economic miracles of our time."[93] Chile became the decisive laboratory for the establishment, more generally, of a transnational post-Fordist economic order which emphasized flexibility, innovation and creative destruction. This new order replaced the Bretton Woods currency framework by privileging the free flow of finance capital as a way of restructuring and disciplining various internal economies. The transformation of internal economic structures by finance capital was accompanied by a general sentiment that excessive popular democracy is detrimental to economic rights and liberties and that market rationality would best determine the distribution of wealth. The neoliberalization of Chile encapsulated the hopes and agenda of American's conservatives to privatize a significant portion of the state to market forces, to deregulate financial services and lower taxation, and above all, to suppress the power of trade unions. However this domestic project to promote economic freedom at home and abroad was fundamentally connected to the restoration of American hegemony.

The Reagan revolution in the United States largely rested on the dual program of domestic economic neoliberalization and a pseudo-Keynesian massive armaments buildup. "The effect of what seemed to be a confused economic policy was," as Grandin argues, "in retrospect, a cohesive transformation of American society and diplomacy – the institutionalizing of a perpetual system of global austerity that rendered political liberalism, both domestic and international, not viable."[94] Arrighi argues that tight monetary policies were designed to resurrect confidence in the United States and its currency. However, austerity had significant repercussions for American domestic industry and led to a significant dismantling of trade unionism, an overarching neoconservative political goal. The great recession of the early 1980s was at the same time an engineered shock treatment that was designed to roll back inflation to the detriment of state welfare, while accentuating class power. Taxation changes primarily favored wealthy classes and financial deregulation opened up finance capital for enormous speculative bubbles over the subsequent thirty years. Moreover, as Loïc Wacquant has shown, this period coincided with the exceptional expansion of the American carceral state through prisons and the criminal justice system to take over from social welfare programs. As he puts it:

> Mapping America's carceral boom after 1973, it became clear that the accelerating retraction of social welfare, leading to the infamous "welfare reform" of 1996, and the explosive expansion of criminal justice were two convergent and complementary shifts toward the punitive regulation of racialized poverty; that disciplinary "workfare" and castigatory "prison-fare" supervise the same dispossessed and dishonored populations destabilized by the dissolution of the Fordist-Keynesian compact and concentrated in the disparaged districts of the polarizing city; and that putting the marginalized fractions of the postindustrial working class under stern tutelage guided by moral behaviorism offers a prime theatrical stage onto which governing elites can project the authority of the state and shore up the deficit of legitimacy they suffer whenever they forsake its established mission of social and economic protection.[95]

The effect of this program of state neoliberalization conjoined with the Reagan "rollback" of Soviet influence, depoliticized such state transformations at home. In essence, the reengineering of a distinctly "neoliberal" American state rested on a project of reestablishing executive and class authority over a population perceived to be ungovernable.

Conclusion

The neoliberalization of the state and society in the United States thus represents the normalization of pervious shock treatments experimented first and foremost within the Chilean (neo)imperial crucible. To be sure, many of the ideas that constitute the façade of neoliberal economic thought originated, as many have shown, in various places and contexts in the West such as the University of Chicago or the emergence of *ordoliberalism* in West Germany.[96] What binds the various strands of "neoliberalism" are "a set of *epistemic* commitments" as Philip Mirowski puts it, that "rallies around a specific vision of the role of knowledge in human affairs."[97] However, the implementation of such "*epistemic* commitments" in state "engineering" projects both in the West and across the global South added as well to a "colonial archive" of knowledge and experience that turns neoliberalism into a "political project" that not only cuts across the international and domestic spheres as a set of economic dispositions for domestic reform, but is crucially contingent for its implementation upon a significant reassertion of domestic authoritarianism.

Ultimately, this normalization of radical economic theories through hegemonic international circuits such as the IMF, the World Bank, academics, journalists, and various semi-private think tanks in the West, gave rise to what Bourdieu and Wacquant have termed a neoliberal vulgate that legitimizes a depoliticized program for structural reform across not only the global South, but also within the North as the only viable program to tackle the twin economic problems of growth and inflation. As opposed to Ikenberry, who draws a straight line from 1945 to the present without so much as noting the significance of the crisis of American hegemony in the 1970s, these years proved pivotal for a reassertion of hegemony through domestic and international (i.e. throughout the global South) neoliberalization. This reassertion could not be accomplished by military means, as witnessed in Vietnam; it had to come through the radical transformation of domestic socio-economic configurations that would privilege specific classes that would realign the South within America's neo-imperial orbit. However, what also needs to be recognized is that this global American hegemonic reassertion was intimately tied to domestic (counter-revolutionary) changes beginning in the 1980s. This conjunction between the international and the domestic is more clearly seen in how ideas, norms and practices are experimented with in certain spaces, travel across international hierarchical circuits, and return as normalized and legitimized.

Notes

1 Arthur M. Schlesinger Jr, *The Cycles of American History* (New York: Mariner Books, 1999 [1986]), 141.
2 Eduardo Galeano quoted in Lawrence Weschler, *A Miracle, a Universe: Settling Accounts with Torturers* (Chicago, IL: University of Chicago Press, 1998), 147.
3 David Rock, "The British in Argentina: From Informal Empire to Post-colonialism," in *Informal Empire in Latin America: Culture, Commerce, and Capital*, ed. Matthew Brown (Malden, MA: Wiley-Blackwell, 2008), 49.
4 Gregory A. Barton and Brett M. Bennet, "Forestry as Foreign Policy: Anglo-Siamese Relations and the Origins of Britain's Informal Empire in the Teak Forests of Northern Siam, 1883–1925," *Itenerario* 34, no. 2 (2010), 67.
5 John Gallagher and Ronald Robinson, "The Imperialism of Free Trade," *The Economic History Review* 6, no. 1 (1953).
6 Ronald Robinson and John Gallagher, *Africa and the Victorians: The Official Mind of Imperialism* (New York: Doubleday, 2000 [1965]).
7 Karuna Mantena, *Alibis of Empire: Henry Maine and the Liberalism of Empire* (Princeton, NJ: Princeton University Press), 6.
8 George Steinmetz, "Imperialism or Colonialism: From Windhoek to Washington, by Way of Basra," in *Lessons of Empire: Imperial Histories and American Power*, eds Craig Calhoun, Frederick Cooper, and Kevin W. More (New York: New Press, 2006), 146.
9 Ann Stoler, "On Degrees of Imperial Sovereignty," *Public Culture* 18, no. 1 (2006), 136.

10 Giovanni Arrighi, "The Social and Political Economy of Global Turbulence," *New Left Review* 20, March–April (2003), 41. For important discussion of the genesis of neoliberalism in the United States and Europe see Mark Blyth, *Great Transformations: Economic Ideas and Institutional Change in the Twentieth Century* (Cambridge: Cambridge University Press, 2002); David Harvey, *A Brief History of Neoliberalism* (Oxford: Oxford University Press, 2005); Monica Prasad, *The Politics of Free Markets: The Rise of Neoliberal Economic Policies in Britain, France, Germany, and the United States* (Chicago, IL: University of Chicago Press, 2006); Greta R. Krippner, *Capitalizing on Crisis: The Political Origins of the Rise of Finance* (Cambridge, MA: Harvard University Press, 2011).

11 Greg Grandin, *Empire's Workshop: Latin America, the United States, and the Rise of the New Imperialism* (New York: Metropolitan Books, 2006), 181.

12 G. John Ikenberry, *Liberal Leviathan: The Origins, Crisis, and the Transformation of the American World Order* (Princeton, NJ: Princeton University Press, 2011).

13 Ibid., 66.

14 For Ikenberry, liberalism, more generally, represents a multifaceted tradition of political-economic thought. Following Michael Doyle, the "liberal vision of order" derives its intellectual influences from three different sources: from Adam Smith and the propagation of economic interdependence; from Immanuel Kant and democratic peace; and from Republicanism and notions of rights and rules that forms the basis of international law and institutions. Fundamental to Ikenberry's understanding of liberalism thus remains notion of "reciprocity and the rule of law." Ibid., 63.

15 Ibid., 70.

16 Ibid., 54. As Ikenberry writes, "The balance of power is actually not as pervasive across historical eras and regional systems as the neorealist logic suggests."

17 Or as Ikenberry puts it: hierarchy is "a basic and enduring feature of world politics." Ibid., 61.

18 Ibid.

19 Ibid., 60, my emphasis.

20 Ibid., 71.

21 Ibid., 71–72.

22 Ibid., 72.

23 Ibid., 175.

24 Ibid., 177.

25 Ibid., 161.

26 Ibid., 64. Or as he writes, "Liberal theories have shared the view that trade and exchange have a modernizing and civilizing effect on states, undercutting illiberal tendencies and strengthening the fabric of international community," 63.

27 Ibid., 4.

28 Ibid., 6, emphasis in the original.

29 Ibid., 265.

30 Further in the text Ikenberry does allude to the current economic crisis and the transition to neoliberalism that occurred in the 1980s:

> The social bargain that was built into the foundation of liberal hegemonic arrangements has given way to a more freewheeling, neoliberal world market system. Under these more recent conditions, liberal order – or at least the market features seem to undercut rather than support the state's ability to make good on its domestic social and political responsibilities.
>
> (Ibid., 287)

But Ikenberry gives the impression that this "neoliberal world market system" appears out of thin air.

31 A striking feature of Ikenberry's text is the persistent use of the term "more or less", which I count 22 times, to describe the ways in which American hegemony operates. For example, "Liberal hierarchy is international order in which the dominant state builds and operates within more or less agreed upon rule and institutions" (ibid., 76). Ikenberry never really defines what he means by "more or less" in his persistent use of the term.

32 Robert Brenner, *The Boom and the Bubble: The US in the World Economy* (New York: Verso, 2003), 14–15; also quoted in Arrighi, "The Social and Political Economy of Global Turbulence," 9.

33 As Brenner writes:

> Because US economic success turned out to be so tightly linked to the success of its rivals and allies, post-war international economic development within the advanced capitalist world could, for a brief time, manifest a relatively high degree of international cooperation – marked by high levels of US aid to and politico-economic support for allies and competitors – even though dominated by the US state and mainly shaped by US interests.
>
> (Brenner, *The Boom and the Bubble*, 15)

34 Ibid., 16.

35 Ibid., 17.

36 Ibid., 18.

37 Robert Brenner, *The Economics of Global Turbulence: The Advanced Capitalist Economies from Long Boom to Long Downturn, 1945–2005* (New York: Verso, 2006), 126–127.

38 Brenner, *The Boom and the Bubble*, 34.

39 Ibid.

40 Ibid., 35.

41 Ibid.

42 As Arrighi writes:

> Brenner's account of the sequence of events that led to the monetarist revolution…is the weakest link in his story of the long downturn … [H]e does not tell us how and why US policies "designed to restore US manufacturing competitiveness" resulted instead in record-breaking trade deficits despite a simultaneous escalation in protectionist measures.

> As Arrighi argues, Brenner's explanations, however, "miss the most fundamental causes of the devastating run on the dollar of 1979–80." Giovanni Arrighi, *Adam Smith in Beijing: Lineages of the Twenty-First Century* (New York: Verso, 2008), 108 n22.

43 Ibid., 133; my emphasis.

44 Ibid.

45 Ibid., 134.

46 Ibid., 136.

47 Giovanni Arrighi, *The Long-Twentieth Century: Money, Power and the Origins of Our Times* (New York: Verso, 2010 [1994]), 331.

48 Ikenberry, *Liberal Leviathan: The Origins, Crisis, and the Transformation of the American World Order*, 71; my emphasis. Of course, what Ikenberry has in mind are Western liberal-democratic states as opposed to recently decolonized states.

49 Arrighi, *The Long-Twentieth Century*, 332; For a pre-Second World War look at American corporate actions in Latin America in the service of American informal

empire see Jason M. Colby, *The Business of Empire: United Fruit, Race, and US Expansion in Central America* (Ithaca, NY: Cornell University Press, 2011).
50 Arrighi, *The Long-Twentieth Century*, 332.
51 Ibid., 333; Or as Arrighi further puts it, "The decline of US power and prestige reached its nadir in the late 1970s with the Iranian Revolution, a new hike in oil prices, the Soviet invasion of Afghanistan, and another serious crisis of confidence in the US dollar." Arrighi, *Adam Smith in Beijing*, 135.
52 Ibid., 159.
53 David Harvey, *Spaces of Global Capitalism: Towards a Theory of Uneven Geographical Development* (New York: Verso, 2006), 47.
54 Arrighi, *The Long-Twentieth Century*, 220.
55 Ibid.
56 Ibid., 221.
57 Ibid.
58 Margaret Thatcher, "Margaret Thatcher, Speech to the Conservative Party Conference, Brighton, 10 October 1980," in *The Broadview Anthology of British Literature: Volume 6b: The Twentieth Century and Beyond: From 1945 to the Twenty-First Century*, ed. Joseph Laurence Black (Buffalo, NY: Broadview Press, 2008), 797.
59 Pierre Bourdieu and Loïc Wacquant, "Newliberal Speak: Notes on the New Planetary Vulgate," *Radical Philosophy* January/February, no. 105 (2001), 2.
60 Ibid., 3.
61 Indeed, in contrast to Bourdieu and Wacquant who see the percolation of this neoliberal vulgate as originating in "the American society of the post-Fordist and post-Keynesian era, the world's only superpower and symbolic Mecca." Ibid., 3.
62 Mark Blyth, *Great Transformations: Economic Ideas and Institutional Change in the Twentieth Century.*
63 David Harvey, *A Brief History of Neoliberalism*, 57.
64 Arrighi, *The Long-Twentieth Century*, 322.
65 Samuel P. Huntington, "The United States," in *The Crisis of Democracy: On the Governability of Democracies*, eds Michel J. Crozier, Samuel P. Huntington, and Joji Watanuki (New York: New York University Press, 1976), 64. As Huntington writes, "People no longer felt the same compulsion to obey those whom they had previously considered superior to themselves in age, rank, status, expertise, character or talents," 75.
66 Harvey, *Spaces of Global Capitalism: Towards a Theory of Uneven Geographical Development*, 25.
67 David Harvey, *The New Imperialism* (Oxford: Oxford University Press, 2005), 63.
68 Jamie Peck, *Constructions of Neoliberal Reason* (Oxford: Oxford University Press, 2010), 20. As Peck argues:

> Neoliberalism defies explanation in terms of fixed coordinates. Rather, it denotes a problem space, together with an accompanying ethos of market complementing regulation. In the most abstract of terms, one can say that neoliberalization refers to a contradictory process of market like rule, principally negotiated at the boundaries of the state, and occupying the ideological space defined by a (broadly) sympathetic critique of nineteenth century laissez faire and deep antipathies to collectivist, planned, and socialized modes of government, especially those associated with Keynesianism and developmentalism.

69 Juan Gabriel Valdés, *Pinochet's Economists: The Chicago School in Chile* (Cambridge: Cambridge University Press, 1995), 2.
70 Naomi Klein, *The Shock Doctrine: The Rise of Disaster Capitalism* (New York: Knopf, 2007).

71 Milton Friedman, *Capitalism and Freedom* (Chicago: Chicago University Press, 2002).
72 Wendy Brown, "Neo-Liberalism and the End of Liberal Democracy," *Theory and Event* 7, no. 1 (2003), paragraph 9. See also Michel Foucault, *The Birth of Biopolitics*, ed. Michel Senellart (New York: Palgrave, 2008).
73 Peck, *Constructions of Neoliberal Reason*, 20.
74 As Valdés writes:

> In Latin America, Chile anticipated by over ten years the stabilization, adjustment, and liberalization processes that are now a generalized feature of the continent ... With a sense of anticipation that might perplex those who regard the developing world as mechanically dependent on events taking place in the central nations, Chilean economists appeared to foresee the final shift in the Keynesian era, as well as the rise to prominence of monetarist policies aimed at correcting monetary imbalances fostered by "statism" during the preceding period.
>
> (Valdés, *Pinochet's Economists: The Chicago School in Chile*, 3)

75 Quoted in Jonathan Haslam, *The Nixon Administration and the Death of Allende's Chile: A Case of Assisted Suicide* (New York: Verso, 2005), 55–56.
76 Valdés, *Pinochet's Economists*, Ch. 2.
77 Mario Sznajder, "Hayek in Chile," in *Liberalism and Its Practice*, eds Dan Avnon and Avner De-Shalit (New York: Routledge, 1999), 43.
78 Luis Corvalán, *El Gobierno De Salvador Allende* (Santiago, Chile: Lom Ediciones, 2003), 124.
79 As Valdés argues throughout his work, the Chicago boys had a deep distrust of democratic governance "which they saw as an obstacle to a free market," Valdés, *Pinochet's Economists*, 253.
80 See especially François Roustang, *Chile under Pinochet: Recovering the Truth* (Philadelphia: University of Pennsylvania Press, 2000).
81 Valdés, *Pinochet's Economists*, 11, my emphasis.
82 Pinochet quoted in Pamela Constable and Arturo Valenzuela, *A Nation of Enemies: Chile under Pinochet* (New York: W. W. Norton, 1993), 160; and in Grandin, *Empire's Workshop: Latin America, the United States, and the Rise of the New Imperialism*, 173. As David Lipton, Jeffrey Sachs, Stanley Fischer and Janos Kornai have argued, "shock treatment" must be comprehensive enough to affect all of society:

> The transition process is a seamless web. Structural reforms cannot work without a working price system; a working price system cannot be put in place without ending excess demand and creating a convertible currency; and a credit squeeze and tight macroeconomic policy cannot be sustained unless prices are realistic, so that there is a rational basis for deciding which firms should be allowed to close. At the same time, for real structural adjustment to take place under the pressures of tight demand, the macroeconomic shock must be accompanied by other measures, including selling off state assets, freeing up the private sector, establishing procedures for bankruptcy, preparing a social safety net, and undertaking tax reform. Clearly, the reform process must be comprehensive.
>
> (Lipton *et al.*, "Creating a Market Economy in Eastern Europe: The Case of Poland," *Brookings Papers on Economic Activity*, no. 1 [1990], 99, quoted in Jack R. Friedman, "Shock and Subjectivity in the Age of Globalization: Marginalization, Exclusion, and the Problem of Resistance," *Anthropological Theory* 7, no. 4 [2007], 428–429)

83 Ibid., 7.
84 "Project files record that CIA collaborators were involved in preparing an initial overall economic plan which has served as the basis for the Junta's most important economic decisions." "Covert Action in Chile: 1963–1973," *Staff Report of the Select Committee to Study Governmental Operations with respect to the Intelligence Activities* (1975), 40; See also Naomi Klein, *The Shock Doctrine*, 71ff.
85 Milton Friedman, *Capitalism and Freedom*, 15. My emphasis.
86 *"El Ladrillo": Bases De La Politica Economica Del Gobierno Militar Chileno* (Santiago, Chile: Centro de Estudios Publicos, 1992), 164.
87 Ibid., 193.
88 John B. Oaks, "Chile's 'Chicago' Pill – II," *New York Times*, May 4, 1979, A33.
89 Valdés, *Pinochet's Economists*, 2.
90 Robert M. Bleiberg, "'The Chicago Boys': Free Markets – as Chile Proves – Are the Way to Economic Growth," *Barron's National Business and Financial Weekly*, February 18, 1980, 7; Valdés, *Pinochet's Economists*, 37.
91 As the Boston Globe columnist David Warsh would summarize the influence of the Chilean model in 1997:

> Portugal and Spain followed Chile's example in the 1970s, as did China, turning loose some markets from its overarching plan. The market-oriented economies of Japan and of the four "Asian dragons" became cynosures as well. The rage for economic liberalization spread to the United Kingdom and the United States. Poland was next, then most of Western and Central Europe. The Berlin Wall came down in 1989. The former Soviet Union broke up. Mexico and the rest of Latin America turned dramatically toward capitalism, as did the rest of nonaligned Asia. Arnold Harberger watched as Chile became a model for the "shock therapy" with which heavily regulated economies were introduced to the industrial world.
> (David Warsh, "Full Circle," *Boston Globe*, January 12, 1997, my emphasis; see also Yves Dezalay and Bryant G. Garth, *The Internationalization of Palace Wars: Lawyers, Economists, and the Contest to Transform Latin American States* [Chicago, IL: University of Chicago Press, 2002], 82)

92 Robin Corey, "Viña del Mar: A Veritable International of the Free-Market Counterrevolution," *Corey Robin*, July 17, 2012, http://coreyrobin.com/2012/07/17/vina-del-mar-a-veritable-international-of-the-free-market-counterrevolution/
93 Quoted in Karin Fischer, "The Influence of Neoliberals in Chile Before, During, and After Pinochet," in *The Road from Mont Pelerin: The Making of the Neoliberal Thought Collective*, eds Philip Mirowski and Dieter Plehwe (Cambridge, MA: Harvard University Press, 2009), 327. This assertion about the ultimate success of neoliberalization in Chile is obviously open to debate. Valdés, for example, argues that in fact "During the subperiods of the Pinochet regime, GDP grew by an annual average of 2.6 percent … [and that] average wages were still less than in 1970." Valdés, *Pinochet's Economists*, 266–267; See also Andrew Farrant, Edward McPhail, and Sebastian Berger, "Preventing the 'Abuses' of Democracy: Hayek, the 'Military Usurper' and Transitional Dictatorship in Chile?" *American Journal of Economics and Society* 71, no. 3 (2012).
94 Ibid., 182.
95 Loïc Wacquant "Three Steps to a Historical Anthropology of Actually Existing Neoliberalism," *Social Anthropology* 20, no. 1 (2012), 67.
96 Foucault, *The Birth of Biopolitics*.
97 Philip Mirowski, "Postface: Defining Neoliberalism," in Mirowski and Plehwe, *The Road from Mont Pelerin*, 417.

Conclusion
Global war comes "home"

The low-intensity warfare tactics of the cold war have found their way to the criminalized inner city.[1]

The latent guerilla warfare in disadvantaged banlieues could spread outside of them and become a civil war.[2]

Introduction

As I argued in Chapter 1, much of international theory is predicated upon an understanding of certain boundaries, both conceptual and practical. International theorists typically attempt to differentiate the international from the set of *intra*-state interactions. Here we have the reification of a particular image of the bounded nineteenth-century European sovereign, each master of its own territory, projected back and forward in time – an aspect of what R. B. J. Walker calls the discourse of eternity. The domestic condition of hierarchy is contrasted with an international ahistorical condition of anarchy between states. Lately, there is an opposing attempt in international theory to theorize the hierarchical stratification of the international system. This attempt includes aspects of the English School and social constructivism, but especially observed in the work of David Lake or John Ikenberry. Each of these approaches emphasizes the specific diffusion of social norms or the emergence of authority relationships that call into question the pristine construction of the hierarchy/anarchy dichotomy so prevalent in realist/neorealist theories. Nonetheless, these approaches typically remain Western-centric. They assume that norm diffusion is a one-way street: specifically, they assume that the periphery remains a passive receptor of norms that have historically emerged in the West. In other words, such approaches to the theorization of international hierarchy do not take into account the historical and contemporary imbrications, feedbacks, reverberations of political, social and institutional norms and practices that were experimented on in what were/are the (neo)imperial laboratories that make up the significant parts of the global order.

What I have attempted to show in the preceding chapters is that we need to be much more attuned to the multidirectional reverberations that result from conditions of domination (particular historical forms of formal and informal imperialism) that have profound effects on domestic institutions and practices. To return to Hoffmann's point made in 1959, international theory must be attentive to what "cuts across" states and not simply the interactions between states. By tracing the ways in which imperial governance resulted in experiments and innovations of violence, social control and new forms of socioeconomics, we can observe the extent to which such subordinated spaces have historically possessed forms of agency that "cut across" and into the "inside" of great powers.

The previous three chapters examined the conjunction between historical changes in the international system and the effects that occurred throughout not only the global periphery but also the center. While I have stressed three different themes that remain crucial for international theory – namely violence, social control or security and political economy – my focus has been on demonstrating the links between international changes (i.e. imperial or hegemonic periods of crisis beginning in the nineteenth century) and the "management" of subaltern and Western populations. Instead of emphasizing the effects that such international changes have on systemic configurations, the number of poles in the international system, for example, or, more generally, on statecraft or foreign policy, I have shown how the materialization of the camp, the colonial surveillance state and neoliberalization were significantly affected by the transnational diffusions taking place across shifting imperial or hegemonic networks. The nineteenth-century experimentation with violence in imperial Africa, the colonization of the American West, and the tectonic shifts in imperial geopolitics during the latter part of the nineteenth century have had fateful implications for the materialization of the concentration camp and the violence perpetuated within Europe during the Second World War; concerns about internal threats in newly industrialized European nation-states provoked the emergence of a modern surveillance state that adapted techniques and technologies developed in imperial domains; the neoliberalization of the global South during the course of the 1970s proved significant for the reassertion of American hegemony, a political project that would be pushed forward by the adoption of a similar neoliberalization in the United States and the United Kingdom. Subordinated peripheries are not passive receptors of norms devised in the imperial West; historically they have proved to be significant "laboratories of modernity" where imperial agents could experiment, innovate and "discover" novel modes and technologies of governing that would undoubtedly prove problematic, at least initially, to implement directly within the metropole. As I have argued in Chapter 1, we should understand the metaphor of the laboratory in the Latourian sense. According to Latour, by forcing the social world to conform to its requirements, the laboratory becomes the vector for defining the parameters of legitimate political and social action. In an analogous way, the (neo)imperial laboratory defines the contours of valid social and political governance. What gets developed, innovated and experimented on in the crucibles of imperial domains becomes perceived as "tried and true" practice, especially in response to conditions of political, social or economic crisis. In this way, the imperial laboratory normalizes new forms of violence, social control, and the reorganization of domestic politico-economic institutions.

Thus the linkages between the international, the domestic, the peripheral and the metropole are much deeper and intense than international theorists usually accept. They involve processes of horizontal as well as vertical diffusion of norms and practices, of material assemblages that connect hierarchical relations between periphery and metropole. However, the relevance of uncovering these processes of co-constitution between metropole and periphery is not just for a deeper awareness of the historical implications of imperial international relations. As I started off describing in the Introduction, the Global War on Terror is itself an intensified contemporary moment of neo-imperial experimentation with significant reverberations not only for the United States itself but also across a wide array of Western states. This is not to say that the processes of militarization of the domestic space underway are novel or specific to the United States. As the epigraphs to this chapter show, the militarization of policing is a long-term process that can be traced back to the American involvement in the Philippines (as McCoy has shown) and is something that is also occurring beyond the United States, for example in France (as Mathieu Rigouste has also shown).

What is perhaps novel about our contemporary period, however, is that our traditional spatial definitions that delineate the applicability of specific forms of violence are becoming increasingly difficult to maintain. As Carlos Galli argues, the very notions of internal and external vis-à-vis state control over territory have essentially lost their meaning.[3] "In the global age," Galli argues:

> modern political spatiality – the State, with all its right and its ability to enclose an internal sphere with order and security, creating a space where "not everything can happen" – has ceased to be fully in effect, challenged as it is by the power of economic flows and the needs of capital, which demand a new politics and which no longer allow the State to be the operative center of political reality and its interpretation.[4]

Threats can no longer be properly demarcated (if they ever were completely) according to a fixed spatial configuration (i.e. the traditional cartography of the Westphalian order of states). What we end up with is a global form of "Empire" possessing neither "interiority" nor "external" edges, laced with a shifting multiplicity of borders, center-less and unstable. What emerges is a planetary condition in which this:

> global Empire [is] locked in a struggle against itself, against anomalous functions that exist within it. In short, it is an Empire whose inner

discontinuity produces conflicts that, no matter where or how they are generated, all have local status, and all of which also fall immediately – with unforeseeable effects – into the Whole.[5]

An effect of this effacement of any notions of inside and outside – something, for example, Carl Schmitt recognized long ago – is that, as Galli puts it, "the Enemy today presents himself as the Disturber, the specter of all that is internal and domestic – as our own wicked caricature, our Double, our Shadow."[6] It is the persistent fear that an amorphous enemy infiltrates the polity, undermining it through persistent and ubiquitous subversion that conditions a specific governmental response.

This concluding chapter thus explores some of the nascent consequences of these (neo)imperial experiences during the better part of a decade of the Global War on Terror, in light of a novel form of spatiality that progressively effaces distinctions between internal and external, metropole and periphery. Experimentation may well occur in Iraq or Afghanistan and reverberate back into the US; but urban American environments may also become laboratories for testing different techniques and technologies by a state that no longer entirely differentiates inside from outside. What defines the intensified pro-liferation of military techniques and technologies at "home" and "abroad" is a concern with the long-term maintenance of American authority.[7] What this results in is a consistent hollowing out of liberal-democratic institutions and the decaying civic participation of the population largely perceived as being a threat to state authority. As Sheldon Wolin puts it, "the superimposition of empire and democracy, the corruption of representative government, the declining status of the citizen, the hegemonic status of American power in the world – suggest that the traditional categories of citizen, democracy, state and power desperately need reformulation."[8]

Global war at home

Since the start of the Global War on Terror the United States military has experimented with doctrinal shifts and technological innovations. Experiments with surveillance technologies, as well as technologies for tracking and liquidating insurgents, increased the reach of American power. Novel programs such as "Tagging, Tracking, and Locating," a special operations program designed to use thermal signatures to track a specific individual over long distances, have been developed by the US military. For example, in the aftermath of the battle of Fallujah in 2004 the US military also developed Joint Expeditionary Forensic Facilities (JEFF), which are vehicles for gathering all sorts of individual data, including biometric, fingerprinting, and DNA information that permit tracking, identifying, and killing insurgents in real time. This allows for real-time decision-making by snipers to determine whether an individual is a friend or foe.[9] Concerns with transnational gangs, criminal networks, or the opaqueness of Third World urban spaces (where new security threats potentially germinate) capture the concern of security services across the Western world. And yet the new doctrines embodied in such terms as "battlespace," "fourth generation warfare," "netwar" – or, more generally as we will see, "counterinsurgency" – are perceived to be adaptable to the domestic urban environment. From the Los Angeles riots of 1992, to hurricane Katrina in New Orleans, the suppression of G8 protests in Seattle and Genoa, to the conflagration in the Parisian *banlieues* in 2005, the domestic state security apparatuses across the developed world have intensified their own militarization by effacing the distinction between internal threats and external ones. As Steven Graham argues, "the US Military's paradigm of urban control, surveillance and violent reconfiguration now straddles the traditional inside/outside binary of cities with the US nation versus cities elsewhere."[10] Indeed, as Graham notes, international security issues that have traditionally occurred between states have captured the local environment as a prime area for securitization.[11] Counterinsurgency doctrines, which many perceive to have saved the American occupation of Iraq in 2007, become a template for rethinking the commonalities between internal criminality and external insurgency, of reasserting legitimate state authority in critical areas such as inner cities, and of increasingly addressing the potential for internal mass mobilization by means of intelligence gathering, surveillance and mass preventative arrests.

These reverberating impacts are especially significant in terms of technological transfers. For example, consider the importance attached to unmanned aerial vehicles for the prosecution of the Global War on Terror. Perhaps no other technological innovation has come to symbolize the capacity to inflict violent death on disparate global "battlefields" from Pakistan to Yemen. There is currently a global arms race in drone warfare that includes Iran and China.[12] And yet UAVs are coming to play a significant role within domestic Western environments: from the monitoring of borders, to their use by the United Kingdom for surveillance during the 2012 Olympics.[13] Drones are, then, the example *par excellence* of the adaptability of contemporary technologies pioneered in military environments for eventual use within Western metropolitan states. More importantly is the fact that drone usage has been authorized against US citizens abroad, as in the case of Anwar al-Awlaki and his 16-year-old son. In this case, President Obama ordered the execution of Awlaki in 2011 in Yemen; Awlaki was accused to being a member of Al-Qaeda and planning attacks against the United States. However, the repercussions of such an extra-judicial drone attack may signify a far-reaching deterioration of constitutional principles that limit state authority. As a representative of the US Congress, Dennis Kucinich, remarked at the time of Awlaki's killing:

> Don't think for a moment that we can do these kinds of things without it having a direct effect here at home. You can't have one America abroad and another one at home. It's all the same. The erosion of democratic values, the erosion of democratic intent all augurs a nation in which the

basic rights of our people can no longer be secured. They are up for the auction of the assassin.[14]

Likewise, expansive use of drones undermines the difference between states of war and peace that define political decisions. As Peter W. Singer notes in a *New York Times* op-ed in 2012, drones allow the state to engage in near-constant warfare without it being effectively understood as warfare.[15] The result is an undermining of democratic accountability concerning the perpetuation of violence abroad.

The American occupations of Iraq and Afghanistan resulted in the significant development of new technological capacities put to the service of a program of social control called counterinsurgency. Indeed, counter-insurgency (COIN) doctrines have made a stunning comeback from the days of the Vietnam War as a way of modulating violence and social control against specific populations, and especially of reestablishing political legitimacy.[16] Counterinsurgency is as much a type of military operation as a particular manner or "style" of conducting that operation.[17] Such a style is based on establishing certain political, social and economic goals: establishing secured territorial areas and the monopoly of violence, promoting commerce and social cohesiveness, attending to the community problems and issues.[18] COIN rests in large part on creating a political and societal consensus to establish a legitimate government apparatus. Legitimacy, as the FM 3–24 Counterinsurgency manual makes clear, is the primary objective (1–113 and 1–115).[19] However, behind this lies an entire infrastructure of violence and internal repression, of conducting surveillance and intelligence-gathering programs designed to map out the population, and of co-opting a larger portion of the population either through monetary or coercive means. Adopting counterinsurgency tactics may appear to be responsive to the needs of a population throughout various "hearts and minds" campaigns, but its application has historically been, as its name implies, a means of suppressing political or structural change. "The purpose of counterinsurgency," Williams writes, "is to prevent any real shift in power."[20] It is designed to neutralize any potential for revolutionary change, or at least a reevaluation of the structural dynamics that create the very conditions of violent discontent.

COIN's ability to resubstantialize a notion of political legitimacy through the co-optation of communities, the establishment of grids and networks of intelligence-gathering apparatuses and the ability to surgically apply violence without alienating an entire population makes it an appealing tactic for fighting crime. In an article entitled "Law and Disorder: The Case for a Police Surge" in the neoconservative magazine the *Weekly Standard*, the criminologist William J. Stuntz argues that the recent experience of the 2007 counterinsurgency surge in Iraq represents a model of criminal control that is entirely applicable to the United States itself.[21] Stuntz's argument rests on the assumption that what was missing in the case of Baghdad and other Iraqi cities was a dramatic increase in "boots on the ground." More military personnel reassured the local population that it was being protected and would ultimately allow civil society to flourish. What proved, according to Stuntz, a means of stabilizing Iraq through a much more forceful strategy of mixing US personnel at the street level, is an obvious recipe for tackling the persistent problem of violent crime in inner cities across the United States. Stuntz writes:

> Most American cities are underpoliced, many of them seriously so. Instead of following the Bush/Petraeus strategy, the United States has sought to control crime by using small police forces to punish as many criminals as possible. As all those who have even a passing familiarity with contemporary crime statistics know, that approach – call it "efficient punishment" – does not work. Like the Army in pre-surge Iraq, the nation's criminal justice system is in a state of crisis. America needs another surge, this one on home territory.[22]

Note here the analogy between the army in a "pre-surge Iraq" and the current situation of the United State's criminal justice system: Stuntz makes his case on the basis of violent crime statistics of American inner cities, though he never compares them to the level of violence in Iraq during the civil war. Moreover, he ignores the fact that the surge in Iraq was accompanied by the formation of vigilante groups to combat Al-Qaeda and other insurgents. Nonetheless, the message is clear. In order to effectively combat criminality at home, adopting the militarized techniques of counterinsurgency (COIN) experimented with abroad represents a more cost-effective way of combating crime than the mass incarceration program enacted over the last three decades. Iraqi insurgents and American criminals are part of the same spectrum of offenses against state authority. Stuntz appears to assume that violent crime is in some way analogous to that of a violent insurgency against an occupying power (i.e. in the United States, criminality is in some way an act of rebellion against the state).

Interestingly enough, this is a theme that is appearing more often within the American policing establishment. In an article entitled "Urban Combat the Petraeus Way: General's Eight-Point Strategy for Crime Counterinsurgency Applied to US Streets," Donald J. Mihalek is more explicit in making the argument that crime is akin to an insurgency: "it is easy to think of criminals as an 'insurgency.'"[23] It is easy enough, because according to this theory, criminality must be understood as a concerted movement to undermine governmental authority, particularly when criminal acts target officers of the law. To the extent that this is the case, the broad range of techniques deployed in the experimental laboratory of occupied Iraq become obvious tools for reasserting domestic state authority.

The idea of applying COIN at home is evidently gaining momentum. In Salinas, California retired Iraqi veterans are advising the local police department on the adoption of COIN methods to counteract drug and gang violence. As Colonel Hy Rothstein notes in a *Washington Post* story on the matter, Salinas is "a little laboratory" in which to test battlefield techniques of population management and control.[24] Reasserting state control, Rothstein admits, and as Mihalek himself argues, rests in part on the psychological operations designed to preclude "negative messages."[25] This means in practice constant interaction with the local population by law enforcement. However, it also implies an increase in the surveillance of the population as a way of preempting criminal activity. The same principles of insurgency management apply in the domestic case in order to dissuade internal subversion.

Likewise, in 2009 in the city of Springfield, Massachusetts, former Green Beret Mike Cutone initiated a police program titled 3C (Counter Criminal Continuum) policing which was directly inspired by his experience in implementing COIN techniques in Iraq. Recently profiled in the American television news program *60 Minutes*, Cutone argues that:

> Insurgents and gang members both want to operate in a failed area, a failed community or a failed state. They know they can live off the passive support of the community, where the community is not going to call or engage the local police.[26]

Cutone's emphasis was on securing the collaboration of the community in reporting criminal activity through outreach programs. Moreover, 3C policing also involved collecting information, from crime rates and types to social and income statistics, into a database to search for patterns. A similar program called Lighthouse was developed to digitally track insurgent data in Afghanistan and Iraq. As Kevin Kit Parker, a biomedical engineering professor at Harvard who developed a program akin to Lighthouse, argues, "We want to make Springfield a laboratory, the way Framingham is for heart disease; let's turn this into a science."[27] What is all the more striking in these examples is the premise that American streets are in fact more amenable to COIN techniques than those of Iraq or Afghanistan because it is easier to collect data and "measure" its effectiveness.

Of course, this raises substantive legal issues: can the same technologies, for example, used in Iraq for tracking people, such as micro-signatures, be implemented within the American constitutional framework? Would biometric information, the adaptation of Total Situational Awareness not violate certain principles against search and seizure? Such constitutional questions will undoubtedly play themselves out in US courts in the future. However, in the meantime, it is becoming apparent that techniques and perceptions emanating from the American experience in Iraq and Afghanistan are progressively being deployed on the streets of American cities. What is more, the Iraq and Afghanistan operations have normalized a set of techniques and the use of certain technologies to tackle problems such as criminality and social marginalization that threaten to undermine state authority.

To be sure, this idea of adopting counterinsurgency techniques within metropolitan spaces as a way of counteracting criminality and reasserting

governmental authority or the use of policing techniques in military campaigns is not, strictly speaking, new or particular to the United States. During
the 1970s, with the Vietnam War and the social upheavals of the 1960s in the
background, "The police needed to reinvent themselves and the first place they
looked for models was the military."[28] Paramilitary units such as SWAT were
invented in a context of militarization while various police departments were
adopting a less confrontational form of crowd control. But as Williams points
out, this seemingly paradoxical situation was actually part and parcel of a
certain adaptation of counterinsurgency doctrines of the time: "Both militarization and community policing arose at the same time, and in response to the
same social pressures."[29] Indeed, a study entitled *The Iron Fist and the Velvet
Glove* by the Center for Research on Criminal Justice in 1975 argued:

> Like the similar techniques developed in the sixties *to maintain the over-
> seas empire (on which many of the new police techniques were patterned)*,
> these new police strategies represent an attempt to streamline and mystify the
> repressive power of the state, not to minimize it or change its direction.
> The forms of repression may change, but their functions remain the same.[30]

Maintaining American empire at home and abroad

In the contemporary United States, the continued widespread fear of internal
subversion and terrorism certainly guides the intensified militarization of
social control and urban space.[31] Concern with homegrown terrorism, transnational criminality, gangs and suchlike, solicits ever-intrusive surveillance
applications that target specific ethnicities or religious groups, and incentivize local
shows of force such as stop-and-frisk in places like New York City. The last
decade has seen the creation of an array of fusion centers throughout the
United States. Designed to accumulate all forms of data (biometric, surveillance, financial, etc.) such centers tie in local law enforcement with federal
security apparatuses. "Suspicious Activity Reports," which potentially include
anything from reports about a person taking photos of bridges or certain
buildings to certain financial transactions, feed the system. To detect criminal
patterns and to preemptively allocate resources, police departments have been
adopting much more powerful computer systems – such as Compstat in
New York City. Preventative arrests have multiplied to preclude organized
protests of important international events on American territory. Edward
Snowden's revelations about the extent to which the National Security Agency
accumulates data demonstrates the incredible growth of domestic surveillance.

The violent suppression of any form of challenge to state authority, particularly at WTO or G8 meetings, or more recently at Occupy Wall Street
protests, is also a consequence of this wider militarization of urban space.[32]
More generally, the intensification of police militarization with the testing and
adaptation of counterinsurgency techniques is part of a much larger perceived
systemic necessity of maintaining American authority at home. At a time

when the Global War on Terror, even if it is no longer called that, represents an indefinite struggle against an amorphous foe and when American military intervention throughout the world may continue indefinitely, it is necessary to maintain a cohesive, well-regulated (with respect to criminal law, in particular) and passive home front. Sheldon Wolin captures this idea when he argues that what is happening in the United States is "the steady marginalization of the demos as social welfare [that is] replaced by corporate welfare, the citizen by the sometime voter" because of a history of engaging in total war and "the acquisition of an empire."[33]

Ashley Dawson draws our attention to the fact that this militarization of urban space is connected with neoliberalism. While many military analysts see the urbanization of conflict over the last decade as a "strategic ploy" to cancel out the technological superiority of the American military, Dawson notes that this argument conveniently ignores "the fundamental causes for a trend that will inevitably become more prominent, given the failure of global elites to broach, let alone answer, the question of how to integrate the surplus humanity of the global South into the global economy."[34] Mike Davis' classic work, *Planet of Slums*, demonstrates the extent to which over the previous three decades transnational structural adjustment programs and the devolution of any kind of social state has resulted in the unparalleled and historic urbanization of the global South.[35] The massification of various urban centers has resulted in an explosion of the informal economy run by a whole host of transnational actors such as crime syndicates and transnational gangs.[36] It has also resulted in an explosion of undocumented immigration from Latin America into the United States, which, for example, has compelled the use of unmanned aerial vehicles on border areas. Dawson's point here is key. Militarization is a way of covering over the "fundamental causes" that have reduced a significant part of humanity to a superfluous status in which military might, whether by proxy or by the US, become the means for exercising social control.

What the neoliberalization of the global North has achieved over the past three decades is precisely the emergence of an internal population that is becoming ever-more marginalized. Unemployed and impoverished, this population serves as a reserve labor pool keeping overall labor costs down. Social insecurity that results from unleashing competitive market forces without government regulation and the minimization any form of social safety net perpetuates a structural underclass. Loïc Wacquant's work shows how the explosion of the carceral state paradoxically accompanies the neoliberalization of the United States.[37] The progressive devolution of the welfare state since the Reagan revolution was accompanied by a heavily segregated and militarized spatiality.[38] Increasingly, the military system is coming into play as well across urban areas in the global South as well as in the North.[39] The analogy drawn here between the poor areas and "war zones" makes it is entirely possible to conceive of an American city like New Orleans after the natural disaster of hurricane Katrina as requiring a similar response to the pacification of Baghdad. Indeed, in the immediate aftermath of Katrina, Kathleen Blanco stated:

> Three hundred of the Arkansas National Guard have landed in the City of New Orleans. These troops are fresh back from Iraq, well trained, experienced, battle tested and under my orders to restore order in the streets. They have M-16s and they are locked and loaded. These troops know how to shoot and kill and they are more than willing to do so if necessary and I expect they will.[40]

The terrifying end of the above statement – "I expect they will" – almost goads these soldiers to use such deadly force. It also reveals quite clearly the imperial after-effects of dehumanization applied to an American population who happen to be black, poor, and located in the vortex of an urban natural disaster. The militarization and carceralization of the American polity are answers to the necessity of maintaining a constant American imperial supremacy. Furthermore, there appears to be nothing on the horizon that might break this vicious circle between empire and the home front.

Notes

1 Elana Zilberg, *Space of Detention: The Making of a Transnational Gang Crisis between Los Angeles and San Salvador* (Durham, NC: Duke University Press, 2011), 71.
2 French General quoted in Didier Fassin, *Enforcing Order: An Ethnography of Urban Policing* (New York: Polity, 2013), 237.
3 Carlo Galli, *Political Spaces and Global War* (Minneapolis: University of Minnesota Press, 2010), 139:

> The external seems to have become the internal, and to have opened up a second front. The West feels forced to respond, and so unleashes technological power against its outside while deploying institutional cunning (also in the form of technology) within its interior. Thus it is that while the machines of imperial technology – spy satellites, Echelon ears, B-2 Stealth bombers, Predator drones, cruise missiles, F-16 Falcons, smart bombs, cluster bombs, daisy-cutters, thermobaric bombs – hunt down and strike enemies in the deserts and the caves of central Asia, the Horn of Africa, and Mesopotamia, the apparatuses of security simultaneously use detectors and interceptors, video cameras and tabulations, as well as an infinite number of checkpoints, seeking to ferret out the infiltrators and the Fifth Columns.

4 Ibid., 157.
5 Ibid., 160.
6 Ibid., 141.
7 Andrew Bacevich, *The New American Militarism: How Americans Are Seduced by War* (New York: Oxford University Press, 2005); Andrew Bacevich, *Washington Rules: America's Path to Permanent War* (New York: Metropolitan Books, 2010); Chalmers Johnson, *Nemesis: The Last Days of the American Republic* (New York:

Metropolitan Books, 2006); Chalmers Johnson, *The Sorrows of Empire: Militarism, Secrecy, and the End of the Republic* (New York: Metropolitan Books, 2004).

8 Sheldon Wolin, *Politics and Vision: Continuity and Innovation in Western Political Thought* (Princeton, NJ: Princeton University Press, 2004), 590.

9 Alfred W. McCoy, *Policing America's Empire: The United States, The Philippines, and the Rise of the Surveillance State* (Madison: University of Wisconsin Press, 2009), 9.

10 Stephen Graham, *Cities under Siege: The New Military Urbanism* (New York: Verso, 2010), 20.

11 Ibid.; see also David Murakami Wood and Jonathan Coaffee, "Security Is Coming Home: Rethinking Scale and Constructing Resilience in the Global Urban Environment to Terrorist Risk," *International Relations* 20, no. 4 (2006).

12 See, for example, Michael J. Boyle, "The Costs and Consequences of Drone Warfare," *International Affairs*89, no. 1 (2013).

13 www.independent.co.uk/news/uk/crime/drones-to-patrol-the-skies-above-olympic-stadium-6267107.html

14 Quoted in Jeremy Scahill, *Dirty Wars: The World Is a Battlefield* (New York: Nation Books, 2013), 367–368.

15 Peter W. Singer, "Do Drones Undermine Democracy?" *New York Times*, SR5, January 22, 2012.

16 Here I define counterinsurgency following the *Counterinsurgency FM-23* manual as:

> Counterinsurgency is those military, paramilitary, economic, psychological and civil actions taken by a government to defeat an insurgency (JP 102). In a counterinsurgency, Host Nation forces and partners operate to defeat armed resistance, reduce passive opposition, and establish or reestablish the legitimacy of the Host Nation's government (FM 30). Counterinsurgency is a proactive approach involving all elements of national power, even down to the tactical level. COIN operations strive to achieve unity of effort amongst many joint, interagency, intergovernmental, and multinational organizations. COIN includes tactical planning; intelligence development and analysis; training; materiel, technical, organizational assistance; advice; infrastructure development; tactical level operations; and information engagement. US forces often lead the US government's counterinsurgency efforts because the US military can quickly project a counterinsurgent force and sustain not only its force but also other agencies.

17 Kristian Williams, "The Other Side of COIN: Counterinsurgency and Community Policing," *Interface: A Journal for and about Social Movements* 3, no. 1 (2011), 83.

18 See in particular David Kilcullen, *Counterinsurgency* (New York: Oxford University Press, 2010).

19 Note especially the Western-centric conceptions of legitimacy. As the authors of the manual argue in 1–114:

> In Western liberal tradition, a government that derives its just powers from the people and responds to their desires while looking out for their welfare is accepted as legitimate. In contrast, theocratic societies fuse political and religious authority; political figures are accepted as legitimate because the populace views them as implementing the will of God. Medieval monarchies claimed 'the divine right of kings.' Imperial China governed with "the mandate of heaven." Since the 1979 revolution, Iran has operated under the "rule

of the jurists [theocratic judges]." In other societies, "might makes right."

20 Williams, "The Other Side of COIN: Counterinsurgency and Community Policing," 85.
21 William J. Stuntz, "Law and Disorder: The Case for a Police Surge," *Weekly Standard*, February 22, 2009.
22 Ibid.
23 Donald J. Mihalek, "Urban Combat the Petraeus Way" (2010 [quoted January 23, 2012]); available from www.tactical-life.com/online/guns-and-weapons/urban-combat-the-petraeus-way/.
24 Karl Vick, "Iraq's Lessons, on the Home Front," *Washington Post*, Sunday November 15, 2009.
25 Ibid.
26 www.cbsnews.com/8301-18560_162-57582859/counterinsurgency-cops-military-tactics-fight-street-crime/
27 Carolyn Y. Johnson, "To Counter Gangs, Springfield Adopts Tactics from War Zones," *Boston Globe*, August 20, 2012; See also Sharon Weinberger, "A Data-Driven War on Crime," *Nature*, April 4, 2012.
28 Williams, "The Other Side of Coin," 91.
29 Ibid., 92.
30 Quoted in ibid., 91, my emphasis.
31 Ashley Dawson, "Combat in Hell: Cities as the Achilles Heel of US Imperial Hegemony," *Social Text* 25, no. 2 (2007), 177.
32 Ibid., 176. See especially Mike Davis, "Fortress Los Angeles: The Militarization of Urban Space," in *Variations on a Theme Park: The New American City and the End of Public Space*, ed. Michael Sorkin (New York: Hill and Wang, 1992).
33 Wolin, *Politics and Vision: Continuity and Innovation in Western Political Thought*, 553.
34 Dawson, "Combat in Hell: Cities as the Achilles Heel of US Imperial Hegemony," 174.
35 Mike Davis, *Planet of Slums* (New York: Verso, 2007).
36 John Hagedorn, *A World of Gangs: Armed Young Men and Gangsta Culture* (Minneapolis: University of Minnesota Press, 2009).
37 Loïc Wacquant, *Punishing the Poor: The Neoliberal Government of Social Insecurity* (Durham, NC: Duke University Press, 2009).
38 See also for example, Katherine Beckett and Steve Herbert, eds, *Banished: The New Social Control in Urban America* (Oxford: Oxford University Press, 2009).
39 Loïc Wacquant, "The Militarization of Urban Marginality: Lessons from the Brazilian Metropolis," *International Political Sociology* 2, no. 1 (2008), 58. Wacquant himself draws links between the intensification of penal repression and neoliberalism by looking at Brazilian favelas as a "living laboratory to uncover the deep logic of punitive containment as political strategy for managing dispossessed and dishonored populations in the polarizing city … " The Brazilian precursor reveals a future in which "urban law-enforcement agencies operate in the manner of border patrols and forces of occupation in poor areas treated as domestic 'war zones' harboring an alien population stripped of the normal protections and privileges of the law," 71.
40 Quoted in Shahrar Ali, "Is There a Justifiable Shoot-to-Kill Policy?" in *Discourses and Practices of Terrorism: Interrogating Terror*, eds Bob Brecher, Mark Devenney, and Aaron Winter (New York: Routledge, 2010), 23.

Bibliography

Acharya, Amitav, and Barry Buzan. *Non-Western International Relations Theory: Perspectives on or Beyond Asia*. London: Routledge, 2010.

Agamben, Giorgio. *Homo Sacer: Sovereign Power and Bare Life*. Stanford, CA: Stanford University Press, 1998.

Agnew, John. "American Hegemony into American Empire? Lessons from the Invasion of Iraq." *Antipode* 35, 5(2003): 871–885.

Amin, Samir. *Eurocentrism*. New York: Monthly Review Press, 1989.

Anderson, Warwick. "Excremental Colonialism: Public Health and the Poetics of Pollution." *Critical Inquiry* 21, 3(1995): 640–669.

Anderson, Warwick. "From Subjugated Knowledge to Conjugated Subjects: Science and Globalization, or Postcolonial Studies of Science." *Postcolonial Studies* 12, 4 (2009): 389–400.

Anderson, Warwick. "Pacific Crossings: Imperial Logics in the United States' Public Health Programs." In *Colonial Crucible: Empire in the Making of the Modern American State*, eds Alfred W. McCoy and Francisco A. Scarano. Madison: University of Wisconsin Press, 2009.

Appadurai, Arjun. *Modernity at Large: Cultural Dimensions of Globalization*. Minneapolis: University of Minnesota Press, 1996.

Arendt, Hannah. "A Reply to Eric Voegelin." In *Essays in Understanding: 1930–1954, Formation, Exile and Totalitarianism*, ed. Jerome Kohn.New York: Schocken, 1994.

Arendt, Hannah. *Eichmann in Jerusalem: A Report on the Banality of Evil*. New York: Viking Press, 1963.

Arendt, Hannah. *The Origins of Totalitarianism*. New York: Harcourt Brace Jovanovich, 1973.

Arnold, David. *Colonizing The Body: State Medicine and Epidemic Disease in Nineteenth-Century India*. Berkeley: University of California Press, 1993.

Arnold, David. "The Colonial Prison: Power, Knowledge, and Penology in Nineteenth-Century India." In *Subaltern Studies Reader, 1986–1995*, eds Ranajit Guha, David Arnold, and David Hardiman.Minneapolis: University of Minnesota Press, 1997.

Arrighi, Giovanni. *Adam Smith in Beijing: Lineages of the 21st Century*. London: Verso, 2007.

Arrighi, Giovanni. *The Long Twentieth Century: Money, Power and the Origins of Our Times*. London: Verso, 1994.

Arrighi, Giovanni. "The Social and Political Economy of Global Turbulence." *New Left Review* 20, (2003): 5–71.

Ashley, Richard. "Neorealism and Its Critics." In *Neorealism and Its Critics*, ed. Robert O. Keohane.New York: Columbia University Press, 1986.

Bacevich, Andrew J.. *The New American Militarism: How Americans Are Seduced by War*. New York: Oxford University Press, 2005.

Bacevich, Andrew J. *Washington Rules: America's Path to Permanent War*. New York: Metropolitan Books, 2010.

Baranowski, Shelley. *Nazi Empire: German Colonialism and Imperialism from Bismarck to Hitler*. Cambridge: Cambridge University Press, 2011.

Barkawi, Tarak, and Mark Laffey. "Retrieving the Imperial: Empire and International Relations." *Millennium: A Journal of International Studies* 31, 01(2002): 109–127.

Barkawi, Tarak, and Mark Laffey. "The Postcolonial Moment In Security Studies.". *Review of International Studies* 32, 2(2006): 329–352.

Barkawi, Tarak. *Globalization and War*. Lanham, MD: Rowman & Littlefield, 2005.

Barton, Gregory A. and Brett M. Bennett. "Forestry as Foreign Policy: Anglo-Siamese Relations and the Origins of Britain"s Informal Empire in the Teak Forests of Northern Siam, 1883–1925." *Itinerario* 34, 2(2010): 65–86.

Bartov, Omer. *Germany's War and the Holocaust: Disputed Histories*. Ithaca, NY: Cornell University Press, 2003.

Bashford, Alison. *Imperial Hygiene: A Critical History of Colonialism, Nationalism and Public Health*. New York: Palgrave Macmillan, 2004.

Baucom, Ian. *Specters of the Atlantic: Finance Capital, Slavery and the Philosophy of History*. Durham, NC: Duke University Press, 2005.

Baucom, Ian. "Township Modernism." In *Beyond the Black Atlantic: Relocating Modernization and Technology*, eds Walter Goebel and Saskia Schabio. London: Routledge, 2006.

Bayly, C. A.. *Empire and Information: Intelligence Gathering and Social Communication in India, 1780–1870*. Cambridge: Cambridge University Press, 1996.

Beckett, Katherine, and Steven Kelly Herbert. *Banished: The New Social Control in Urban America*. Oxford: Oxford University Press, 2010.

Beckley, Michael. "China's Century? Why America's Edge Will Endure." *International Security*, 36, 3(2011): 41–78.

Beier, J. Marshall. "Beyond Hegemonic State(ment)s of Nature: Indigenous Knowledge and Non-State Possibilities in International Relations." In *Power, Postcolonialism and International Relations: Reading Race, Gender and Class*, eds Geeta Chowdhry and SheilaNair.London: Routledge, 2014.

Bell, Duncan. "Race and International Relations: Introduction." *Cambridge Review of International Affairs* 26, 1(2013): 1–4.

Berman, Russell A. *Enlightenment or Empire: Colonial Discourse in German Culture*. Lincoln, NE: University of Nebraska Press, 1998.

Bhabha, Homi. "Of Mimicry and Man: The Ambivalence of Colonial Discourse." In *Tensions of Empire: Colonial Cultures in a Bourgeois World*, eds Frederick Cooper and Ann Laura Stoler.Berkeley: University of California Press, 1997.

Bhambra, Gurminder K. *Rethinking Modernity: Postcolonialism and the Sociological Imagination*. Basingstoke: Palgrave, 2007.

Blaut, James M. *The Colonizer's Model of the World: Geographical Diffusionism and Eurocentric History*. New York: Guilford Press, 1993.

Bloxham, Donald. *The Final Solution: A Genocide*. Oxford: Oxford University Press, 2009.

Blyth, Mark. *Great Transformations: Economic Ideas and Institutional Change in the Twentieth Century*. New York: Cambridge University Press, 2002.

Bourdieu, Pierre, and Loïc Wacquant. "New Liberal Speak: Notes on the New Planetary Vulgate." *Radical Philosophy* 105(2001): 1–5.

Boyle, Michael J. "The Costs and Consequences of Drone Warfare." *International Affairs* 89, 1(2013): 1–29.

Brenner, Robert. *The Boom and the Bubble: The US in the World Economy.* London: Verso, 2002.

Brenner, Robert. *The Economics of Global Turbulence.* London: Verso, 2006.

Brown, Wendy. "Neo-Liberalism and the End of Liberal Democracy." *Theory and Event* 7, 1(2003).

Bull, Hedley, and Adam Watson. *The Expansion of International Society.* Oxford: Clarendon Press, 1984.

Bull, Hedley. "Justice and International Relations." In *Hedley Bull on International Society*, eds Kai Alderson and Andrew Hurrell. New York: Palgrave, 1984.

Bull, Hedley. *The Anarchical Society: A Study of Order in World Politics.* New York: Columbia University Press, 2002.

Burbank, Jane, and Frederick Cooper. *Empires in World History: Power and the Politics of Difference.* Princeton, NJ: Princeton University Press, 2010.

Buret, Eugene. *De la misère des classes laborieuses en Angleterre et en France.* Paris: Paulin, 1840.

Butler, Stuart M. "The Enterprise Zone as a Political Animal," *Cato Journal* 2, 2 (1982): 373–390.

Buzan, Barry, and George Lawson. "The Global Transformation: The Nineteenth Century and the Making of Modern International Relations." *International Studies Quarterly*, 3(2013): 620–635.

Buzan, Barry, and Richard Little. "Reconceptualizing Anarchy: Structural Realism Meets World History." *European Journal of International Relations* 2, 4(1996): 403–438.

Buzan, Barry, OleWaever, and Jaap H. de Wilde. *Security: A New Framework of Analysis.* Boulder, CO: Lynne Rienner, 1998.

Buzan, Barry. "The English School: An Underexploited Resource in IR." *Review of International Studies* 27, 3(2001): 471–488.

Callahan, William A. "Nationalising International Theory: Race, Class and the English School." *Global Society* 18, 4(2004): 305–323.

Callwell, Major C. E. *Small Wars: Their Principles and Practice.* Urbana, IL: Tales End Press, 2013.

Carnegie, Andrew. *The Empire of Business.* New York: Doubleday, Page & Co., 1902.

Cbsnews.com. "Text of Bush Speech", 2014. www.cbsnews.com/stories/2003/05/01/iraq/main551946.shtml.

Centro de Estudios Publicos, ed., *"El Ladrillo": Bases de la Politica Economica del Gobierno Militar Chileno.* Santiago, Chile: Centro de Estudios Publicos, 1992.

Césaire, Aime. *Discourse on Colonialism.* New York: Monthly Review Press, 2000.

Chakrabarty, Dipesh. *Provincializing Europe: Postcolonial Thought and Historical Difference.* Princeton, NJ: Princeton University Press, 2000.

Chatterjee, Partha. "More on Modes of Power and the Peasantry." In *Selected Subaltern Studies*, eds Ranajit Guha and Gayatri Chakravorty Spivak. New York: Oxford University Press, 1988.

Cho, Kyungjin. "The Culture of Boom-and-Bust and the Duty Free Zone: A Struggle to Find Iquique's Place in the Chilean Nation-State." Ph.D. dissertation, University of Chicago, 2004.

Clark, Ian. *Legitimacy in International Society.* Oxford: Oxford University Press, 2005.

Coaffee, Jon, and David Murakami Wood. "Security Is Coming Home: Rethinking Scale and Constructing Resilience in the Global Urban Response to Terrorist Risk." *International Relations* 20, 4(2006): 503–517.

Cole, Simon A.. *Suspect Identities: A History of Fingerprinting and Criminal Identification.* Cambridge, MA: Harvard University Press, 2001.

Conrad, Sebastian. *German Colonialism: A Short History.* Cambridge: Cambridge University Press, 2012.

Constable, Pamela, and Arturo Valenzuela. *A Nation of Enemies: Chile Under Pinochet.* New York: Norton, 1993.

Cooley, Alexander. *Logics of Hierarchy: The Organization of Empires, States and Military Occupation.* Ithaca, NY: Cornell University Press, 2005.

Cooper, Frederick, and Ann Laura Stoler, eds *Tensions of Empire: Colonial Cultures in a Bourgeois World.* Berkeley: University of California Press, 1997.

Corvalan, Luis. *El Gobierno de Salvador Allende.* Santiago, Chile: LOM Ediciones, 2003.

Cox, Robert W. "Social Forces, States and World Orders: Beyond International Relations Theory." *Millennium: Journal of International Studies* 10, 2(1981): 126–155.

Dalrymple, William. *The Last Mughal.* New York: Alfred A. Knopf, 2007.

Darby, Phillip, and Albert J. Paolini. "Bridging International Relations and Postcolonialism." *Alternatives: Global, Local and Political* 19(1994), 371–397.

Darwin, John. *The Empire Project: The Rise and Fall of the British World System, 1830–1970.* Cambridge: Cambridge University Press, 2009.

Davis, Mike. *Planet of Slums.* London: Verso, 2006.

Dawson, Ashley. "Combat in Hell: Cities as the Achilles Heel of US Imperial Hegemony." *Social Text* 25, 2(2007): 169–180.

Deudney, Daniel. *Bounding Power: Republican Security Theory from the Polis to the Global Village.* Princeton, NJ: Princeton University Press, 2007.

Dezalay, Yves, and Bryant G. Garth. *The Internationalization of Palace Wars: Lawyers, Economists and the Contest to Transform Latin American States.* Chicago, IL: University of Chicago Press, 2002.

Dickerson, James. *Inside America's Concentration Camps: Two Centuries of Interment and Torture.* Chicago: Lawrence Hill Books, 2010.

Dirks, Nicholas B. "Foreword." In *Colonialism and Its Forms of Knowledge*, by Bernard S. Cohn. Princeton, NJ: Princeton University Press, 1996.

Douglas, Mary. *Purity and Danger: An Analysis of Concepts of Pollution and Taboo.* New York: Praeger, 1966.

Doyle, Michael W.. *Empires.* Ithaca, NY: Cornell University Press, 1986.

Du Bois, W. E. B.. *The World and Africa.* New York: International Publishers, 1972.

Elliot, J. H. "*How They Made the Empire*, by J. H. Elliott." *New York Review of Books,* 2011. www.nybooks.com/articles/archives/2011/aug/18/how-they-made-empire/.

Erichsen, Casper Wolf. "Forced Labor in the Concentration Camp on Shark Island." In *Genocide in German South-West Africa: The Colonial War of 1904–1908 and Its Aftermath*, eds Jürgen Zimmerer and Joachim Zeller. London: Merlin Press, 2007.

Fanon, Frantz. *The Wretched of the Earth.* New York: Grove Press, 1965.

Farrant, Andrew, EdwardMcPhail, and Sebastian Berger. "Preventing the 'Abuses' of Democracy: Hayek, The 'Military Usurper' and Transitional Dictatorship in Chile?" *American Journal of Economics and Sociology* 71, 3(2012): 513–538.

Fassin, Didier. *Enforcing Order: An Ethnography of Urban Policing*. Cambridge: Polity Press, 2013.

Ferguson, Niall. *Colossus: The Rise and Fall of the American Empire*. New York: Penguin Press, 2004.

Finnemore, Martha. "Norms, Culture, And World Politics: Insights From Sociology's Institutionalism." *International Organization* 50, 02(1996): 325–347.

Fischer, Karen. "The Influence of Neoliberals in Chile Before, During, and After Pinochet," In *The Road from Mont Pelerin: The Making of the Neoliberal Thought Collective*, eds Philip Mirowski and Dieter Plehwe.Cambridge, MA: Harvard University Press, 2009.

Fortescue, William. *France and 1848: The End of Monarchy*. London: Routledge, 2005.

Foster, Ann L. "Prohibiting Opium in the Philippines and the United States: The Creation of the Interventionist State." In *Colonial Crucible: Empire in the Making of the Modern American State*, eds Alfred W. McCoy and Francisco A. Scarano. Madison: University of Wisconsin Press, 2009.

Foucault, Michel. *Discipline and Punish: The Birth of the Prison*. New York: Pantheon Books, 1977.

Foucault, Michel. *Power/Knowledge: Selected Interviews and Other Writings, 1972–1977*. New York: Pantheon Books, 1980.

Foucault, Michel. *Society Must Be Defended*. New York: Picador, 2003.

Foucault, Michel. *The Archaeology of Knowledge*. New York: Routledge, 2002.

Foucault, Michel. *The Birth of Biopolitics*. New York: Palgrave Macmillan, 2008.

Frazier, Lessie Jo. *Salt in the Sand: Memory, Violence and the Nation-State in Chile, 1890 to the Present*. Raleigh, NC: Duke University Press, 2007.

Friedman, Jack R. "Shock and Subjectivity in the Age of Globalization Marginalization, Exclusion, and the Problem of Resistance." *Anthropological Theory* 7, 4 (2007): 421–448.

Friedman, Milton. *Capitalism and Freedom*. Chicago: University of Chicago Press, 1962.

Fuchs, Christian. "Political Economy and Surveillance Theory." *Critical Sociology* 39, 5(2013): 671–687.

Galeano, Eduardo. *Days and Nights of Love and War*. New York: Monthly Review Press, 1983.

Gallagher, John, and Ronald Robinson. "The Imperialism of Free Trade." *Economic History Review* 6, 1(1953): 1–15.

Galli, Carlo. *Political Spaces and Global War*. Minneapolis: University of Minnesota Press, 2010.

George, Jim. *Discourses of Global Politics: Critical Reintroduction to International Politics*. Boulder, CO: Lynne Rienner, 1994.

Gerwarth, Robert, and Stephan Malinowski. "Hannah Arendt's Ghosts: Reflections on the Disputable Path from Windhoek to Auschwitz." *Central European History* 42, 2(2009): 279–300.

Gilpin, Robert. *War and Change in World Politics*. Cambridge: Cambridge University Press, 1981.

Gilroy, Paul. *Postcolonial Melancholia*. New York: Columbia University Press, 2005.

Go, Julian. *Patterns of Empire: The British and American Empires, 1688 to the Present*. Cambridge: Cambridge University Press, 2011.

Gordon, Michael R. and Bernard E. Trainor. *Cobra II: The Inside Story of the Invasion and Occupation of Iraq*. New York: Pantheon Books, 2006.

Gouda, Frances. "Mimicry and Projection in the Colonial Encounter: The Dutch East Indies/Indonesia as Experimental Laboratory, 1900–1942." *Journal of Colonialism and Colonial History* 1, 2(2000).

Gould, Stephen Jay. *The Mismeasure of Man*. New York: Norton, 1981.

Graham, Stephen. *Cities Under Siege: The New Military Urbanism*. London: Verso, 2010.

Grandin, Greg. *Empire's Workshop: Latin America, The United States and the Rise of the New Imperialism*. New York: Metropolitan Books, 2006.

Gusterson, Hugh. *People of the Bomb: Portraits of America's Nuclear Complex*. Minneapolis: University of Minnesota Press, 2004.

Hagedorn, John. *A World of Gangs: Armed Young Men and Gangsta Culture*. Minneapolis: University of Minnesota Press, 2008.

Hall, Peter M. "Enterprise Zones: A Justification", *International Journal of Urban and Regional Research*, 6, 3(1982): 416–421.

Handler, Richard. *Nationalism and the Politics of Culture in Quebec*. Madison: University of Wisconsin Press, 1988.

Haraway, Donna. "Situated Knowledges: The Science Question in Feminism and the Privilege of Partial Perspective." *Feminist Studies* 14, 3(1988): 575–599.

Harding, Sandra. *Sciences from Below: Feminisms, Postcolonialities, and Modernities*. Raleigh, NC: Duke University Press, 2008.

Hardt, Michael, and Antonio Negri. *Empire*. Cambridge, MA: Harvard University Press, 2000.

Hardt, Michael and Antonio Negri. *Multitude*. New York: The Penguin Press, 2004.

Harvey, David. *A Brief History of Neoliberalism*. New York: Oxford University Press, 2005.

Harvey, David. *Spaces of Global Capitalism: A Theory of Uneven Georgraphical Development*. London: Verso, 2006.

Harvey, David. *The New Imperialism*. Oxford: Oxford University Press, 2003.

Haslam, Jonathan. *The Nixon Administration and the Death of Allende's Chile*. London: Verso, 2005.

Heyningen, Elizabeth van. "A Tool for Modernisation? The Boer Concentration Camps of the South African War, 1900–1902." *South African Journal of Science* 106, 5-6(2010): 52–61.

Hobsbawm, E. J. *The Age of Empire, 1875–1914*. New York: Pantheon Books, 1987.

Hobson, John M. *The Eastern Origins of Western Civilization*. Cambridge: Cambridge University Press, 2004.

Hoffmann, Stanley H. "International Relations: The Long Road to Theory." *World Politics* 11, 3(1959): 346–377.

Home, Robert K. *Of Planting and Planning: The Making of British Colonial Cities*. London: Routledge, 2013.

Hull, Isabel V. *Absolute Destruction: Military Culture and the Practice of War in Imperial Germany*. Ithaca, NY: Cornell University Press, 2005.

Huntington, Samuel. "The United States." In *The Crisis of Democracy: On the Governability of Democracies*. New York: New York University Press, 2014.

Ikenberry, G. John. *Liberal Leviathan: The Origins, Crisis and Transformation of the American World Order*. Princeton, NJ: Princeton University Press, 2011.

Inayatullah, Naeem, and David L. Blaney. *International Relations and the Problem of Difference*. New York: Routledge, 2004.

Jackson, Patrick Thaddeus. *The Conduct of Inquiry in International Relations*. New York: Routledge, 2011.

Jackson, Robert H. *Quasi-States: Sovereignty, International Relations and the Third World.* Cambridge: Cambridge University Press, 1990.

Jaeger, Hans-Martin. "UN Reform, Biopolitics, and Global Governmentality." *International Theory* 2, 1(2010): 50–86.

Jennings, Eric Thomas. *Curing the Colonizers: Hydrotherapy, Climatology, and French Colonial Spas.* Durham, NC: Duke University Press, 2006.

Johansen, Bruce E., and Barry Pritzker. *Encyclopedia of American Indian History.* Santa Barbara, CA: ABC-CLIO, 2008.

Johnson, Chalmers. *Nemesis: The Last Days of the American Republic.* New York: Metropolitan Books, 2006.

Johnson, Chalmers. *The Sorrows of Empire: Militarism, Secrecy and the End of the Republic.* New York: Metropolitan Books, 2004.

Jones, Daniel Stedman. *Masters of the Universe: Hayek, Friedman, and the Birth of Neoliberal Politics.* Princeton, NJ: Princeton University Press, 2012.

Kaplan, Martha. "Panopticon in Poona: An Essay on Foucault and Colonialism." *Cultural Anthropology* 10, 1(1995): 85–98.

Kaplan, Robert D. *Imperial Grunts: On the Ground with the American Military, from Mongolia to the Philippines to Iraq and Beyond.* New York: Random House, 2005.

Kayaoglu, Turan. "Westphalian Eurocentrism in International Relations Theory." *International Studies Review* 12, 2(2010): 193–217.

Keene, Edward. *Beyond the Anarchical Society: Grotius, Colonialism and Order in World Politics.* Cambridge: Cambridge University Press, 2002.

Kennedy, Paul M. *The Rise and Fall of the Great Powers.* New York: Random House, 1987.

Keohane, Robert O. and Joseph S. Nye. *Power and Interdependence.* Boston: Little, Brown, 1977.

Khagram, Sanjeev, James V. Riker, and Kathryn Sikkink. *Restructuring World Politics: Transnational Social Movement, Networks and Norms.* Minneapolis: University of Minnesota Press, 2002.

Kiernan, V. G.. *America: The New Imperialism, From White Settlement to World Hegemony.* London: Zed Press, 1978.

Kilcullen, David. *Counterinsurgency.* Oxford: Oxford University Press, 2010.

Klein, Naomi. *The Shock Doctrine: The Rise of Disaster Capitalism.* New York: Metropolitan Books/Henry Holt, 2007.

Koselleck, Reinhart. "Neuzeit: Remarks on the Semantics of Modern Concept of Movement." In *Futures Past: On the Semantics of Historical Time.* New York: Columbia University Press, 2004.

Koselleck, Reinhart. "'Progress' and 'Decline': An Appendix to the History of Two Concepts." In *The Practice of Conceptual History: Timing Concepts, Spacing Concepts.* Stanford, CA: Stanford University Press, 2002.

Koselleck, Reinhart. "'Space of Experience' and 'Horizon of Expectation': Two Historical Categories." In *Futures Past: On the Semantics of Historical Time.* New York: Columbia University Press, 2004.

Koselleck, Reinhart. "Time and History." In *The Practice of Conceptual History: Timing Concepts, Spacing Concepts.* Stanford, CA: Stanford University Press, 2002.

Kotek, Joel, and Pierre Rigoulot. *Le siècle des camps: emprisonnement, détention, extermination, cent ans de mal absolu.* Paris: Jean-Claude Lattes, 2000.

Krippner, Greta R. *Capitalizing on Crisis: The Political Origins of the Rise of Finance.* Cambridge, MA: Harvard University Press, 2011.

Lake, David A. *Hierarchy in International Relations*. Ithaca, NY: Cornell University Press, 2009.

Larner, Wendy, and William Walters. *Global Governmentality: Governing International Spaces*. New York: Routledge, 2004.

Latour, Bruno, and Steve Woolgar. *Laboratory Life: The Construction of Scientific Facts*. Princeton, NJ: Princeton University Press, 1986.

Latour, Bruno. "Give Me a Laboratory and I Will Raise the World." In *Science Observed: Perspectives on the Study of Science*. London: Sage, 1983.

Latour, Bruno. *Politics of Nature: How to Bring the Sciences into Democracy*. Cambridge, MA: Harvard University Press, 2004.

Latour, Bruno. *The Pasteurization of France*. Cambridge: Harvard University Press, 1988.

Le Cour Grandmaison, Olivier. *Coloniser, exterminer: sur la guerre et l'état colonial*. Paris: Fayard, 2005.

Lempereur, Nathalie, Jean-Louis Schlegel, and Olivier Mongin. "What Is Postcolonial Thinking? – Achille Mbembe. An Interview with Achille Mbembe." Eurozine.Com, 2014. www.eurozine.com/articles/2008-01-09-mbembe-en.html.

Lester, Alan. *Imperial Networks: Creating Identities in Nineteenth Century South Africa and Britain*. London: Routledge, 2001.

Levi, Primo. *The Drowned and the Saved*. New York: Summit Books, 1988.

Lim, Bl Cua. *Translating Time: Cinema, the Fantastic and Temporal Critique*. Durham, NC: Duke University Press, 2009.

Linklater, Andrew. "Realism, Marxism and Critical International Theory." *Review of International Studies* 12, 4(1986): 301–312.

Lipschutz, Ronnie D. "Global Civil Society and Global Governmentality: Or, the Search for Politics and the State Amidst the Capillaries of Social Power." In *Power in Global Governance*, eds Michael Barnett and Raymond Duvall.Cambridge: Cambridge University Press, 2005.

Lipton, David, JeffreySachs, StanleyFischer, and Janos Kornai. "Creating a Market Economy in Eastern Europe: The Case of Poland." *Brookings Papers on Economic Activity* 1(1990): 75–147.

Lock, Margaret M., and Vinh-Kim Nguyen. *An Anthropology of Biomedicine*. Oxford: Wiley-Blackwell, 2010.

Long, David, and Brian C. Schmidt. *Imperialism and Internationalism in the Discipline of International Relations*. Albany: State University of New York Press, 2005.

Lyon, David. *The Electronic Eye: The Rise of Surveillance Society*. Minneapolis: University of Minnesota Press, 1994.

Lyons, Claire L., and John K. Papadopoulos. *The Archaeology of Colonialism*. Los Angeles, CA: Getty Research Institute, 2002.

Magubane, Zine. "Simians, Savages, Skulls, and Sex: Science and Colonial Militarism in Nineteenth-Century South Africa." In *Race, Nature, and the Politics of Difference*, eds Donald S. Moore, Jake Kosek, and Anand Pandian. Durham, NC: Duke University Press, 2003.

Mann, Michael. *Incoherent Empire*. London: Verso, 2003.

Mantena, Karuna. *Alibis of Empire: Henry Main and the Ends of Liberal Imperialism*. Princeton, NJ: Princeton University Press, 2010.

Mantena, Karuna. "Genealogies of Catastrophes: Arendt on the Logic and Legacy of Imperialism." In *Politics in Dark Times: Encounters with Hannah Arendt*, ed. Seyla Benhabib.Cambridge: Cambridge University Press, 2010.

Marks, Paula Mitchell. *In a Barren Land: American Indian Dispossession and Survival.* New York: William Morrow, 1998.

Mazower, Mark. *Hitler's Empire: How the Nazis Ruled Europe.* New York: Penguin Press, 2008.

Mbembe, A. "Necropolitics." *Public Culture* 15, 1(2003): 11–40.

Mbembe, A. *On the Postcolony.* Berkeley: University of California Press, 2001.

McCoy, Alfred W., and Francisco Antonio Scarano, eds *Colonial Crucible: Empire in the Making of the Modern American State.*Madison: University of Wisconsin Press, 2009.

McCoy, Alfred W. *Policing America's Empire: The United States, the Philippines and the Rise of the Surveillance State.* Madison: University of Wisconsin Press, 2009.

Mearsheimer, John J. "Imperial by Design." *The National Interest*, Jan-Feb (2011).

Mearsheimer, John J. *The Tragedy of Great Power Politics.* New York: Norton, 2001.

Mehta, Uday Singh. *Liberalism And Empire: A Study in Nineteenth Century British Liberal Thought.* Chicago, IL: University of Chicago Press, 1999.

Meyer, John W., John Boli, George M.Thomas, and Francisco O. Ramirez. "World Society and the Nation-State." *American Journal of Sociology* 103, 1(1997): 144–181.

Mezzadra, Sandro and Federico Rahola. "The Postcolonial Condition: A Few Notes on the Quality of Historical Time in the Global Present.". *Postcolonial Text* 2, 1 (2005).

Mihalek, Donald. "Urban Combat the Petraeus Way." *Tactical Life*, 2010. www.ta ctical-life.com/online/guns-and-weapons/urban-combat-the-petraeus-way/.

Mintz, Sidney Wilfred. *Sweetness and Power: The Place of Sugar in Modern History.* New York: Viking, 1985.

Mirowski, Philip. "Postface: Defining Neoliberalism." In *The Road from Mont Pelerin: The Making of the Neoliberal Thought Collective*, eds Philip Mirowski and Dieter Plehwe.Cambridge, MA: Harvard University Press, 2009.

Mitchell, Timothy. *Colonising Egypt.* Berkeley: University of California Press, 1988.

Mitchell, Timothy. *Rule of Experts: Egypt, Techno-politics, Modernity.* Berkeley: University of California Press, 2002.

Moses, A. Dirk. *Empire, Colony, Genocide: Conquest, Occupation and Subaltern Resistance in World History.* New York: Berghahn Books, 2008.

Muhlhahn, Klaus. "The Concentration Camp in Global Historical Perspective." *History Compass* 8, 6(2010): 543–561.

Munkler, Herfried. *Empires.* Cambridge: Polity Press, 2007.

Netz, Reviel. *Barbed Wire: An Ecology of Modernity.* Middletown, CT: Wesleyan University Press, 2004.

Netzloff, Mark. *England's Internal Colonies: Class, Capital and the Literature of Early Modern English Colonialism.* New York: Palgrave Macmillan, 2003.

Onuf, Nicholas. *The Republican Legacy in International Thought.* Cambridge: Cambridge University Press, 1998.

Osiander, Andreas. *Before the State: Systemic Political Change in the West from the Greek to the French Revolution.* Oxford: Oxford University Press, 2007.

Owen, John M. *The Clash of Ideas in World Politics: Transnational Networks, States and Regime Change, 1520–2010.* Princeton, NJ: Princeton University Press, 2010.

Packer, George. *The Assassins' Gate: America in Iraq.* New York: Farrar, Straus and Giroux, 2005.

Pagden, Anthony. *The Fall of Natural Man: The American Indian and the Origins of Comparative Ethnology.* Cambridge: Cambridge University Press, 1982.

Parenti, Christian. *The Soft Cage: Surveillance in America from Slavery to the War on Terror.* New York: Basic Books, 2003.

Peck, Jamie. *Constructions of Neoliberal Reason.* Oxford: Oxford University Press, 2010.

Perelman, Michael. *The Invention of Capitalism: Classical Political Economy and the Secret History of Primitive Accumulation.* Durham, NC: Duke University Press, 2000.

Perkinson, Robert. *Texas Tough: The Rise of America's Prison Empire.* New York: Metropolitan Books, 2010.

Pick, Daniel. *Faces of Degeneration: A European Disorder, 1848–1918.* Cambridge: Cambridge University Press, 1989.

Pocock, J. G. A. *The Machiavellian Moment: Florentine Political Thought and the Atlantic Republican Tradition.* Princeton, NJ: Princeton University Press, 1975.

Prasad, Monica. *The Politics of Free Markets: The Rise of Neoliberal Economic Policies in Britain, France, Germany and the United States.* Chicago, IL: University of Chicago Press, 2006.

Pratt, Mary Louise. *Imperial Eyes: Travel Writing and Transculturation.* New York: Routledge, 1992.

Priest, Dana, and William M. Arkin. *Top Secret America: The Rise of the New American Security State.* New York: Little, Brown, 2011.

Quijano, Anibal. "Coloniality of Power and Eurocentrism in Latin America." *International Sociology* 15, 2(2000): 215–232.

Redfield, Peter. "Foucault in the Tropics: Displacing the Panopticon." In *Anthropologies of Modernity: Foucault, Governmentality and Life Politics*, ed. Jonathan Xavier Inda.Malden, MA: Blackwell Publishing, 2005.

Rigouste, Mathieu. *L'ennemi interieur.* Paris: La Découverte, 2009.

Robin, Corey. "Via Del Mar: A Veritable International of the Free-Market Counterrevolution." *Corey Robin*, 2012. http://coreyrobin.com/2012/07/17/vina-del-mar-a-veritable-international-of-the-free-market-counterrevolution/.

Robinson, Ronald Edward, and John Gallagher. *Africa and the Victorians: The Climax of Imperialism.* London: Macmillan, 1961.

Rock, David. "The British in Argentina: From Informal Empire to Postcolonialism." In *Empire in Latin America: Culture, Commerce, and Capital*, ed. Matthew Brown. Malden, MA: Wiley-Blackwell, 2008.

Rosanvallon, Pierre. *La société des égaux.* Paris: Seuil, 2011.

Rothberg, Michael. *Multidirectional Memory: Remembering the Holocaust in the Age of Decolonization.* Stanford, CA: Stanford University Press, 2009.

Roustang, Francois. *Chile Under Pinochet: Recovering the Truth.* Philadelphia: University of Pennsylvania Press, 2000.

Ruggie, John Gerard. "Continuity and Transformation in the World Polity: Toward a Neorealist Synthesis." *World Politics* 35, 2(1983): 261–285.

Rushdie, Salman. *Imaginary Homeland: Essays and Criticism 1981–1991.* New York: Penguin Books, 1992.

Saada, Emannuelle. "The History of Lessons: Power and Rule in Imperial Formations." *Items and Issues: Social Science Research Council* 4, 4(2003): 10–17.

Sabaratnam, Meera. "IR in Dialogue … But Can We Change the Subjects? A typology of Decolonising Strategies for the Study of World Politics.". *Millennium – Journal of International Studies* 39, 3(2011): 781–803.

Said, Edward W. *Orientalism.* New York: Vintage Books, 1979.

Sala-Molins, Louis. *Dark Side of The Light*. Minneapolis: University of Minnesota Press, 2006.

Salman, Michael. "Nothing Without Labor: Penology, Discipline, and Independence in the Philippines under United States Rule." In *Discrepant Histories: Translocal Essays on Filipino Cultures*, ed. Vicente L. Rafael.Philadelphia, PA: Temple University Press, 1995.

Sarvary, Katalin. "No Place for Politics? Truth, Progress and the Neglected Role of Diplomacy in Wendt"s Theory of History." In *Constructivism and International Relations: Alexander Wendt and His Critics*, eds Stefano Guzzini and Anna Leander.London: Routledge, 2006.

Scahill, Jeremy. *Dirty Wars: The World Is a Battlefield*. New York: The Nation Books, 2013.

Schaller, Dominik J. "From Conquest to Genocide: Colonial Rule in German Southwest Africa and German East Africa." In *Empire, Colony, Genocide: Conquest, Occupation, and Subaltern Resistance in World History*, ed. A. Dirk MosesNew York: Berghahn Press, 2008.

Schlesinger, Arthur M.. *The Cycles of American History*. Boston, MA: Houghton Mifflin, 1986.

Schmidt, Brian C.. *The Political Discourse of Anarchy: A Disciplinary History of International Relaions*. Albany: State University of New York Press, 1998.

Schmidt, Donald E. *The Folly of War: American Foreign Policy, 1898–2005*. New York: Algora Publishing, 2005.

Schmitt, Carl. *The Nomos of the Earth in the International Law of the Jus Publicum Europaeum*. New York: Telos Press, 2003.

Schroeder, Paul W. "Necessary Conditions and World War I as an Unavoidable War." In *Explaining War and Peace: Case Studies and Necessary Condition Counterfactuals*, eds Jack S. Levy and Gary Goertz.New York: Routledge, 2007.

Schweller, Randall L. *Deadly Imbalances: Tripolarity and Hitler's Strategy of World Conquest*. New York: Columbia University Press, 1998.

Scott, David. "Colonial Governmentality." In *Anthropologies of Modernity: Foucault, Governmentality and Life Politics*, ed. Jonathan Xavier Inda. Malden, MA: Blackwell Publishing, 2005.

Scott, James C. *Seeing Like a State: How Certain Schemes to Improve the Human Condition Have Failed*. New Haven, CT: Yale University Press, 1998.

Sengoopta, Chandak. *Imprint of the Raj: How Fingerprinting Was Born in Colonial India*. London: Macmillan, 2003.

Shilliam, Robbie. "Race and Research Agendas." *Cambridge Review of International Affairs* 26, 1(2013): 152–158.

Shohat, Ella, and Robert Stam. *Unthinking Eurocentrism: Multiculturalism and the Media*. New York: Routledge, 1994.

Singer, J. David. "The Level-of-Analysis Problem in International Relations." *World Politics* 14, 1(1961): 77–92.

Singer, Peter W. "Do Drones Undermine Democracy?" *New York Times*, January 21, 2012.

Smith, Iain R., and Andreas Stucki. "The Colonial Development of Concentration Camps (1868–1902)." *Journal of Imperial and Commonwealth History* 39, 3(2011): 417–437.

Smith, Steve. "The United States and the Discipline of International Relations: Hegemonic Country, Hegemonic Discipline." *International Studies Review* 4, 2(2002):
67–85.

Smith, Woodruff D. *The Ideological Origins of Nazi Imperialism*. New York: Oxford
University Press, 1986.

Snyder, Jack. "Myths of Empires and Strategies of Hegemony." In *Lessons of Empire:
Imperial Histories and American Power*, eds Craig Calhoun, Frederick Cooper, and
Kevin W. Moore. New York: The New Press, 2006.

Snyder, Timothy. *Bloodlands: Europe Between Hitler and Stalin*. New York: Basic
Books, 2010.

Sofsky, Wolfgang. *The Order of Terror: The Concentration Camp*. Princeton, NJ:
Princeton University Press, 1997.

Spivak, Gayatri. "Subaltern Studies: Deconstructing Historiography." In *Selected
Subaltern Studies*, eds Ranajit Guha and Gayatri Chakravorty Spivak. New York:
Oxford University Press, 1988.

Spurr, David. *The Rhetoric of Empire: Colonial Discourse in Journalism, Travel Writing, and Imperial Administration*. Durham, NC: Duke University Press, 1993.

*Staff Report of the Select Committee to Study Governmental Operations with respect to
the Intelligence Activities. Covert Action In Chile: 1963–1973*. Washington, DC: US
Congress, 1975.

Steinmetz, George. "Imperialism or Colonialism: From Windhoek to Washington, By
Way of Basra." In *Lessons of Empire: Imperial Histories and American Power*, eds
Craig Calhoun,Frederick Cooper, and Kevin W. Moore.New York: New Press,
2006.

Steinmetz, George. "Return to Empire: The New US Imperialism in Comparative
Historical Perspective." *Sociological Theory* 23, 4(2005): 339–367.

Stepan, Nancy Leys. "Race and Gender: The Role of Analogy in Science." Isis 77, 2
(1986): 261–277.

Stoler, Ann Laura, and Frederick Cooper. "Between Metropole and Colony:
Rethinking a Research Agenda." In *Tensions of Empire: Colonial Cultures in a
Bourgeois World*. Berkeley: University of California Press, 2014.

Stoler, Ann Laura. *Capitalism and Confrontation In Sumatra's Plantation Belt, 1870–
1979*. New Haven, CT: Yale University Press, 1985.

Stoler, Ann Laura. *Carnal Knowledge and Imperial Power: Race and the Intimate in
Colonial Rule*. Berkeley: University of California Press, 2002.

Stoler, Ann Laura. "On Degrees of Imperial Sovereignty." *Public Culture* 18, 1(2006):
125–146.

Stoler, Ann Laura. *Race and the Education of Desire: Foucault's History of Sexuality
and the Colonial Order of Things*. Durham, NC: Duke University Press, 1995.

Street, James H. "Values in Conflict: Developing Countries as Social Laboratories,".
Journal of Economic Issues 18, 1(1984): 633–641.

Stuntz, William J. "Law and Disorder: The Case for a Police Surge." *The Weekly
Standard* 14, 22, February 23 (2009):19–25.

Suzuki, Shogo. *Civilization and Empire: China and Japan's Encounter with European
International Society*. London: Routledge, 2009.

Sznajder, Mario. "Hayek in Chile." In *Liberalism and Its Practice*, eds Dan Avnon and
Avner de-Shalit. New York: Routledge, 1999.

Teschke, Benno. *The Myth of 1648: Class, Geopolitics and the Making of Modern
International Relations*. London: Verso, 2003.

The Independent. "Drones to Patrol the Skies Above Olympic Stadium," 2011. www.independent.co.uk/news/uk/crime/drones-to-patrol-the-skies-above-olympic-stadium-6267107.html.

Thomas, Ronald R. *Detective Fiction and the Rise of Forensic Science.* Cambridge: Cambridge University Press, 1999.

Tilley, Helen. *Africa as a Living Laboratory: Empire, Development and the Problem of Scientific Knowledge, 1870–1950.* Chicago: University of Chicago Press, 2011.

Towns, Ann E. *Women and States: Norms and Hierarchies in International Politics.* Cambridge: Cambridge University Press, 2010.

Traverso, Enzo. *The Origins of Nazi Violence.* New York: New Press, 2003.

Valdes, Juan Gabriel. *Pinochet's Economists: The Chicago School of Economics in Chile.* Cambridge: Cambridge University Press, 1995.

Vitalis, Robert. "The Noble American Science of Imperial Relations and its Laws of Race Development." *Comparative Studies in Society and History* 52, 4(2010): 909–938.

Volk, Christian. "The Decline of Order: Hannah Arendt and the Paradoxes of the Nation-State." In *Politics in Dark Times: Encounters with Hannah Arendt,* ed. Seyla Benhabib. Cambridge: Cambridge University Press, 2010.

Wacquant, Loïc. *Punishing the Poor: The Neoliberal Government of Social Insecurity.* Durham, NC: Duke University Press, 2009.

Wacquant, Loïc. "The Militarization of Urban Marginality: Lessons from the Brazilian Metropolis." *International Political Sociology* 2, 1(2008): 56–74.

Wacquant, Loïc. "Three Steps to a Historical Anthropology of Actually Existing Neoliberalism." *Social Anthropology* 20, 1(2012): 66–79.

Walker, R. B. J. *Inside/Outside: International Relations as Political Theory.* Cambridge: Cambridge University Press, 1993.

Wall, Tyler, and Torin Monahan. "Surveillance and Violence from Afar: The Politics of Drones and Liminal Security-scape." *Theoretical Criminology* 15, 3(2011): 239–254.

Wallerstein, Immanuel. "Eurocentrism and Its Avatars: The Dilemmas of Social Science." *New Left Review* 226(1997): 93–108.

Waltz, Kenneth N. *Theory of International Politics.* Reading, MA: Addison-Wesley, 1979.

Ward, Kerry. *Networks of Empire.* Cambridge: Cambridge University Press, 2009.

Watson, Adam. *The Evolution of International Society: A Comparative Historical Analysis.* London: Routledge, 1992.

Wendt, Alexander, and Daniel Friedheim. "Hierarchy Under Anarchy: Informal Empire and the East German State." *International Organization* 49, 4(1995): 689–721.

Wendt, Alexander. *Social Theory of International Politics.* Cambridge: Cambridge University Press, 1999.

Weschler, Lawrence. *A Miracle, a Universe: Settling Accounts with Torturers.* New York: Pantheon Books, 1990.

Wight, Martin. *Systems of States.* Leicester: Leicester University Press, 1977.

Wilder, Gary. *The French Imperial Nation-State: Negritude and Colonial Humanism between the Two World Wars.* Chicago: Chicago University Press, 2005.

Williams, Kristian. "The Other Side of the COIN: Counterinsurgency and Community Policing." *Interface* 3, 1(2011): 81–117.

Wolf, Eric R. *Europe and the People Without History.* Berkeley: University of California Press, 1982.

Wolin, Sheldon S. *Politics and Vision: Continuity and Innovation In Western Political Thought.* Princeton, NJ: Princeton University Press, 2004.

Wood, Ellen Meiksins. *Empire of Capital.* London: Verso, 2003.

Woodward, C. Vann. *The Strange Career of Jim Crow*. New York: Oxford University Press, 1974.

Yenne, Bill. *Indian Wars: The Campaign for the American West*. Yardley, PA: Westholme Publishing, 2006.

Zilberg, Elana. *Space of Detention: The Making of a Transnational Gang Crisis Between Los Angeles and San Salvador*. Durham, NC: Duke University Press, 2011.

Zinoman, Peter. *The Colonial Bastille: A History of Imprisonment in Vietnam, 1862–1940*. Berkeley: University of California Press, 2001.

Zinoman, Peter. "The History of the Modern Prison and the Case of Indochina." In *Figures of Criminality in Indonesia, the Philippines, and Colonial Vietnam*, ed. Vicente L. Rafael. Ithaca, NY: Cornell University Southeast Asia Program Publications, 1999.

Index

Trinidad 7
Trotha, Lothar von 65

uncivilized 65, 96
underclass 80, 137
unionism 11, 120
unipolarity 6, 107
United States Iraq, 2–3, 6; 11–12, 15,
20; Alfred McCoy on 34; 43, 50;
rise of in 19th century 53–5;
counterinsurgency in Philippines 57,
60, 63; 69, 75; adoption of
fingerprinting 86; 91, 93–5, 98,
100–101, 104–106, 108, 111–12,
114–16, 119–21, 123, 125–27, 129–34,
136–37, 139
urbanization 13, 65, 137
utopian 69

vagrants 78, 82
Valdés, Juan Gabriel 14, 116–17, 119,
125–27
Vick, Karl 140
Vietnam 104–105, 108, 111–12, 114,
122, 133, 136
Viña del Mar 120, 127
Vinh-Kim, Nguyen 37, 41, 51
Vitalis, Robert 21–2, 43
Voegelin, Eric 72
volksdeutsche 69
Volksschädling 70

Wacquant, Loic on neoliberal vulgate,
114; on prisonfare 121–22, 137; 125,
127, 140
Walker, R.B.J. 18, 42, 128
Wall, Tyler 12
Wallerstein, Immanuel 43
Waltz, Kenneth 17–19, 41–2, 46
Ward, Kerry 14

warfare colonial warfare 23, 53, 60–2,
65–66, 69–70, 73, 75–6; 39, 100, 102,
128, 132–33, 139
Warsh, David 127
Washington Post 3
Watanuki, Joji 125
Watson, Adam 26, 45
Weber, Max 18, 30; on surveillance, 78–79
Weimar 58
Weinberger, Sharon 140
Weltpolitik 73
Weschler, Lawrence 122
Westphalian State System 18, 26, 28, 95,
130
Weyler, Valeriano 62–3
Wight, Colin 45
Wilde, Jaap de 42
Wilder, Gary 5, 13
Williams, Kristian 80, 133, 136, 139–40
Wilson Administration 91–2
Winter, Aaron 140
Wolf, Eric 43, 46, 76
Wolin, Sheldon 131, 137, 139–40
Wood, Ellen Meiksins 12, 139
Woodward, C. Vann 92, 100
Woolgar, Steve 50
World Polity Institutionalism 29–30, 47
World Trade Organization 136

Yemen 132
yen (Japanese currency) 109
Yenne, Bill 62, 75
Yom Kippur War 112

Zilberg, Elana 138
Zimmerer, Jürgen 76
Zinoman, Peter 98–9
zoē 58
zones (imperial) 11, 17, 30, 40–1, 59, 62,
102